Lecture Notes in Artificial Intelligence   7837

Subseries of Lecture Notes in Computer Science

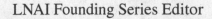

T0202561

Mehdi Dastani   Jomi F. Hübner
Brian Logan (Eds.)

Programming Multi-Agent Systems

10th International Workshop, ProMAS 2012
Valencia, Spain, June 5, 2012
Revised Selected Papers

 Springer

Volume Editors

Mehdi Dastani
Utrecht University, Intelligent Systems Group
Utrecht 3508 TB, The Netherlands
E-mail: m.m.dastani@uu.nl

Jomi F. Hübner
Federal University of Santa Catarina
Department of Automation and Systems Engineering
Florianópolis, 88040-900, Brazil
E-mail: jomi@das.ufsc.br

Brian Logan
University of Nottingham, School of Computer Science
Nottingham, NG8 1BB, UK
E-mail: brian.logan@nottingham.ac.uk

ISSN 0302-9743   e-ISSN 1611-3349
ISBN 978-3-642-38699-2   e-ISBN 978-3-642-38700-5
DOI 10.1007/978-3-642-38700-5
Springer Heidelberg Dordrecht London New York

Library of Congress Control Number: 2013939791

CR Subject Classification (1998): I.2.9, I.2.11, I.2, D.1, D.2

LNCS Sublibrary: SL 7 – Artificial Intelligence

Typesetting: Camera-ready by author, data conversion by Scientific Publishing Services, Chennai, India

Printed on acid-free paper

Springer is part of Springer Science+Business Media (www.springer.com)

Preface

These are the proceedings of the International Workshop on Programming Multi-Agent Systems (ProMAS 2012), the tenth of a series of workshops. Over the last decade, the ProMAS workshop series has provided a venue for state-of-the-art research in programming languages and tools for the development of multi-agent systems. ProMAS aims to address both theoretical and practical issues related to developing and deploying multi-agent systems. It has provided a forum for the discussion of techniques, concepts, requirements and principles central to multi-agent programming technology, including the theory and application of agent programming languages, the specification, verification and analysis of agent systems, and the implementation of social structures in agent-based systems. Many of these concepts and techniques have subsequently found widespread application in agent programming platforms and systems.

For the tenth edition of ProMAS, we received 14 submissions which were reviewed by members of the Program Committee. Of these papers, ten were accepted for presentation during the worksop and included in this proceedings volume after being improved by the authors based on the reviewers' comments and discussion at the workshop. We are pleased to be able to present proceedings with high-quality papers covering a wide range of topics in multi-agent system programming languages, including language design and efficient implementation, agent communication, and robot programming.

In addition to regular papers, this volume includes six papers from the Multi-Agent Programming Contest 2012 (MAPC). The practical experience with non-trivial problems provided by the Multi-Agent Programming Contests has been invaluable in improving some of the best-known platforms for multi-agent programming. The paper from Michael Köster, Federico Schlesinger, and Jürgen Dix presents the contest organization and the main results. The following papers are from the participants and report their specific strategies and results.

We would like to thank the ProMAS Steering Committee for giving us the opportunity to organize this workshop. We also want to express our gratitude to the Program Committee members and additional reviewers, to the participants of the workshops, and especially to the authors for their original contributions. We thank the organizers of the AAMAS conference for hosting and supporting the organization of the ProMAS workshops since the first edition in 2003.

We hope the ProMAS community continues to contribute to the design of programming languages and tools that are both principled and at the same time practical for "industrial-strength" multi-agent systems development.

February 2013

Mehdi Dastani
Jomi F. Hübner
Brian Logan

Organization

The 10th International Workshop on Programming Multi-Agent Systems (ProMAS-2012) took place with the 11th International Conference on Autonomous Agents and Multiagent Systems (AAMAS 2012) in Valencia, Spain, on June 5, 2012.

Organizing Committee

Mehdi Dastani	Utrecht University, The Netherlands
Jomi F. Hübner	Federal University of Santa Catarina, Brazil
Brian Logan	University of Nottingham, UK

Steering Committee

Rafael H. Bordini	Federal University of Rio Grande do Sul, Brazil
Mehdi Dastani	Utrecht University, The Netherlands
Juergen Dix	Clausthal University of Technology, Germany
Amal E.F. Seghrouchni	University of Paris VI, France

Program Committee

Natasha Alechina	University of Nottingham, UK
Lacramioara Astefanoaei	Laboratoire d'Informatique de Grenoble, France
Matteo Baldoni	University of Turin, Italy
Olivier Boissier	Ecole des Mines de St Etienne, France
Juan Botia Blaya	University of Murcia, Spain
Lars Braubach	University of Hamburg, Germany
Rem Collier	University College Dublin, Ireland
Louise Dennis	University of Liverpool, UK
Vladimir Gorodetsky	Russian Academy of Sciences, Russia
Francisco Grimaldo	Universitat de Valencia, Spain
James Harland	RMIT, Australia
Koen Hindriks	Delft University of Technology, The Netherlands
Benjamin Hirsch	Technical University of Berlin, Germany
Max Knobbout	Utrecht University, The Netherlands
João Leite	Universidade Nova de Lisboa, Portugal
Viviana Mascardi	Genova University, Italy
Philippe Mathieu	University Lille 1, France
John-Jules Ch. Meyer	Utrecht University, The Netherlands

Jorg Muller	Clausthal University of Technology, Germany
Peter Novák	Czech Technical University, Czech Republic
Alexander Pokahr	University of Hamburg, Germany
Alessandro Ricci	University of Bologna, Italy
Birna van Riemsdijk	Delft University of Technology, The Netherlands
Ralph Ronnquist	Intendico, Australia
Sebastian Sardina	RMIT University, Australia
Ichiro Satoh	NII, Japan
Michael Ignaz Schumacher	University of Applied Sciences Western Switzerland, Sierre, Switzerland
Kostas Stathis	Royal Holloway, University of London, UK
Bas Steunebrink	University of Lugano, Switzerland
John Thangarajah	RMIT, Australia
Pankaj Telang	Cisco, USA
Wamberto Vasconcelos	University of Aberdeen, UK
Jørgen Villadsen	DTU Informatics, Denmark
Neil Yorke-Smith	American University of Beirut, Lebanon and SRI International, USA
Yingqian Zhang	Delft University of Technology, The Netherlands

Additional Reviewers

Antonin Komenda
Matthias Knorr
Andrea Santi

Table of Contents

eJason: An Implementation of Jason in Erlang*

Álvaro Fernández Díaz, Clara Benac Earle, and Lars-Åke Fredlund

Babel Group. Universidad Politécnica de Madrid, Spain
{avalor,cbenac,fred}@babel.ls.fi.upm.es

Abstract. In this paper we describe eJason, a prototype implementation of Jason, the well-known agent-oriented programming language, in Erlang, a concurrent functional programming language. The reason for choosing Erlang as the implementation vehicle is the surprising number of similarities between Jason and Erlang, e.g., both have their syntactical roots in logic programming, and share an actor-based process and communication model. Moreover, the Erlang runtime system implements lightweight processes and fast message passing between processes. Thus, by mapping Jason agents and agent-to-agent communication onto Erlang processes and Erlang process-to-process communication, we can create a very high-performing Jason implementation, potentially capable of supporting up to a hundred thousand concurrent actors. In this paper we describe in detail the implementation of Jason in Erlang, and provide early feedback on the performance of the implementation.

1 Introduction

Among the different agent-oriented programming languages, AgentSpeak [13] is one of the most popular ones. It is based on the BDI architecture [14,17], which is central in the development of multiagent systems. AgentSpeak allows the implementation of rational agents by the definition of their *know-how*, i.e. how each agent must act in order to achieve its goals. AgentSpeak has been extended into a programming language called Jason [7,9]. Jason refers to both the AgentSpeak language extension and the related interpreter that allows its execution in Java. Thus, Jason is an implementation of AgentSpeak that allows the construction of multiagent systems that can be organized in agent infrastructures distributed in several hosts. It allows the interfacing to the JADE Framework [5,6], thus generating multiagent systems fully compliant to FIPA [1,12] specifications. To effortlessly distribute the agent infrastructure over a network, the use of the SACI [11,2] middleware is suggested. Jason has been designed to address the desirable properties of rational agents identified in [16]: autonomy, proactiveness, reactiveness and social ability. In the rest of the paper we assume that the reader is familiar with Jason [9].

A significant new trend in processor architecture has been evident for a few years. No longer is the clock speed of CPUs increasing at an impressive rate,

---

* This work has been partially supported by the following projects: DESAFIOS10 (TIN2009-14599-C03-00) and PROMETIDOS (P2009/TIC-1465).

M. Dastani, J.F. Hübner, and B. Logan (Eds.): ProMAS 2012, LNAI 7837, pp. 1–16, 2013.

rather we have started to see a race to supply more processor elements in main-stream multi-core CPU architectures coming from Intel and AMD. Initially, the software industry has been slow in reacting to this fundamental hardware change, but today, utilising multiple cores is the only way to improve software system performance. With traditional programming languages (such as Java, C, C++, etc.) writing bug-free concurrent code is hard, and the complexity grows quickly with the number of parallel tasks. As a result, alternative languages, with less error-prone concurrency primitives, are attracting more attention.

Following this trend, the Erlang programming language [3,10] is gaining momentum. The usage has increased, and among the users are large organisations like Facebook, Amazon, Yahoo!, T-Mobile, Motorola, and Ericsson. The most prominent reasons for the increased popularity of Erlang are lightweight concurrency based on the actor model, the powerful handling of fault tolerance, the transparent distribution mechanisms, the generic OTP design patterns, and the fact that the language has functional programming roots leading to a small, clean code base.

In this paper we report on our experience translating the Jason programming language to Erlang. The similarities between Jason and Erlang – both are inspired by Prolog, both support asynchronous communication among computational independent entities (agents/processes) – make the translation rather straightforward. By implementing Jason in Erlang we offer the possibility to Erlang programmers of using an agent-oriented programming language like Jason integrated in Erlang. To Jason programmers, the approach gives them the possibility of executing their code in the Erlang runtime system, which is particularly appropriate for running robust multiagent systems with a large number of concurrent and distributed agents.

Moreover, as the syntax of Erlang is inspired by Prolog [1], e.g., having atoms beginning with a lowercase letter, and single-assignment variables beginning with an uppercase letter, etc., we hope to reduce the conceptual gap for a Jason programmer interested in modifying the Jason meta-level (e.g., changing the selector functions, and implementing actions) by adopting Erlang, compared to having to use Java. Perhaps even more interesting is the potential for introducing Erlang programmers to the world of BDI programming through this new Jason implementation. This is a group of programmers already used to thinking of programming systems composed of independent communicating agents (or in the terminology of Erlang, processes), and superficially familiar with the syntax of Jason. To us it appears that the conceptual gap between programming agents in Jason, and functions and processes in Erlang, is smaller than for many other programming languages (Java).

A prototype of the implementation of Jason in Erlang is available at

$$git://github.com/avalor/eJason.git$$

The rest of the paper is organized as follows. Before explaining the translation, the main characteristics of Erlang are briefly described in Sect. 2. Then, in

---

[1] Not surprisingly, as the first implementation of Erlang was written in NU Prolog [4]

Sect. 3 the translation of the Jason constructs, the Jason reasoning cycle, the process orchestration of eJason, and the current limitations of the approach are explained. Some early benchmarks results for the eJason prototype are reported in Sect. 4. Finally, a summary of our conclusions and items for future work appear in Sect. 5.

2   Erlang

Erlang [3,10] is a functional concurrent programming language created by Ericsson in the 1980s. The chief strength of the language is that it provides excellent support for concurrency, distribution and fault tolerance on top of a dynamically typed and strictly evaluated functional programming language. It enables programmers to write robust and clean code for modern multiprocessor and distributed systems. In this section we briefly describe the key aspects of Erlang.

2.1   Functional Erlang

In Erlang basic values are: integers, floats, atoms (starting with a lowercase letter), bit strings, binaries, and funs (to create anonymous functions), and process identifiers (pids). The compound values are lists and tuples. Erlang syntax includes a record construct which provides syntactic sugar for accessing the elements of a tuple by name, instead of by position. Functions are first class citizens in Erlang. For example, consider the declaration of the function factorial that calculates the factorial of a number.

```
factorial(0) -> 1;
factorial(N) when N > 0 -> N * factorial(N - 1).
```

As in Prolog, variable identifiers (N) start with a capital letter, and atoms (factorial) with a lowercase letter. Like Prolog, Erlang permits only single assignment to variables.

As virtually all functional programming languages, Erlang supports higher order functions.

2.2   Concurrent and Distributed Erlang

An Erlang system (see Fig. 1) is a collection of Erlang nodes. An Erlang node (or Erlang Run-time System) is a collection of processes, with a unique node name. Communication is asynchronous and point-to-point, with one process sending a message to a second process identified by its pid. Messages sent to a process are put in its message queue, also referred to as a mailbox. Informally, a mailbox is a sequence of values ordered by their arrival time. Mailboxes can in theory store any number of messages. Although mailboxes are ordered, language constructs permit retrieving messages from the process mailbox in arbitrary order.

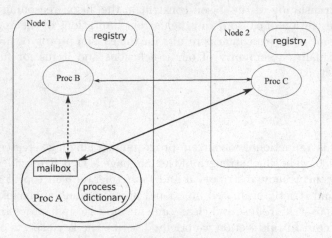

Fig. 1. An Erlang multi-node system

As an alternative to addressing a process using its pid, there is a facility for associating a symbolic name with a pid. The name, which must be an atom, is automatically unregistered when the associated process terminates. Message passing between processes in different nodes is transparent when pids are used, i.e., there is no syntactical difference between sending a message to a process in the same node, or to a remote node. However, the node must be specified when sending messages using registered names, as the pid registry is local to a node.

A unique feature of Erlang that greatly facilitates building fault-tolerant systems is that processes can be "linked together" in order to detect and recover from abnormal process termination. If a process P_1 is linked to another process P_2, and P_2 terminates with a fault, process P_1 is automatically informed of the failure of P_2. It is possible to create links to processes at remote nodes.

As an integral part of Erlang, the OTP library provides a number of very frequently used design patterns (behaviours in Erlang terminology) for implementing robust distributed and concurrent systems. The most important OTP design patterns are generic servers that implement client/server architectures, and supervisors, to build robust systems. Other OTP design patterns implement, for instance, a publish-subscribe mechanism, and a finite state machine.

3   Implementing Jason in Erlang

This section describes the implementation of a subset of Jason in Erlang.

3.1   A Simple Running Example in Jason

To illustrate the implementation of Jason in Erlang, we use the example in Fig. 2, which illustrates the main syntactical elements of the Jason language.

```
init_count(0).                                              (a)
max_count(2000).                                            (b)

next(X,Y) :-  Y = X + 1.                                    (c)

!startcount.                                                (d)

+!startcount : init_count(X) <- +actual_count(X);          (e)
                       !count.

+!count: actual_count(X) & max_count(Y) & X < Y <-         (f)
                 ?next(X, NewCount);
                 -+actual_count(NewCount);
                 !count.


+!count: actual_count(X) & max_count(Y)& X >= Y <-         (g)
                 .print("Terminated count").
```

Fig. 2. A simple Jason agent

This somewhat artificially programmed agent is a *counter*, which prints a message when finished. The initial beliefs of the agent are (a), representing that the agent believes the initial value to be zero, and (b), representing that the agent believes that it has to count up to 2000. There is one rule (c), expressing the successor relation for numbers. The agent's initial goal (d) is to start counting. There are three plans (e), (f) and (g). Plan (e) initializes the actual counter by adding a new belief to the agent's belief base and introduces a new achievement goal !count. That goal can be achieved by plans (f) and (g), whose context's are disjoint and, thus, can never be considered as applicable plans at the same time. When plan (g) is executed, which occurs when the agent has counted up to its limit, it prints a message and the agent remains waiting as there are no more events. We kindly direct the reader to [9] for a complete definition of the Jason programming language and its interpreter, as a detailed description of the different features of Jason lies beyond the scope of this paper.

3.2   An Overview of the Implementation

Jason is both a programming language which is an extension of AgentSpeak, and an interpreter of this programing language in Java. The constructs of the Jason programming language can be separated into three main categories: beliefs, goals and plans. The Jason interpreter runs an agent program by means of a reasoning cycle that provides the operational semantics of the agent. This semantics has been formalised and can be found in [9].

The translation of beliefs and goals to Erlang is rather straightforward since they represent the knowledge of an agent, rather than its behaviour (with the exception of rules). Common Erlang data types and functions are used to translate these Jason constructs to Erlang. Initially we used the third party software ERESYE [15] (ERlang Expert SYstem Engine) to implement the belief base of each agent. ERESYE is a library to write expert systems and rule processing engines using the Erlang programming language. It allows to create multiple engines, each one with its own facts and rules to be processed. We decided to use this software as the term storage service due to its capabilities to store Erlang terms and to also retrieve them using pattern matching. Nevertheless, due to the way in which we used this software, the resulting Jason implementation was rather inefficient. Therefore we decided to implement our own belief base. This later implementation represents the belief base of each agent as a list of ground terms. The translation of beliefs, goals and rules to Erlang is explained in Sect. 3.3

The implementation of plans is more convoluted due to their dynamic nature. Every plan is composed by one or more formulas that must be evaluated sequentially. However, the formulas in a plan may not all be executable in the same reasoning cycle. The representation of plans in Erlang, and their execution by a tail-recursive Erlang function, is explained in Sect. 3.4.

A higher-level view of the different Erlang *processes* implementing the Jason reasoning cycle [9] and the communication between them is described in Sect. 3.5, while Sect. 3.6 provides the details. Basically, the reasoning cycle of each agent is handled by a different Erlang process.

Finally Sect. 3.7 enumerates the limitations of eJason, with respect to implementing the full Jason language, at the time of writing this paper.

3.3   Translation of Jason Beliefs and Goals into Erlang

Here we describe how the different constructs for representing and inferring knowledge of Jason are implemented.

Variables. To represent the bound and unbound variables of a plan we use a variable valuation that is updated as variables become bound to values. Concretely, a valuation for a plan is represented by an Erlang tuple where values are associated with distinct variables ordered according to the order in which these variables first occur in the plan. For instance, a possible valuation for the second plan (f) in Fig. 2 would be $\{0, 2000, '\_'\}$, thus binding X to 0, Y to 2000 and leaving NewCount unbound.

Beliefs. Every agent possesses its own belief base, i.e., each agent can only access and update its own belief base. In a first version of eJason, we used ERESYE in the following manner. Each agent ran its own ERESYE engine, which spawned three Erlang processes for each belief base. Early experiments showed that this implementation was rather inefficient. For instance, the eJason implementation of the counter example could only handle around four thousand agents.

An alternative is to use a single ERESYE engine for all agents, and provide some means to isolate the beliefs of each agent from everyone else's. We discarded this approach because the autonomy of agents would have been compromised. For instance, a failure in the ERESYE engine would cause a failure in the belief base of all agents. Therefore, we decided to implement our own belief base in a separate module, named *beliefbase*, which provides the functionality to access and update a belief base without having to create a separate Erlang process. As explained earlier, this belief base is represented as a list of Erlang terms, where each term in the list corresponds to a different belief.

A belief, i.e., either an atom or a ground formula, is represented in eJason as an Erlang tuple. An atom belief is represented in Erlang as the tuple containing the atom belief itself, e.g., {*atom_belief*}. A ground formula belief is represented by an Erlang tuple with three elements. The first element is the name of the predicate, the second is a tuple which enumerates the arguments of the predicate, and the third is a list containing a set of annotations. Each annotation can either be an atom or a predicate and is represented in the same manner as a belief. As an example, the belief base of the running example (with an added annotation):

```
init_count(0).
max_count(2000)[source(self)].
```

is translated to the following Erlang term:

```
{ init_count, {0}, [] }.
{ max_count, {2000}, [ {source,{self},[]} ] }.
```

Rules. Each rule in Jason is represented as an Erlang function. This function, when provided with the proper number of input parameters, accesses the belief base, if necessary, and returns a function that can be used to compute, one at a time, all the terms that both satisfy the rule and match the input pattern.

Goals. Goals are represented in the same way as beliefs. Nevertheless, they are never stored in isolation, but as part of the body of an event, as specified below.

Events. As we have not yet implemented perception of the agent environment, events always correspond to the explicit addition or deletion of beliefs, or the inclusion of achievement and test goals. An event is composed of an event body, an event type, and a related intention. The event body is a tuple that contains two elements. The first element is one of the atoms {*added_belief, removed_belief, added_achievement_goal, added_test_goal*}. The second element is a tuple that represents the goal or belief whose addition or deletion generated the event. The event type is either the atom *internal* or the atom *external*, with the obvious meaning. The related intention is either a tuple, as described below, or the atom *undefined* to state that the event has no related intention. The only internal events that possess a related intention are the events corresponding to the addition of goals, as their intended means will be put on top of that intention. The intended means for the rest of events will often generate new intentions.

When a relevant plan for the event is selected, the list of Erlang functions that execute the formulas in its body is added either on top of a related intention or as a brand new intention (e.g. in the case of external events). For instance, consider the following formulas in the body of a plan belonging to some intention *Intention*:

```
+actual_count(NewCount);
?next(X, NewCount);
```

The events generated after their respective execution would be:

```
{event, internal, {added_belief,
                  {actual_count,{NewCount}, []} }, undefined }

{event, internal, {added_test_goal,
                  {next, {X, NewCount}, []} }, Intention}
```

For the sake of clarity, the variable *Intention* appears as placeholder for the real representation of the corresponding related intention.

3.4   Implementing Jason Plans in Erlang

Body of a Plan. Every Jason plan is composed by one or more formulas that must be evaluated in a sequence. However, these formulas are not all necessarily evaluated during the same reasoning cycle of the agent, e.g., due to the presence of a subgoal that must be resolved by another plan. To be able to execute the formulas separately, each formula is implemented by a different Erlang function. Then, the representation of the body of a Jason plan is a list of Erlang functions. Each of these functions implements the behaviour of a different formula from the Jason plan. The order of these functions in the list is the same order of the body formulas they represent. The implementation and processing of the formulas in a plan body is the most intricate task in the implementation of Jason in Erlang.

Plans. A Jason plan is represented by a record having three components: a *trigger*, a *context* and *body*. The trigger element is a function which, applied to the body of an event, returns either the atom *false* if the plan does not belong to the set of relevant plans for the event or the tuple {*true,InitialValuation*}, where *InitialValuation* provides the bindings for the variables in the trigger. The context is a function which, when applied to the initial valuation obtained from the trigger, returns a function used to compute, one by one, the possible valuations for the variables in the trigger and context that satisfy the context. Finally, the body element is the list of Erlang functions that implement the body of the plan, as described before.

As an example, consider the plan for agent *counter*:

```
+!startcount : init_count(X) <- +actual_count(X);
                                 !count.
```

The *plan* record generated for the plan above is

```
{plan, fun start_count_trigger/1,
       fun start_count_context/1,
       [Fun1, Fun2]}
```

where the `start_count_trigger/1` and `start_count_context/1` functions implement the trigger and the context respectively. The list at [`Fun1`,`Fun2`] represents the plan body, where `Fun1` implements the formula `+actual_count(X)` and `Fun2` implements the formula `!count`.

Intentions. The stack of partially instantiated plans that compose each of the Jason intentions is represented as a list of Erlang records. Each of these records is composed of four elements. The first element is the event that triggered the plan. This element is kept as a meta-level information that can be accessed by the intention selection function. For instance, we could give priority to the execution of intentions whose partially instantiated plan on top of the stack resolves a test goal. The second element is the plan record chosen by the option selection function and, again, is intended to serve as a meta-level information accessible by the intention selection function. The third element is a tuple that represents the intended means of the intention plan, i.e. the bindings for the variables in the partially instantiated plan. The fourth element is a list of Erlang functions, representing the formulas of the partially instantiated plan that have not been executed yet. If an intention is selected for execution, the record for the partially instantiated plan on top of it (i.e. the first element of the list that represents the intention) is obtained. Then, the function at the head of the list of Erlang functions in the fourth element of this record is applied to the current variable valuation. Finally, this last function is removed from the list. This process amounts to processing the formula on top of the intention stack as is required by the specification in [9].

Selection Functions. The event, plan and intention selection functions for a MAS can be customised by providing new implementations (in Erlang) of the functions `selectEvent`, `selectPlan` and `selectIntention`.

3.5   Process Orchestration and Communication

The multiagent system generated by the translation from Jason to Erlang maps each agent to an Erlang process, all executing on the same Erlang node. Each Erlang agent process can be accessed using either its process identifier, or the name of the Jason agent. The name of the agent is associated with the Erlang process using the Erlang process registry. In the case where multiple agents are created with the same name, an integer (corresponding to the creation order) is appended to the registered name to keep such names unique. An item for future work is to extend Jason with new mechanisms to create multiple agents from the same agent definition, and to associate symbolic names with such agents, as the present mechanisms are somewhat unwieldy.

The communication between agents is implemented using Erlang message passing. As an example, consider a system where the agent *alice* sends different messages to agent *bob* by executing the internal action formulas:

```
.send(bob, tell, counter(3)}
```

```
.send(bob, untell, price(coffee,300))
```

```
.send(bob, achieve, move_to(green_cell))
```

The actions are mapped to the following Erlang expressions:

```
bob ! {communication,alice,{tell,{counter,{3},[]}}}.
```

```
bob ! {communication,alice,{untell,{price,{coffee,300},[]}}}.
```

```
bob ! {communication,alice,{achieve,{move_to,{green_cell},[]}}}).
```

The Erlang expression `Receiver ! Message` deposits `Message` into the mailbox of agent `Receiver`. The atom *communication* is used to declare the message type. It is included in the implementation to enable processes to exchange other types of messages, possibly not related to agent communication, in a future extension of eJason.

Agent *bob* can process the different messages sent by *alice* by checking its mailbox, which is performed automatically in every iteration of the reasoning cycle. The Erlang expression that retrieves the message from the process mailbox:

```
receive
  {communication,Sender,{Ilf,Message}} ->
    case Ilf of
      tell ->      ... %% Process tell message
      untell ->    ... %% Process untell message
      achieve ->   ... %% Process achieve message
    end.
```

These examples show how easily the agent communication between Jason agents can be implemented in Erlang. The simple yet efficient process communication mechanism of Erlang is one of the principal motivations to implement Jason agents using the Erlang programming language.

In the example above, all the agents are located in the same MAS architecture; messaging between agents in different architectures would be easy to support too, and would not require the use of a communication middleware like SACI. However, such an extension is not yet implemented in eJason.

3.6   Representing the Jason Reasoning Cycle in Erlang

The Jason reasoning cycle [8] must of course be represented in eJason. We implement the reasoning cycle using an Erlang function `reasoningCycle` with a single parameter, an Erlang record named *agentRationale*, which represents the current state of the agent. The elements of this record are: an atom that specifies the name of the agent, a list that stores the events that have not yet been processed, the list of executable intentions for the agent, the list of executable plans, a list of the terms that compose the agent belief base, and three elements (`selectEvent`, `selectPlan` and `selectIntention`) bound to Erlang functions implementing event, plan and intention selection for that particular agent (in this manner each agent can tailor its selection functions; appropriate defaults are provided).

Below a sketch of the `reasoningCycle` function is depicted, providing further details on how eJason implements the reasoning cycle of Jason agents:

```
reasoningCycle(OldAgent) ->
    Agent = check_mailbox(OldAgent),                            (1)
    #agentRationale
       {events = Events,
        belief_base = BB,
        agentName = AgentName,
        plans = Plans,
        intentions = Intentions,
        selectEvent = SelectEvent,
        selectPlan = SelectPlan,
        selectIntention = SelectIntention} = Agent,

    {Event,NotChosenEvents} = SelectEvent(Events),              (2)
    IntendedMeans =
      case Event of
        [] -> []; %% No events to process
        _ ->
          RelevantPlans = findRelevantPlans(Event,Plans),       (3)
          ApplicablePlans = unifyContext(BB, RelevantPlans),    (4)
          SelectPlan(ApplicablePlans)                           (5)
      end,
    AllIntentions = % The new list of intentions is computed
        processIntendedMeans(Event,Intentions,IntendedMeans),
    case SelectIntention(AllIntentions) of                      (6)
        {Intention,NotChosenIntentions} ->
            Result = executeIntention(BB,Intention),            (7)
            NewAgent =                                          (8)
              applyChanges
              (Agent#agentRationale
                 {events = NotChosenEvents,
                  intentions = NotChosenIntentions},
                 Result),
            reasoningCycle(NewAgent);                           (9)
    end.
```

This record is updated during the execution of each reasoning cycle:

(1) At the beginning of each reasoning cycle, the agent checks its mailbox and processes its incoming messages, adding new events.

(2) The event selection function included in the *agentRationale* record is applied to the list of events also included in the same record. The result of the function evaluation is an Erlang record of type *event*. This record represents the unique event that will be processed during the current reasoning cycle.

(3) The function trigger of every plan is applied to the body of the selected event. For every distinct valuation returned by a trigger function, a new plan is added to the list of *relevant plans*. Each relevant plan is represented by a *plan* record along with a valuation for the parameter variables.

(4) Next, the context function of each relevant plan is evaluated. The result of each function application is either an extended valuation, possibly binding additional variables, or the failure to compute a valuation that is consistent with both the trigger and the context. For each remaining valuation, a new plan is added to the set of applicable plans. Each applicable plan is represented by a set of variable bindings along with a *plan* record.

(5) The plan selection function is applied to the list of applicable plans. The result obtained is an applicable plan that represents the new intended means to be added to the list of intentions.

(6) The intention selection function is applied to the list of executable intentions. It selects the intention that will be executed in the current reasoning cycle. Note that, as specified by the Jason formal semantics, this intention may not necessarily be the intention that contains the intended means for the event processed at the beginning of the reasoning cycle.

(7) The first remaining formula of the plan that is at the head of the chosen intention is evaluated. The result of evaluating a function may generate new internal or external events, e.g. by adding a new belief to the belief base.

(8) The new events generated are added to the list of events stored in the *agentRationale* record representing the state of affairs of the agent. If the formula evaluated was the last one appearing in a plan body, the process implementing the plan body terminates. If, moreover, the plan that finished was the last remaining plan in the corresponding intention, the intention itself is removed from the list of executable intentions.

(9) Finally a new reasoning cycle is started by repeating steps 1-9 with the new updated *agentRationale* record.

3.7   Jason Subset Currently Supported

eJason currently supports only a subset of the Jason constructs needed to implement complex multi-agent systems. However, we foresee no major difficulties in adding the additional features not currently supported, and expect to do so in the near future. The features of the Jason language not currently supported are the following:

1. **Belief annotations.** Even though our Jason parser accepts code with belief annotations, these annotations are not taken into account when resolving plans (e.g., when checking whether a plan context is satisfied).
2. **Annotations on plan labels.** The meta-level information associated with plans is removed during the lexical analysis.
3. **Plan failure handling.** Whenever a plan fails, e.g., because test goal in the plan body cannot be successfully resolved, the whole intention that the plan belongs to is dropped. Moreover, no new event is generated as a result of the plan failure.
4. **Environment.** The environment of eJason programs is not currently modelled. Therefore, no external actions, except console output, are allowed and no perception phase is required.
5. **Distribution.** There is no support for distributed agents.
6. **Communication.** The only illocutionary forces that are properly processed are *tell*, *untell* and *achieve*. Messages with any other kind of illocutionary force are ignored and dropped from the mailbox of the agent.
7. **Library of internal actions.** The only internal actions considered are ".print" (to display text on the standard output) and ".send" (to interact with other agents in the same multiagent system).
8. **Unbound plan triggers.** The trigger of every plan must be either an atom or a predicate (whose parameters do not need to be bound) but never a variable.
9. **Decomposition operator.** The binary operator "=..", used to (de)construct literals (i.e. predicates and terms), is not accepted by the parser.
10. **Code order.** The grammar accepted by the parser is similar to the simplified one presented in Appendix 1 of [9]. Therefore, the source code to be translated must state first the initial beliefs and rules, followed by the initial goals and, finally, the different plans.
11. **Multiagent system architecture.** There is only one kind of agent infrastructure implemented. It runs all the agents in a multiagent system within the same Erlang node.

4   Experiments

To test the performance of eJason, we use two simple Jason programs. The first is the counter example of Fig. 2 in Section 3.1. The second represents an agent that outputs two greeting messages on the console. To add some complexity to the behaviour, the contents of those messages are obtained from the set of beliefs of the agent using queries which have both bound and unbound variables. The examples were run using different numbers of homogeneous agents, i.e., all the agents behaved the same. All of them were run under Ubuntu Linux version 10.04 in a computer with two 2.53 GHz processors. With these examples, we want to measure the execution time of the generated MAS and their scalability with respect to the number of agents in the system.

Table 1. Execution times for the counter multiagent system

Number of Agents	Jason Execute Time (magnitude)	eJason Execution Time (milliseconds)
10	milliseconds	2
100	milliseconds	46
1000	seconds	181
10000	minutes	1916
100000	not measurable	18674
500000	not measurable	97086
800000	not measurable	165522

Table 2. Execution times for the greetings multiagent system

Number of Agents	Jason Execute Time (magnitude)	eJason Execution Time (milliseconds)
10	milliseconds	1
100	milliseconds	15
1000	seconds	143
10000	minutes	1550
100000	not measurable	154415
300000	not measurable	484371

The preliminary results are presented in Tables 1 and 2.

The results indicate that the multiagent systems generated by eJason scale to some hundreds of thousands of agents with an average execution time of a few seconds. Regarding the multiagents systems generated by Java-based Jason, we can see that they required more time to execute (the exact time quantities could not be precisely measured) and that it was not possible to increase the number of agents over a few thousands (in the cases labeled as *not measurable* a java.lang.OutOfMemoryError exception was raised).

Clearly these are only preliminary findings as more thorough benchmarking is needed.

5   Conclusions and Future Work

In this paper we have described a prototype implementation of eJason, an implementation of Jason, an agent-oriented programming language, in the Erlang concurrent functional programming language. The implementation was rather straightforward due to the similarities of Jason and Erlang. eJason is able to generate Erlang code for a significant subset of Jason. Early results are promising, as the multiagent systems running under the Erlang runtime system can make use of the Erlang lightweight processes to compose systems of thousands of agents, where the process generation, scheduling, and communication introduce a negligible overhead. We also describe and motivate some of the implementation decisions taken during the design and implementation phases, such as e.g. the use of the ERESYE tool during an early stage and its later replacement.

Clearly, the similarities between the capabilities of agents and the Erlang processes are many, with the exception of the support for programming rational reasoning in Jason. We believe that the existence of eJason can help attract Erlang programmers to the MAS community, by providing them a convenient and largely familiar platform in which to program rational agents, while being able to implement the rest (adapting interpreter meta behaviour, and actuators for the environment) in Erlang itself. Moreover we believe that the MAS community can benefit from having access to the efficient concurrency and distribution capabilities of Erlang, while maintaining backward compatibility with legacy code, and without the need to develop a new agent-based language.

Clearly, as eJason is still a prototype, there are numerous areas for future work and improvement. The subset of Jason implemented at the moment is quite small; it is, for example, necessary to add support for belief annotations and plan labeling. Moreover, we plan to add support in eJason for robust distributed agent architectures. An essential item for near future work is the implementation of a means for agents to act on their environment. We intend to make eJason agents capable to cause changes in their environment using actions programmed either in Java or Erlang, i.e., there should be no need to rewrite the large body of existing Java code for Jason environment handling. Besides, we expect to be able to use the agent inspection mechanisms already implemented in e.g. JEdit.

Another item for future work includes prototyping extensions to Jason; we believe that eJason is a good platform on which to perform such experiments. Finally we also intend to experiment with model checking, applied on the resulting Erlang code, to verify Jason multiagent systems.

References

1. Foundation for Intelligent Physical Agents, Agent Communication Language, http://www.fipa.org/specs/fipa00061/SC00061G.html
2. Simple Agent Communication Infrastructure, http://www.lti.pcs.usp.br/saci/
3. Armstrong, J.: Programming Erlang: Software for a concurrent world. The Pragmatic Bookshelf (2007)
4. Armstrong, J., Virding, R., Williams, M.: Use of Prolog for developing a new programming language. In: Proc. of the International Conference on Practical Application of Prolog (1992)
5. Bellifemine, F., Bergenti, F., Caire, G., Poggi, A.: JADE - a Java agent development framework. In: Bordini, R.H., Dastani, M., Dix, J., El Fallah-Seghrouchni, A. (eds.) Multi-Agent Programming. Multiagent Systems, Artificial Societies, and Simulated Organizations, vol. 15, pp. 125–147. Springer (2005)
6. Bellifemine, F.L., Caire, G., Greenwood, D.: Developing Multi-Agent Systems with JADE. Wiley Series in Agent Technology. Wiley (April 2007)
7. Bordini, R.H., Hübner, J.F.: BDI agent programming in agentSpeak using *jason*. In: Toni, F., Torroni, P. (eds.) CLIMA 2005. LNCS (LNAI), vol. 3900, pp. 143–164. Springer, Heidelberg (2006)

8. Bordini, R.H., Fisher, M., Visser, W., Wooldridge, M.: Verifying multi-agent programs by model checking. Journal of Autonomous Agents and Multi-Agent Systems 12, 2006 (2006)
9. Bordini, R.H., Wooldridge, M., Hübner, J.F.: Programming Multi-Agent Systems in AgentSpeak using Jason. Wiley Series in Agent Technology. John Wiley & Sons (2007)
10. Cesarini, F., Thompson, S.: Erlang Programming. O'Reilly Media (2009)
11. Hübner, J.F.: Um modelo de reorganização de sistemas multiagentes. PhD thesis, Universidade de São Paulo, Escola Politécnica, Brazil (2003) (in Portuguese)
12. O'Brien, P.D., Nicol, R.C.: FIPA - Towards a Standard for Software Agents. BT Technology Journal 16, 51–59 (1998)
13. Rao, A.S.: AgentSpeak(L): BDI agents speak out in a logical computable language. In: Van de Velde, W., Perram, J.W. (eds.) MAAMAW 1996. LNCS, vol. 1038, pp. 42–55. Springer, Heidelberg (1996)
14. Rao, A.S., Georgeff, M.P.: BDI agents: From theory to practice. In: Proceedings of the first Interntional Conference on Multi-Agent Systems, ICMAS 1995, pp. 312–319 (1995)
15. Di Stefano, A., Gangemi, F., Santoro, C.: ERESYE: artificial intelligence in erlang programs. In: Sagonas, K.F., Armstrong, J. (eds.) Erlang Workshop, pp. 62–71. ACM (2005)
16. Wooldridge, M., Jennings, N.R.: Intelligent agents: Theory and practice. Knowledge Engineering Review 10(2), 115–152 (1995)
17. Wooldridge, M.: Reasoning about rational agents. MIT Press (2000)

Conceptual Integration of Agents with WSDL and RESTful Web Services

Lars Braubach and Alexander Pokahr

Distributed Systems and Information Systems
Computer Science Department, University of Hamburg
Vogt-Kölln-Str. 30, 22527 Hamburg, Germany
{braubach,pokahr}@informatik.uni-hamburg.de

Abstract. Agent communication has been standardized by FIPA in order to ensure interoperability of agent platforms. In practice only few deployed agent applications exist and agent technology remains a niche technology that runs its own isolated technology stack. In order to facilitate the integration of agents with well-established and used technologies the connection of agents with web services plays an important role. This problem has traditionally been tackled by creating translation elements that accept FIPA or web service requests as input and produce the opposite as output. In this paper we will show how a generic integration of web services can be achieved for agents that follow our active components approach. Active components allow encapsulating agent behavior in black box components that may act as service providers and consumers with explicit service interfaces. Thus, the integration approach will directly make use of these services. Concretely, the presented approach aims at answering two important questions. First, how can specific functionality of an existing agent system be made available to non-agent systems and users? Second, how can an agent system seamlessly integrate existing non agent functionality? The first aspect relates to the task of service publication while the latter refers to external service invocation. In this paper a generic conceptual approach for both aspects will be presented and it will be further shown how a specific integration with both WSDL and RESTful web services can be achieved. Example applications will be used to illustrate the approach in more details.

1 Introduction

One prime objective of the FIPA standards is ensuring interoperability between different agent platforms by defining e.g. the message format and communication protocols. As these standards have been made over 10 years ago they could not foresee that in practice agent technology would not be adopted to a high degree so that interoperability between agent systems is not a key concern nowadays. In practice, also the need for interoperability between different kinds of technological systems was present for a long time and with web services a set of standards has emerged that is generally accepted and has already proven its usefulness within many industry projects.

M. Dastani, J.F. Hübner, and B. Logan (Eds.): ProMAS 2012, LNAI 7837, pp. 17–34, 2013.
© Springer-Verlag Berlin Heidelberg 2013

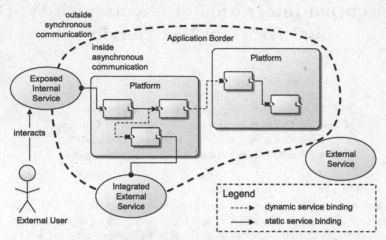

Fig. 1. Motivating scenario

From a developer perspective, standards-based interconnections are important for two main reasons (cf. Fig. 1). First, specific functionality that is needed by the software to be built could be available from another vendor as a service. Hence, it would be beneficial if it is possible to seamlessly integrate such existing functionality in the agent system and hence let it reuse this outbound knowledge. Second, it should be possible to expose functionality of a newly built application in a standardized way, such that it can be easily incorporated in other external applications. Both aspects, accessing external functionality and exposing functionality to external applications, call for *openness*, i.e. open and standardized interfaces for encapsulating the accessed or exposed functionality in programming language and middleware independent way.

This paper tackles the question, how existing web service standards and models can be integrated into agent platforms, or more specifically:

- How can (partial) functionality be exposed as web service to external system users on demand (cf. Figure 1, left)?
- How can existing web services be integrated as functionality inside of the system in an agent typical way (cf. Figure 1, bottom)?

The rest of this paper is structured as follows. Next, Section 2 gives a background of the active components programming model. The web service integration concept is described in Section 3. Illustrative examples in Section 4 show how the concept is put into practice. Related work is discussed in Section 5, before the paper closes with conclusions and an outlook in Section 7.

2   Active Components Fundamentals

The service component architecture (SCA) is a recent standard, proposed by several major industry vendors including IBM, Oracle and TIBCO, that aims at

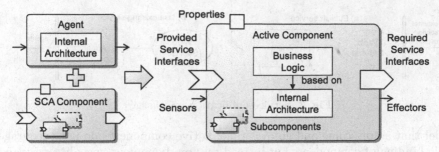

Fig. 2. Active component structure

providing a high-level design approach for distributed systems [9]. SCA fosters clearly structured and hierarchically decomposed systems by leveraging service orientation with component concepts. In an SCA design a distributed system is seen as set of interacting service providers and consumers that may reside on possibly different network nodes. Each component may act as service provider and consumer at the same time and defines its interfaces in terms of provided and required services in line with the traditional component definition of [15]. From a conceptual point of view SCA simplifies the construction of distributed systems but also has inherent limitations that delay widespread adoption.

Two aspects are especially crucial. First, even though a system is seen as set of interacting components, these components are rather statically connected with so called wires between required and provided services. The underlying assumption is that at deployment time all component instances are known and can be directly bound together. This assumption is not true for many systems with components or devices appearing or vanishing at runtime. Second, the interactions between components are supposed to be synchronous. This keeps the programming model simple but may lead to concurrency problems in case component services are accessed by multiple service requesters at the same time. Low level mechanisms like semaphores or monitors have to be employed to protect the component state from inconsistencies, but these mechanisms incur the danger of deadlocks if used not properly.

Active components build on SCA and remedy these limitations by introducing *multi-agent concepts* [3,12,13]. The general idea consists in using the actor model as fundamental world model for SCA components [8]. This means that components are independently behaving actors that do not share state and communicate only asynchronously. In this way concurrency management can be embedded into the infrastructure freeing developers from taking care of ensuring state consistency of components.[1] As it is fundamental property of the actor

---

[1] Asynchronous communication helps avoiding technical deadlocks. Of course, at the application layer circular waits can be created making the components wait on each other. In contrast, to a technical deadlock, in this case no system resources (threads) are bound to the waiting entities. Furthermore, the "application deadlocked" components remain responsive and can answer other incoming service requests or act proactively.

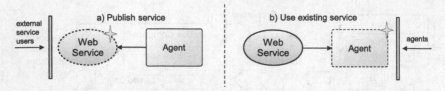

Fig. 3. Service publication and usage

model that actors come and go over time, active components do not encourage static binding of components but instead rely on dynamic service discovery and usage. In Fig. 2 an overview of the synthesis of SCA and agents to active components is shown. It can be seen that the outer structure of SCA components is kept the same and the main difference is the newly introduced internal architecture of components. The internal architecture of active components is used to encode the proactive behavior part of a component that can be specified additionally to provided service implementations. More details about the integration can be found in [3].

3   Web Service Integration Concept

In this section the overall integration concept as well as more detailed design choices will be presented. In Fig. 3 the ideas of publication and usage are sketched. The publication (cf. Fig. 3a) assumes that an agent is present that wants to make available some part of its functionality as web service for external users. The publication process thus has to ensure that a proper web service is generated and made available. In contrast, the usage approach (cf. Fig. 3b) aims at making accessible an existing web service to other agents from a multi-agent system. Here, the service functionality has to be wrapped in an agent conform manner, i.e. here a new agent is created for a service.

3.1   Making Functionality Accessible as Web Service

In order to make functionality of an application available to external system users, component services can be dynamically published at the runtime of the system. In general, it has to be determined when, where and how a service should be published. A common use case consists in performing the service publication according to the lifecycle state of the underlying component service. For this reason, per default, service publication and shutdown is automatically checked for when a component service is started or ended. The component inspects the provided service type descriptions for publish information and indirectly uses this information to publish/shutdown the service via delegation to the infrastructure. The publish information is composed of four aspects: *publish type*, *publish id*, *mapping* and *properties*. To support arbitrary kinds of service publications such as REST (Representational State Transfer) [5] and WSDL (Web Services Description Language) [17] the component uses the publish type from the service

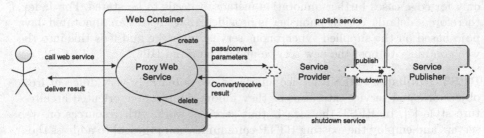

Fig. 4. Web Publishing

specification to dynamically look up a suitable service publisher (cf. Figure 4). This is done by iterating over all available service publishers until one is found that supports the requested publish type. In case a suitable publisher could be found it is instructed to publish or retreat the component service. Otherwise the publication has failed and an exception is raised within the service provider component. As an additional task the publisher may also support the advertisement of the newly deployed service within a service registry that can be accessed from external users. The service user can use the service information from the registry to locate the service and issue requests to it. The service itself acts as a proxy, which forwards the request the actual service provider and waits for a reply. The service provider executes the service domain logic and returns the service results to the proxy which in turn delivers it to the external user. It has to be noted that the incoming web service request is synchronous and therefore blocks until the internal asynchronous component service processing has been finished. In the following it will be shortly explained how WSDL and REST publishing work.

WSDL Publisher. Conceptually, a direct correspondence between methods of the component service and the operations of the WSDL service is assumed, i.e. both services are syntactically and semantically equivalent with one minor exception. The exception is that WSDL services are mostly assumed to be synchronous whereas component services follow the actor model and are asynchronous. Therefore, publishing a component service requires the original asynchronous service interface being rewritten as synchronous version. Based on this interface the proxy web service component can be automatically generated using dynamic class creation using bytecode engineering or Java dynamic proxies.

Publishing a WSDL service is supported extensively in Java environments and also directly within the JDK. Most web containers like Axis2 and JDK internal lightweight container allow publishing annotated Java pojos (plain old java objects, i.e. simple objects). The container automatically reads the Java interface of the pojo and uses the additional annotation information to produce a WSDL description of the service. Java types are mapped using JAXB[2] databinding to corresponding or newly created XML schema types. In normal cases the message signatures of the Java interface are sufficient for creating the WSDL and

---

[2] http://jaxb.java.net/

only for edge cases further annotation metadata needs to be stated. For Jadex, therefore a default WSDL publisher is provided that creates an annotated Java pojo based on the supplied synchronous service interface and feds this into the web container to host the new service under the given URL.

REST Publisher. REST service interfaces are potentially very different from object oriented service interfaces as they follow the resource oriented architecture style [5]. In REST the idea is that services work with resources on web servers and employ the existing HTTP communication protocol to address these resources via URIs. In addition, REST proposes special semantics to the different kinds of HTTP requests, e.g. a GET request should be used to retrieve a resource and PUT to create a new one. Taking this into account, a one-to-one mapping between method signatures of the object oriented service interface and REST methods is not directly possible or the ideal result.[3] Hence, the idea is to allow a very flexible mapping between both kinds of representations. In general, three different types of mappings are supported ranging from fully automatic, over semi automatic with additional mapping information to completely manual descriptions. Mapping information that needs to be generated encompasses the set of methods that should be published and for each method the following information:

- URL: i.e. the address that can be used to reach the service method. Typically, the URL of a service method is composed of two sections. The first section refers to the service itself and the second section refers to the method. This scheme treats methods as subresources of the service resource. In case multiple methods with the same name but different signatures exist it has to be ensured that different URLs are produced.
- Consumed and produced media types: REST services are intended to be usable from different clients such as browsers or other applications. These clients may produce and consume different media types such as plain text, XML or JSON. The REST service can be made accepting and producing different media types without changing the service logic by using data converters like JAXB for XML and Jackson[4] for JSON. The conversions from and to the transfer formats are done automatically via the REST container infrastructure respecting the given media types.
- Parameter types: i.e. the parameter types the rest service expects and the return value type it produces. In the simplest case these types directly

---

[3] It has to be noted that characteristics like stateless interactions and cacheability, which are often associated with REST services, do not render REST useless for implementing multi-agent interactions. First, the web resources in REST are stateful being subject of creation, manipulation and deletion. Second, cacheability means that operations should be idempotent, which is achieved when e.g. mapping parts of an interaction protocol to the HTTP request types GET and HEAD. Given that for each stateful interaction a new REST resource is created both properties can be preserved.

[4] http://jackson.codehaus.org/

correspond to the object oriented parameter types of the underlying service interface but often RESTful APIs intend to use basic string parameters in the URL encoded format of HTTP. If there is a mismatch between the object oriented and the RESTful interface, parameter mappers can be employed that transparently mask the conversion process. It has to be noted that the transformation of parameter values is n:m, meaning that n input values of the component service need to be mapped to m parameters of the REST service. Therefore, it has to be ensured that as well more than less parameters can be generated from the incoming value set. Parameter type generation is done in addition to conversions with regard to the consumed and produced media types.

– HTTP method type: REST defines specific meanings for HTTP method types like put, get, post, delete that roughly correspond to the CRUD (create, retrieve, update, delete) pattern. This means that different HTTP method types should be used depending on the action that should be executed on a web resource. Mapping these types from a method signature is hardly possible as the method semantics is not available to the mapper. Nevertheless, using other HTTP methods than originally intended is not prohibited per se. Possible negative effects that may arise concern efficiency as some of the method types are considered being idempotent so that existing HTTP caching can further be used.

The architecture of the REST publisher is more complex than the WSDL publisher. It partitions work into two phases. In the first phase the given component service interface is analyzed with respect to the methods that should be generated and how these should be represented in REST. For this purpose it is first checked if the developer provided custom mapping data via an annotated interface or a (possibly abstract) base class or if no mapping information has been given at all. If no mapping information is available, the publisher will use all interface methods and guess their REST interpretation. The same will be done for an annotated interface and all abstract methods if a base class was used. All given public non-abstract methods of a base class with REST annotations will be kept so that the user implementations are not be touched. The used heuristics for automatic method generation is very simple and tries to determine the different REST characteristics (according to the descriptions above) especially including the REST method type. To determine the REST method type the parameter and return value types are considered. As a default, the generator tries to interpret methods as GET and only assumes POST, if GET is not possible, e.g., due to complex data types, which could not be sent in GET requests. The generator is thus currently limited to using GET and POST methods and requires the developer to add specific mapping information if other types shall be used. Therefore, the generator has been developed as extension point for the REST publisher so that it can be easily exchanged with an enhanced version if necessary. Nonetheless, our experience with REST publication is that for more complicated services a dedicated mapping should be crafted manually by

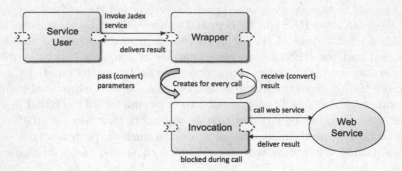

Fig. 5. Web Service Invocation

developer and the generator is mainly helpful for simple services and for rapid prototyping REST publications during manual development.

The result is a list of methods with exact descriptions how these methods should be created in REST. This list is passed on to the second stage in which a Java class is generated for the REST service via bytecode engineering. The generator first creates Java method signatures using the method name and parameter types produced in the first phase. Afterwards, it creates Java annotations for the REST specific mapping information according to the JAX-RS specification[5]. The publisher can directly pass this class to the REST container, which ensures that the service is made available.

3.2 Integrating Existing Web Services

Integrating web services aims at making usable existing functionalities as component services (cf. Fig. 5). In this way access to external functionalities can be masked and be used in the same way as other middleware services. Challenges in this integration are mainly limited to the question how an external service can be adequately mapped to the middleware and how it can be made accessible to service clients. The conceptual approach chosen is based on wrapper components, which act as internal service providers for the external functionality. A wrapper component offers the external functionality as provided service with an interface that on the one hand mimics the original service interface and on the other hand complies to the asynchronous requirements of the middleware, i.e. in the simplest case the internal interface is the asynchronous version of the external interface. The implementation of the provided service is represented by a specific forward mechanism that dispatches the call to the external web service. To resolve the synchronous/asynchronous mismatch a decoupled invocation component is used. For each service call such an invocation component is created, which is solely responsible to perform the synchronous operation. While the operation is pending the invocation component remains blocked, but as it has no other duties than performing the call this is not troublesome.

---

[5] http://jax-rs-spec.java.net/

This pattern keeps the wrapper component responsive and lets it accepting concurrent service invocations without having to wait until the previous call has returned.

WSDL Wrapper. The WSDL wrapper component heavily relies on the existing JAX-WS technology stack.[6] One core element of this stack is a tool called *wsimport* that is used to automatically generate Java data and service classes for a given WSDL URL. The generated code can directly be used to invoke the web service from Java. Based on this generated code the asynchronous service interface has to be manually defined relying on the generated data types for parameters. For this reason no further parameter mappings need to be defined. The wrapper component itself declares a provided service with this interface and uses a framework call to dynamically create the service implementation.

REST Wrapper. The REST wrapper is based on JAX-RS technology but currently does not employ automatic code generation.[7] Instead, the asynchronous component service interface has to be created manually based on the REST service documentation. The interface definition should abstract away from the REST resource architecture and give it a normal object oriented view. The mapping of the component service towards the REST service is done with a mapping file represented as annotated interface. This annotated interface contains all methods of the original service interface and adds mapping information for the same types of information that already have been used for publishing, i.e. for each method the URL for the REST call, the consumed and produced media types, parameter and result mappings as well as the HTTP method type. The wrapper component definition is done analogously to the WSDL version with one difference. Instead of using a generated service implementation, the REST wrapper uses a dynamic proxy that uses the mapping interface to create suitable REST invocations.

4   Example Applications

In this section the publish and invocation web service integration concept will be further explained by using small example applications. The domain used to show how service publication can be achieved is a simple banking service, which offers operations for account management. For simplicity reasons it has been stripped down to one method called *getAccountStatement*, which is used to fetch an account statement viable for a specifiable date range. Integration of external services is shown using a WSDL geolocation service for IP addresses and the Google REST chart API.

---

[6] http://jax-ws.java.net/

[7] Automatic code generation can only be used for REST services that supply a web application description (WADL file) of themselves that represents the pendant to the WSDL file of an XML web service. Similar to wsimport, a tool called wadl2java is available that is able to create Java classes for data types and services of the REST service. A problem is that WADL has not reached W3C standard status and also is not in widespread use in practice.

```
01:  public interface IBankingService {
02:    public IFuture<AccountStatement> getAccountStatement(Date begin, Date end);
03:  }
04:
05:  public interface IWSBankingService {
06:    public AccountStatement getAccountStatement(Date begin, Date end);
07:  }
08:
09:  @Agent
10:  @ProvidedServices(@ProvidedService(type=IBankingService.class,
11:    implementation=@Implementation($component)
12:    publish=@Publish(publishtype="ws", publishid="http://localhost:8080/banking",
13:     mapping=IWSBankingService.class)
14:  public class BankingAgent implements IBankingService {
15:    ...
16:  }
```

Fig. 6. Java code for publishing a WSDL service

4.1   WSDL Publishing

Figure 6 shows how the service publication is specified in the Jadex active components framework. The existing component service interface *IBankingService* (lines 1-3), which uses asynchronous future return values[8] (see line 2) is augmented with a synchronous interface *IWSBankingService* (lines 5-7) providing the same methods. In the component definition (lines 9-16) the declaration of the provided service (lines 10-13) is extended with the publish information (lines 12, 13) specifying the target URL and the newly defined synchronous interface (line 12). In the publish information the publish type is set to WSDL web services (*ws*). In this example, the banking service is implemented by the component itself (line 14), which is stated in the provided service declaration using the predefined variable *$component* (similar to *this* in Java).

4.2   REST Publishing

As introduced earlier, REST publishing is supported in fully automatic, semi automatic and manual modes. In Figure 7 the fully automatic variant is shown, which is similar to the WSDL variant but doesn't require a synchronous interface to be manually derived. In contrast to the example above, the publish type is set to REST services (*rs*, line 8). The fully automatic mode uses internal heuristics to generate appropriate REST methods, which is difficult in many cases. Hence, additional mapping information can be supplied in both other modes. For this purpose an annotated Java interface or (abstract) class can be employed.

---

[8] A future [14] represents the result of an asynchronous computation, i.e. the future object is immediately returned to the caller will contain the real result value when it has been computed. The caller can use the future to check if the result already has been produced or use a listener to get a notification when this happens.

```
01:  public interface IBankingService {
02:    public IFuture<AccountStatement> getAccountStatement(Date begin, Date end);
03:  }
04:
05:  @Agent
06:  @ProvidedServices(@ProvidedService(type=IBankingService.class,
07:    implementation=@Implementation($component)
08:    publish=@Publish(publishtype="rs",publishid="http://localhost:8080/banking")))
09:  public class BankingAgent implements IBankingService {
10:    ...
11:  }
```

Fig. 7. Java code for publishing a REST service

```
01:  public interface IRSBankingService {
02:    @GET
03:    @Path("getAS/")
04:    @Produces(MediaType.TEXT_HTML)
05:    @MethodMapper(value="getAccountStatement",params={Date.class, Date.class})
06:    @ParametersMapper(@Value(clazz=RequestMapper.class))
07:    @ResultMapper(@Value(clazz=BeanToHTMLMapper.class))
08:    public String getAccountStatement(Request request);
09:  }
```

Fig. 8. REST publish mapping information

In case of an interface the method signatures are enhanced with REST annotations as shown in Figure 8. It can be seen that a method *getAccountStatement()* with one parameter of type *Request* (line 8) is delegated to a component service method with the same name but other parameter types. The method mapper annotation is used to specify the target method (line 5) and additional parameter and result mapper can be added to transform the corresponding values (lines 6 and 7). In this case a request mapper is used to extract two dates from a request and the result is generated as HTML using a simple bean property mapper. This example also shows the difference between parameter and media types. The Java return type in this example is string but the additional produces annotation (line 4) tells the client that it can expect HTML.

If even more flexibility is needed, instead of an interface a class can be used (not shown). In this class it is possible to add abstract methods and annotate them in the same way as in the interface. Additionally, other non abstract methods can be implemented with arbitrary domain logic to bring about service functionalities. If no generation is wanted, the wrapper class can also be implemented completely by the programmer.

In Fig. 9 a screenshot of the banking REST web interface is shown. This web site is produced by a banking agent with a publish annotation as shown above. This interface is automatically generated by the *getServiceInfo()* method and is per default linked to the root resource URL of the service (here localhost:8080/banking1/). It can be seen that the web site contains a new part for

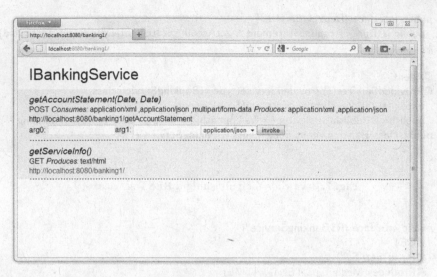

Fig. 9. Banking REST web service screenshot

```
01:  public interface IGeoIPService {
02:     public IFuture<GeoIP> getGeoIP(String ip);
03:  }
04:
05:  @Agent
06:  @ProvidedServices(@ProvidedService(type=IGeoIPService.class,
07:     implementation=@Implementation($component.createServiceImplementation(
08:     new Mapping(GeoIPService.class)))
09:  public class GeoIPAgent {
10:     ...
11:  }
```

Fig. 10. Java code for invoking a WSDL service

each service method with basic information about it, i.e. the method signature, REST call details, the URL and a form with input fields for all parameters. According to the media types the service method is able to consume a choice box is added to allow the user specifying in which format the input string shall be interpreted. This can be seen in the *getAccountStatement()* method, which accepts JSON and XML. Currently, the result value of a method call is produced in the same media type as the request but it is easily possible to add another control that allows to request the service to produce an alternative format.

4.3   WSDL Invocation

WSDL service invocation is illustrated using a geo IP service, which offers a method to determine the position of an IP address. After having generated the Java classes for data types and service using *wsimport*, based on the generated

```
01:  public interface IChartService {
02:    public IFuture<byte[]> getBarChart(int width, int height, double[][] data,
03:       String[] labels, Color[] colors);
04:  }
05:
06:  public interface IRSChartService {
07:    @GET
08:    @Path("https://chart.googleapis.com/chart/")
09:    @Produces(MediaType.APPLICATION_OCTET_STREAM)
10:    @ParametersMapper(@Value(clazz=ChartParameterMapper.class))
11:    @ResultMapper(@Value(clazz=ChartResultMapper.class))
12:    public IFuture<byte[]> getBarChart(int width, int height, double[][] data,
13:       String[] labels, Color[] colors);
14:    ...
15:  }
16:
17:  @Agent
18:  @ProvidedServices(@ProvidedService(type=IChartService.class,
19:    implementation=@Implementation($component.createServiceImplementation(
20:    IRSChartService.class))
21:  public class ChartAgent {
22:    ...
23:  }
```

Fig. 11. Java code for invoking a REST service

service interface an asynchronous version needs to be defined (cf. lines 1-3 in Figure 10). In the component declaration (lines 5-11) a provided service is specified using the asynchronous service interface (line 6) and an automatically generated implementation (lines 7-8). The framework method that is called to create the implementation takes as argument the wsimport generated service class.

4.4   Rest Invocation

REST invocation is exemplified using the Google chart API, which can be used to create chart images of different types for a given data set. The implementation is shown in Figure 11. It consists of the asynchronous service interface (lines 1-4), the REST service mapping (lines 6-13) and the chart component definition (lines 17-23). For illustration purposes the component interface is reduced to one method that can be used to create a bar chart. The method expects the width and height of the image to produce, possibly multiple data series, label texts and series colors as input and produces an png image as output. The mapping is defined within an interface called *IRSChartService* (lines 6-15). It declares that the generated REST call uses HTTP GET on the google chart URL. In addition, parameter mappers for in- and output values need to be employed (lines 10-11, mapper code not shown) as the REST API expects a specific textual encodings for the data. The component implementation is very similar to the WSDL variant with exception of the mapping definition in terms of an interface.

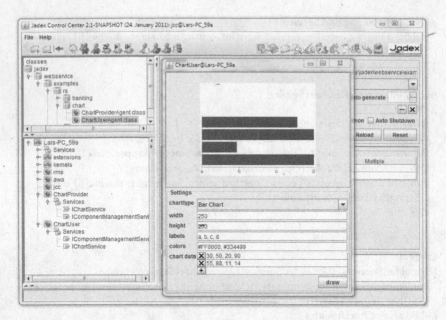

Fig. 12. Chart application screenshot

Fig. 12 shows a chart application screenshot. In the background the Jadex control center window of the platform is displayed while in the foreground the chart window is shown. The application consists of two agents. The *ChartProvider* agent that takes over the wrapper role and offers an *IChartService* instance and on the other hand the *ChartUser* agent which own the graphical user interface for entering chart requests and displaying the resulting chart graphics. On the lower left hand side of the control center the running agent instances with required and provided services are depicted. It can be seen that the *ChartProvider* offers an *IChartService* and the *ChartUser* requires an *IChartService*. The processing is done as follows. After a user has entered some configuration data in the chart window including e.g. width and height of the target image, series data, and colors, and issued a chart request via pressing the draw button, the chart user agent fetches its required chart service (which is dynamically searched on request) and calls the *getBarChart()* method. The service call is received by the user agent, which automatically transfers it to a REST call and hands it over to the external REST provider. The result is passed back to the user agent which displays the corresponding chart in the window for the user.

5   Related Work

In this section, the features of the approach proposed in this paper will be discussed with respect to the following areas of related work: 1) *programming level frameworks*, i.e. APIs and tools that ease the usage of web services from inside a general purpose programming language like Java, 2) *middleware extensions* that aim at a conceptual integration between web services and agent middleware and 3) *SCA standards and implementations* that, although they don't focus on asynchronous programming, are an important conceptual inspiration of this work.

The approach presented in this paper is unique with respect to the simultaneous conceptual treatment of both directions of web service integration: publication and access. Treating both the same way has advantages e.g. with regard to developers only having to learn one API for both aspects. Programming level frameworks such as JAX-WS and Axis2[9] also follow this direction to the advantage of the programmer. E.g. in JAX-WS the developer can use the same techniques to generate Java classes and interfaces from an existing WSDL or vice versa, regardless if she wants to publish or access a web service. Interestingly, the conceptual integrations of *middleware extensions* focus usually on only one aspect. E.g. in the area of agent platforms, [6,11,2] are examples for dealing with exposing agent services as web services. On the contrary [16,10] discuss web service invocation from agents. The ProActive middleware [1] provides support both for web service invocation as well as web service publication. Yet, only the publication part provides a conceptual integration into the ProActive programming model by allowing to directly expose methods of ProActive objects as web services. The invocation part on the other hand is merely a set of utility classes comparable to other programming level frameworks. In [7] a transparent usage of web services as interoperability enabler for agents is fostered. They present an extension for JADE, which is based on the idea of having agents with a head and body, meaning that the cognitive agent part can be complemented with a web service body. This leads to an infrastructure, in which communication of agents is conceptually based on FIPA ACL, but can be technically transformed to web service invocations via SOAP. In addition, the approach also aims at bridging organizational borders by supporting content semantics via ontologies. Unlike the aforementioned approaches, the SCA standards treat service publication and invocation at the same conceptual level. Due to the prevalent synchronous programming model, SCA lacks an additional wrapper level for decoupling caller and callee during service invocation or execution.

Another important aspect of the approach presented here is the unified treatment of WSDL and RESTful web services. Most existing integration work is devoted to WSDL web services, e.g. [6,11,10,16] in the agent area and also implemented in ProActive. The main reason for this is probably the explicitly typed nature of the WSDL that lends itself to automatic code generation. REST on the other hand is much more free in the way a service is defined and used and thus requires more manual implementation or mapping specification. Publication of REST services is treated in [2], although they only support a simplistic mapping of only one operation per service. Similar to the conceptual middleware extensions, most programming level frameworks focus on one type of web service, with many standards (JAX-WS and JAX-RS) and non-standards based implementations being available for each type. One exception is Apache CXF[10],

---

[9] http://axis.apache.org/axis2/java/core/
[10] http://cxf.apache.org/

that incorporates APIs for RESTful as well as WSDL services. Yet, CXF does not aim at unification for the programmer, but at implementing the different available standards. The SCA standards only deal with WSDL web services and define a *ws* binding for provided and required SCA component services. Some available SCA implementation like Tuscany[11] and Frascati[12] additionally offer proprietary support for RESTful services. Yet, both require JAX-RS annotations in the service implementations that hinder a transparent usage of the same component functionality as WSDL and REST service.

In summary, the approach presented in this paper picks up earlier work on web services support for agent platforms, incorporates and extends existing ideas from SCA and combines a unified treatment of REST and WSDL with a conceptual model for an agent-style asynchronous provision and invocation of services.

6   Discussion and Current Limitations

In this paper a solution for the publication and invocation of web services has been presented. In constrast to other agent approaches it is not based on message conversions between an agent language (FIPA) and a web service language (SOAP or HTTP in case of REST). Instead, due to the more object oriented nature of active components, it becomes possible to directly use Java interfaces as service specifications, which closes the gap between services and agents to a large extent and is an improvement of the status-quo with respect to usability from a developer's perspective. The conceptual approach resembles the SCA proposal in this respect closely and extends it for agents. On basis of the service interfaces different annotations have been conceived making publication and invocation of web services a simple and rather descriptive task. Despite its advantages, the approach is not easily transferrable to other purely message based agent platforms like JADE. Although, the general ideas of publication and invocation could be kept, the explicit object oriented service representation is missing and an additional API layer would have to be introduced that is able to convert between service invocations and the agent's internal architecture. E.g. for JADE agents, the publication of a web service could mean that a corresponding agent behavior is instantiated for each service invocation. The behavior could then be implemented, like other JADE agent behaviors, as a simple Java class that encodes the agent's execution logic for reacting to the service invocation.

The approach in this paper also has some limitations that represent interesting topics of possible further work. With respect to service publication currently only service publishers exist that are able to publish a service on a web container that resides at the same host as the agent platform. In many business scenarios, it would be desirable having publishers that can deploy a service on a dedicated web container as in many cases web access is restricted from outbound computers to a specific web server instance. Another limitation consists in using only

---

[11] http://tuscany.apache.org/
[12] http://wiki.ow2.org/frascati/Wiki.jsp?page=FraSCAti

synchronous web services as support for asynchronous solutions is steadily increasing. Ultimate goal would be preserving the asynchronous service interfaces so that no substantial difference between Jadex and web service inferfaces exist any longer. Recent developements such as Ajax, Comet, Servet-API 3.0 etc. underline that in the web area stronger support for long lasting and asynchronous interactions gains traction. Concretely, regarding WSDL services, with JAX WS 2.0 it is already possible to automatically generate asynchronous service methods and also create asynchronous clients. Similarily, with the upcoming JAX RS 2.0 specification the same will be supported for for Java REST services.

7   Conclusions and Outlook

Web services are important for interoperability and extensibility as they allow integrating external functionality into applications as well as developed functionality being integrated in external applications. This paper focuses on web services support for agent platforms.

The proposed model provides a conceptual integration for both the publication of application functionality as web service as well as the invocation of external web services. To avoid dependencies between the implementation of application functionality and specific web services technology such as WSDL or REST, the model incorporates two important abstraction layers. First, the wrapper and invocation agents map a synchronous external web service interface to an asynchronous one and register the mapped service description transparently inside the middleware, such that external and internal services can be access in the same way. Second, publish services take care of exposing internal services as external web services and different publish services for REST and WSDL technology allow the same internal services to be transparently published using these different approaches.

The integration concept has been implemented as part of the open source active components platform Jadex[13]. Besides the simple examples presented in this paper, the web services integration is currently being put into practice in a commercial setting that deals with business intelligence processes and activities in heterogeneous company networks [4].

References

1. Baduel, L., Baude, F., Caromel, D., Contes, A., Huet, F., Morel, M., Quilici, R.: Programming, Deploying, Composing, for the Grid. In: Grid Computing: Software Environments and Tools. Springer (January 2006)
2. Betz, T., Cabac, L., Wester-Ebbinghaus, M.: Gateway architecture for Web-based agent services. In: Klügl, F., Ossowski, S. (eds.) MATES 2011. LNCS, vol. 6973, pp. 165–172. Springer, Heidelberg (2011)

---

[13] http://jadex.sourceforge.net/

3. Braubach, L., Pokahr, A.: Addressing challenges of distributed systems using active components. In: Brazier, F.M.T., Nieuwenhuis, K., Pavlin, G., Warnier, M., Badica, C. (eds.) Intelligent Distributed Computing V. SCI, vol. 382, pp. 141–151. Springer, Heidelberg (2011)
4. Braubach, L., Pokahr, A.: Developing Distributed Systems with Active Components and Jadex. Scalable Computing: Practice and Experience 13(2), 3–24 (2012)
5. Fielding, R.T.: Architectural styles and the design of network-based software architectures. PhD thesis (2000) AAI9980887
6. Greenwood, D., Buhler, P., Reitbauer, A.: Web service discovery and composition using the web service integration gateway. In: Proceedings of the IEEE International Conference on e-Technology, e-Commerce, and e-Services (EEE 2005), pp. 789–790. IEEE Computer Society (2005)
7. Karaenke, P., Schuele, M., Micsik, A., Kipp, A.: Inter-organizational interoperability through integration of multiagent, web service, and semantic web technologies. In: Fischer, K., Müller, J.P., Levy, R. (eds.) ATOP 2009 and ATOP 2010. LNBIP, vol. 98, pp. 55–75. Springer, Heidelberg (2012)
8. Karmani, R., Shali, A., Agha, G.: Actor frameworks for the jvm platform: a comparative analysis. In: Proceedings of the 7th International Conference on Principles and Practice of Programming in Java, PPPJ 2009, pp. 11–20. ACM, New York (2009)
9. Marino, J., Rowley, M.: Understanding SCA (Service Component Architecture), 1st edn. Addison-Wesley Professional (2009)
10. Nguyen, X.T., Kowalczyk, R.: WS2JADE: Integrating web service with jade agents. In: Huang, J., Kowalczyk, R., Maamar, Z., Martin, D., Müller, I., Stoutenburg, S., Sycara, K. (eds.) SOCASE 2007. LNCS, vol. 4504, pp. 147–159. Springer, Heidelberg (2007)
11. Overeinder, B., Verkaik, P., Brazier, F.: Web service access management for integration with agent systems. In: Proceedings of the 2008 ACM Symposium on Applied Computing (SAC), Fortaleza, Ceara, Brazil, March 16-20, pp. 1854–1860 (2008)
12. Pokahr, A., Braubach, L.: Active Components: A Software Paradigm for Distributed Systems. In: Proceedings of the 2011 IEEE/WIC/ACM International Conference on Intelligent Agent Technology (IAT 2011). IEEE Computer Society (2011)
13. Pokahr, A., Braubach, L., Jander, K.: Unifying agent and component concepts - jadex active components. In: Dix, J., Witteveen, C. (eds.) MATES 2010. LNCS, vol. 6251, pp. 100–112. Springer, Heidelberg (2010)
14. Sutter, H., Larus, J.: Software and the concurrency revolution. ACM Queue 3(7), 54–62 (2005)
15. Szyperski, C., Gruntz, D., Murer, S.: Component Software: Beyond Object-Oriented Programming, 2nd edn. ACM Press and Addison-Wesley (2002)
16. Varga, L.Z., Hajnal, Á.: Engineering web service invocations from agent systems. In: Mařík, V., Müller, J.P., Pěchouček, M. (eds.) CEEMAS 2003. LNCS (LNAI), vol. 2691, pp. 626–635. Springer, Heidelberg (2003)
17. World Wide Web Consortium (W3C). Web Services Description Language (WSDL) (June 2007)

Agent Programming Languages Requirements for Programming Autonomous Robots

Pouyan Ziafati[1,3], Mehdi Dastani[3],
John-Jules Meyer[3], and Leendert van der Torre[1,2]

[1] SnT, University of Luxembourg
[2] CSC, University of Luxembourg
[3] Intelligent Systems Group, Utrecht University
{pouyan.ziafati,leon.vandertorre}@uni.lu,
{M.M.Dastani,J.J.C.Meyer}@uu.nl

Abstract. This paper presents four requirements for BDI-based agent programming languages to facilitate the implementation of autonomous robot control systems. The first requirement is to support the integration of these languages with robotic frameworks. The second requirement is real-time reaction and response to events. The real-time reactivity problem in the BDI architecture is discussed and a distributed BDI architecture is proposed to approach this problem. The third requirement is to extend the BDI architecture with sensory management components for the management of sensory events and detecting complex events. The fourth requirement is the representation of complex plans and the coordination of the parallel execution of plans. These requirements are derived from an extensive survey of current autonomous robot programming tools and architectures and a study of a home-care application scenario for the NAO robot.

Keywords: Agent Programming Languages, Cognitive Robotics.

1 Introduction

Recent advances in robotic perception, actuation and software engineering have enabled robots to perform complex tasks such as baking a cake [3]. However, to achieve complex goals in an unstructured and dynamic environment, a robot needs a deliberative behavior to reason about its objectives to select appropriate actions. Various agent programming languages (APLs) such as 2APL [10], AgentSpeak(L), [1] and Jason [5] (see [4] for a survey) have been developed to implement autonomous systems with deliberative behaviors. Deliberative behavior in these languages is implemented based on the BDI (Belief-Desire-Intention) architecture [29,30] inspired by the BDI model of human practical reasoning [21]. However, the application domains of such languages so far have been mainly limited to cognitive software agents in simulated toy examples. Current agent programming languages reveal various shortcomings when applied in robotics [20,33].

M. Dastani, J.F. Hübner, and B. Logan (Eds.): ProMAS 2012, LNAI 7837, pp. 35–53, 2013.
© Springer-Verlag Berlin Heidelberg 2013

The recent availability of affordable autonomous robots such as NAO humanoid robot[1] and open-source robotic frameworks such as ROS[2] facilitates research on APLs in autonomous robotics. Robotics provides an important and challenging domain to research on design and development of APLs. Moreover, APLs might facilitate the development of autonomous robots beyond the support provided by current robot programming languages. Our research aim is to provide a systematic support of autonomous robot programming for APLs in general and for 2APL in particular. We work on a home-care application scenario for the NAO robot as a test bed.

This paper discusses the problem of developing a robot's control (i.e. decision-making) component in APLs to control and coordinate the robot software processes. It contributes by presenting four requirements for APLs to support the implementation of a robot's control component. The first requirement is related to the integration of a control component, developed in an APL, in a robot's software framework. An APL should support the interaction of the robot's control component with its other components. ROS is introduced as today's de facto standard robotic framework to be supported by APLs. The second requirement addresses how APLs can support the development of a control component operating in real-time. Distributed BDI architecture is proposed to approach the reactivity problem in BDI architecture. The third requirement discusses the support needed from APLs to manage and process sensory events received by the robot's control component. The fourth requirement presents the need for the representation of complex plans, to synchronize the execution of a robot's actions in complex arrangements, and for coordinating the parallel execution of the robot's plans including resource management and handling conflicting plans.

Exploring our home-care robot application scenario presented in section 2, we faced the problems of real-time control, sensory event management, plan execution control and integration with other robot's software components as basic shortcomings of current APLs to support programming autonomous robots. To provide a systematic analysis of APLs' requirements for autonomous robot programming, this paper provides a through survey of various robot programming tools and architectures. Generalizing from the approaches taken by current robotic programming tools and architectures, the paper presents a set of requirements to address the above problems in APLs. The presented requirements are limited to single robotic applications. Multi-robot scenarios impose other requirements on APLs for coordination, cooperation and communication between robots which have been left for further research.

The remainder of this paper is organized as follows. Section 2 presents a running example. Section 3 discusses the integration with robotic frameworks and introduces ROS. Section 4 is devoted to the discussion of real-time reactivity. Section 5 presents the need to support the development of sensory management components to process sensory events. Section 6 discusses the required plan execution control capabilities. Section 7 Concludes the paper.

---

[1] http://www.aldebaran-robotics.com/en/
[2] http://www.ros.org

2 Running Example

Araz and Mori are old and have Alzheimer. Moreover, Mori is under medication. To help them living easier and increase their safety, their children have bought them a NAO robot personal assistant. NAO helps them by performing the following tasks:

1. T1: To remind Mori to take drug A every morning at 10 am. To remind Mori, NAO calls, "Take drug A Mori". When NAO hears the response back, "OK, I will take A", it considers the task as successfully finished.
2. T2: To check if drug A is finished. Drug A's color is red and is placed in a white box. NAO should check the box every afternoon to see if there are enough A in the box. If drug A is finished, NAO asks Mori if he has already ordered. Otherwise, it orders itself by sending an email to drugstore.
3. T3: To open the door if a visitor rings the bell. NAO checks the visitor face from the door camera; if it recognizes the face, it opens the door by pressing the OPEN_DOOR_BUTTON. Otherwise it informs Araz and Mori by calling, "A stranger is behind the door". In this case, the task is finished when NAO hears the response back, "Ok, I check it".
4. T4: To frequently check if there is any trash (a black cube) on the table and throw it to the trash can.
5. T5: To remind Araz and Mori about the places of their personal objects. E.g. Mori goes in front of the NAO's camera or introduces himself by saying, "It's Mori" and asks NAO, "Remember my key is on the desk". He can later ask NAO, "Where is my key?". NAO should answer, "On the desk".
6. T6: To bring drinks from the kitchen table on users requests.
7. T7: If Araz or Mori calls, "Help!", NAO should call for emergency assistance by pressing a RED_BUTTON placed in the the room. Also in T1 and T3, If NAO communicates with Araz/Mori for 3 times and does not hear the response back, NAO calls for emergency assistance as it might be sign of a dangerous situation.

2.1 Analysis of the Example

Implementation of the NAO control component poses various challenges to APLs.
– Integration with Robotic Software: the NAO software composed of many components such as face-recognition, voice-recognition, object-recognition, move-base and grasp-controller. The control component should interact with these components to receive sensory data and to configure and control their operations.
– Sensory Data Management: the control component receives streams of events such as recognized faces, phrases and objects, and events of the robot's and users' locations in time. Such sensory data should be managed and processed to extract relevant information to the control component operations.
– Plan Execution Control: Some NAO's plans such as going and checking if there are enough drug A in the box requires complex sequential and parallel arrangements of action executions synchronized in time and based on

conditional and floating contingencies. Moreover, plans such as helping the user and serving drinks are conflicting and cannot be executed in parallel. NAO's resources should be managed, conflicts between plans should be resolved based on plan priorities, and the failure, suspension or abortion of a plan should be properly handled.

– Real-Time Reactivity: in addition to scheduling plans based on their priorities and deadlines, the control component should react to events in real-time. E.g. It should recognize the user help request and react to it within a second.

3   Integration with Robotic Frameworks

A robot's software functional layer is composed of a large number of components to provide different robot's action and perception capabilities and processing algorithms such as image processing, path planning and motion control. In order to cope with ever growing scale and scope of robotic software, a wide variety of robotic frameworks has been developed to facilitate the development, re-use and maintainability of the functional layer modules [19,16]. Advantages of these frameworks include: providing standard interfaces for accessing heterogeneous robotic hardwares; facilitating robotic software development and reuse by component based software development technique; providing software development tools such as programming environments; and providing open-source repositories of robotic softwares.

A robot's control component developed in an APL needs to interact with functional layer modules to receive sensory data and to control and coordinate their operations. To facilitate the use of APLs for developing robotic control systems, these languages should support the programming of a control component interactions with functional layer modules developed in robotic frameworks. This requires suitable interfaces to integrate with existing robotic frameworks. Such interfaces ideally provide built-in support for communication and control mechanisms of robotic frameworks in general, and in particular ROS which has become the de facto standard open-source robotic framework.

ROS (Robot Operating System)[34] is a flexible framework for developing a robotic functional layer. The ROS repository has an ever increasing number of state-of-the-art software packages for interfacing various robotic hardware, and for performing different robotic tasks such as SLAM, image processing, etc. Providing access to such advanced robotic software packages significantly eases the rapid prototyping and development of complex robotic applications. Using ROS, functional layer modules (i.e. nodes) can be developed in different languages such as C++, Python and Java. These modules can be started, killed, and restarted at runtime and communicate with each other in a peer-to-peer fashion. Several different styles of communication between modules are provided, including synchronous service based (i.e. request/reply) interaction, asynchronous publish-subscriber based streaming of data, and key-value based storage/retrieval of data on/from a central server. ROS modules communicate by exchanging messages based on a simple standard language similar to C language data structures.

ROS supports robotic simulators such as Stage, Gazebo and MORSE. Moreover ROS has been integrated with many other robotic frameworks such as Open-RAVE, Orocos, and Player.

To integrate with ROS, we have developed an environment interface for 2APL which facilitates the implementation of interacting with ROS components using ROS communication mechanisms. We have used ROS to create a functional layer for NAO, providing basic robotic capabilities such as face recognition, voice recognition and a number of high-level actions such as sit-down(), stand-up(), turn-neck(O) and walk-to(X,Y). Using 2APL and ROS, we have developed a demo application in which movements of NAO are controlled by voice. Also NAO can be commanded to remember the face of a user and whenever a user greets NAO, if NAO recognizes the user's face, it greets the user by his/her name.

4 Real-Time Reactivity

Providing a proper balance between deliberation and reaction has been always a major concern in research on robotic control systems [12,22,32]. On the one hand, a complex deliberation capability is desired for an autonomous robot to generate plans to achieve its goals, taking into account its limited resources, and on the other hand, it requires a time-bounded reactivity to events from its dynamic environment. Time-bounded reactivity to events can be essential for a robot's safety, its functionalities and the safety of its environment. Similar to the work of Ingrand and Coutance [18], the real-time properties we consider for a BDI control component are the reaction time (i.e. the maximum delay between the arrival of an event to the control component and when the control component takes it into account), and the response time (i.e. the maximum delay between the event arrival and when the execution of its corresponding plan is finished or rejected).

The real-time control problem of our concern here is not the real-time low-level actuation control such as a robot's end-effector trajectory tracking. Such real-time behavior is expected from the robot's functional layer. However, the real-time operation and responsiveness of the robot's control layer, controlling and coordinating the functional layer, is important as well.

Example 1. Consider the case that NAO's control component should react to the user's help request within a second from receiving such a request. It would be unacceptable if the NAO would respond to a request only after finishing its current task, or more generally would react with a long delay.

This section discusses how the reactivity problem is addressed in various robotic architectures and provides an insight about how to approach this issue in the BDI architecture.

4.1 Sense-Plan-Act

In the BDI deliberation cycle, it is desirable to update beliefs with the new information (i.e. percepts) made available during the last cycle, to process events and goals to choose the best course of plans to follow, and to execute the plans. If each deliberation cycle processes all available percepts, events and goals and executes all generated plans, the BDI architecture resembles much the sense-plan-act paradigm which was the base of early examples of robot control architectures such as Shakey [26]. The sense-plan-act architecture embeds the deliberative component of a robot at the heart of the robot's control loop. The problem is that in dynamic environments, a generated plan might become invalid before the plan can be fully executed. Moreover, while a robot is deliberating, it is unable to react to events.

To decrease the reaction time in BDI architecture, one could apply a selection function to process only a subset of input events in each deliberation cycle. However, this can lead to the starvation of some events, if other events preferred by such a selection function occur in some high frequency. One could also execute only a subset of actions of generated plans in each cycle. However this can not be an efficient strategy and may lead to the starvation of plans due to the deliberation cycle computational cost. Moreover, even the time needed for executing a single blocking external action might be long enough to pose an unacceptable increase in the deliberation cycle reaction time.

4.2   Behavior-Based

Following the failure of the sense-plan-act paradigm in controlling robots and pioneered by the Brooks' subsumption architecture [6], behavior-based robotics aims to drive a robot's control behavior without an explicit representation of the robot's world model. In this paradigm, rather than having a planning capability or an explicit goal-oriented behavior, a robot's behavior is emerged as the sum result of a set of concurrent and distributed behaviors.

Although behavior-based robotics has shown to be successful in programming complex robots, the control and coordination problem of the concurrent and possibly competing behaviors in such architectures is still an open challenge. To tackle this problem, state of the art behavior-based architectures such as iB2C [28] and DBN [23] provide different action selection mechanisms and modularization techniques. This allows creating modules of hierarchies of behaviors implementing a robot's high-level behaviors. However, these works do not address how the possible conflicts between the behaviors in lower-levels of the hierarchies of different high-level behaviors can be efficiently resolved, which in turn decreases the re-usability of behavior modules when to be executed concurrently. Moreover, the lack of explicit representation of the state in a robot's program reduces its readability and makes its debugging difficult. Although much can be learned from behavior-based robotics, specially for developing a robot's functional layer, the application of such approach in building autonomous robots with complex conflicting goals is in question and hence it is not further discussed in this paper.

4.3 Three Layered Architecture

To provide a deliberation capability and at the same time preserving reactivity, robotic research has come up with different hybrid architectures. Perhaps the most well known and used hybrid architecture is the classic three layered architecture [12,17]. This architecture is composed of 3 components. A functional component interfacing with hardware and providing low-level perception and action capabilities. A deliberative component producing plans to achieve a robot's goals and supervising the temporal execution of plans. Finally, an executive (i.e. sequencer) which resides between the other two and its main functionality is context-dependent execution of plans generated by the deliberative component. It refines plans into low-level actions that can be executed to control modules of the functional component, reacts to events and provides limited monitoring and plan failure recovery mechanisms.

The design principle behind the three layered architecture is to encapsulate the time-consuming deliberation processes into a deliberative component and increase reactiveness by providing a separate executive component with a much faster reaction time than that of the deliberative component. However, as mentioned in [22], the use of different models, syntax and semantics in different layers leads to some design and implementation issues. Firstly, the redundancy of maintaining common information in separate worldmodels in deliberative and executive components causes additional overhead in maintaining the system and can lead to inconsistencies between the two. Secondly, diagnostics of plan failures can be difficult as the deliberative component might not have relevant information about the failure causes. Thirdly, the plan execution might be less efficient because the executive does not have a global view of the plan. Due to these and other reasons, it is desirable to avoid the decomposition of the control layer into heterogeneous components.

4.4 Distributed Control Architectures

To address the problem of heterogeneous control components in hybrid architectures, state of the art research on robotic control architectures proposes different approaches to develop a distributed control layer under a unified framework, two representatives of such are described below.

T-REX. T-REX [32] provides a unified framework for interleaved deliberation (i.e. planning) and execution (i.e. sensing and action). T-REX control architecture comprises a set of coordinated concurrent control loops named reactors, and a functional layer encapsulating a robot low-level functionalities. Reactors maintain their own view of the world and have their own control functionalities and temporal properties (i.e. lookahead window for deliberation and deliberation latency), therefore allow for partitioning a control problem in both functional and temporal horizons. T-REX has a central and explicit notion of time which allows execution of all reactors to be synchronized by an internal clock, ensuring the current state of the control system to be kept consistent and complete.

The unit of time in T-REX is a tick, defined in external units on a per application basis. A deliberation time for each reactor in T-REX is bounded by its own deliberation latency, which is defined as a number of ticks. When a deliberation requires more than one tick, it should be defined as a proper sequence of steps to allow for interleaving synchronization (i.e. information exchange) in each tick.

ContrACT. The programming model of ContrACT [27] decomposes a robot control software into a set of controllable modules. Modules are independent real-time software tasks, which, depending on their types, use different communication models such as blocking/non-blocking and publish-subscribe/request-reply to communicate with each other. Some modules are reactive to events they receive, named asynchronous, and others are executed periodically, named synchronous. There is also a single scheduler module, implementing a scheduling algorithm to schedule the synchronous modules according to a set of constraints defined on the module itself (e.g. duration of the execution) and on composition of modules (e.g. precedence constraints, shared resources mutual exclusion, etc). To achieve this scheduling, the scheduler module works with operating system priorities and activation requests sent to modules.

4.5   Real-Time APLs

This section discusses the real-time properties of AgentSpeak(RT) [39] as of the state of the art research on real-time agent programming languages. However, the presented arguments are general and similarly applicable to other works such as PRS [18]. AgentSpeak(RT) extends an agent's intentions (i.e. generated plans) with deadlines, specifying the time by which the agent should respond to events, and with priorities, specifying the relative importance of responding to particular events. In each deliberation cycle, the agent commits to a priority-maximal set of intentions which is a maximally feasible set of intentions while preferring higher priority intentions.

The deliberation cycle of AgentSpeak(RT) consists of the sequential application of the following four functions. The $evt()$ function generates a set of events based on the agent's percepts P and external goals G received during the last cycle. For each of these events, the $opt()$ function generates a set of applicable plans and chooses one of them. The $sched()$ function merges the new generated plans and existing plans and returns a set of feasible plans in deadline order. Finally, the $exec()$ function executes the first action of the first plan in the schedule. Under certain conditions, it can be shown that the execution time of the AgentSpeak(RT)'s deliberation cycle is bounded by a constant δ_c. The upper-bound on the deliberation cycle depends on different factors including the maximum number of events that can be generated by $evt()$ and the maximum expected execution time (i.e. t_{max}) of any action in the agent program.

The upper-bound on the AgentSpeak(RT) reaction time is at least δ_c as an event (e.g. an external goal) which arrives just after starting the evaluation of $evt()$ could be only recognized (i.e. read from the input buffer) after the current deliberation cycle is passed. This means all events caused from the percepts and goals received during the last cycle should be processed, corresponding plans should be generated, selected and scheduled, and an action is executed before recognizing the new arrived event. The question is what if an important event should be serviced in a short time such that having the possible delay of δ_c for its recognition is unacceptable? The following presents two initial ideas to approach the problem of real-time reactivity in APLs.

4.6   Interrupting the Deliberation Cycle

To increase the reactivity, one possible approach is to interrupt the deliberation cycle from its normal operation on arrival of an event. As described above, the upper bound on the reaction time is directly related to t_{max}, the upper-bound on actions' execution times. To decrease the reaction time caused by t_{max}, even if it was possible to decompose a long running action into a sequence of actions with smaller execution times, that would cause such long running action to be executed within a larger number of deliberation cycles rather than executed normally by one. This in turns reduces the efficiency due to the computational cost caused by executing extra deliberation cycles that might result the corresponding plan to miss its deadline. Interrupting the deliberation cycle in some cases can be useful to address this issue. To illustrate this, the following discusses two such cases that interrupting the deliberation cycle during the execution of an external action can be beneficial.

In the first case, consider that an external action is executed by another computational resource than the one used by the deliberation cycle. While the action is being executed and the deliberation cycle is waiting for the result, the arrival of a new event interrupts the deliberation cycle, a plan is generated in response, and it is evaluated whether a priority-maximal set of intentions from the current set of plans (including the newly generated one) can be scheduled (not necessary in the deadline order) if the current action is allowed to finish its execution. If it is determined that a priority-maximal set can be only scheduled by immediate execution of another plan, the current action (and corresponding plan) is aborted to allow the execution of the other.

In the second case, consider that an action and the agent deliberation cycle share the same computational resource. In this case, it depends on the application whether interrupting the deliberation cycle by arrival of a new event is desirable, as the action, being currently executed, should be interrupted to handle the interrupt (i.e. to generate plan for the new event and evaluate the schedule). Only then it can be determined if the interrupt was necessary or not. If the newly arrived event is of the highest priority, needs to be executed immediately and there is no other plan with the same priority in the current schedule, it can be shown that the interrupt is always necessary for committing to a priority-maximal set. However, in the general case, one cannot know in advance whether the interrupt is necessary before re-scheduling and needs to decide heuristically on application basis when to enable the interrupt. Nevertheless, systematic and clean support of interrupting the deliberation cycle provided with a precise operational semantics can be beneficial in improving the reactiveness of the deliberation cycle and hence deserves further investigation.

4.7 Distributed BDI Architecture

On the one hand, a central control component based on sense-plan-act paradigm would most probably fail to satisfy reactivity requirements of a robot. On the other hand, while the behavior-based robot programming paradigm facilitates developing robots with robust behaviors and high degrees of reactivity, development and debugging of a robot's program in this paradigm becomes increasingly more difficult as the complexity of the robot's tasks increases. At the same time, hybrid architectures which decompose a robot control system into heterogeneous control components with different levels of reactivity are not well suited and lead to various design and development issues. Therefore, state of the art research on design of robotic control architectures propose unified frameworks for development of distributed robot control systems.

To ensure reactivity, the deliberation cycle in BDI architecture interleaves planning and action execution. However, this comes with the cost of the starvation of events and plans. We discussed how the use of interrupts can be advantageous to partly address this issue, however the benefits of the interrupt are in limited cases and more importantly, it complicates the operational semantics of an agent and its programming. Therefore, we believe that one of the most suitable approach to the problem of reactivity when implementing a robot control system in a BDI architecture is to follow the lessons from decades of robotic research and decompose the control system into a set of distributed BDI-based control components under a unified framework. In addition to possibly providing better support to modularity, re-usability and more easier and efficient use of parallel and distributed computing resources, and hence, better software development experience, a distributed BDI-based control architecture in particular can provide an effective solution, when the nature of a problem allows for its decomposition into a set of tasks with different priorities and real-time constraints. For example one control component can be devoted to deliberate and generate plans for the long-term mission of a robot and the other can be devoted to handle current goals and events in real-time. Another example is NAO which only needs to guarantee real-time response when its user asks for help. Here, a BDI-based control component with the highest priority on robot resources can be devoted to handle such situation.

In a distributed setting, a set of control components with different levels of computational complexity (i.e. deliberation capabilities) can be utilized to provide solutions for different tasks according to their real-time requirements. Some BDI-based control components can be devoted to implement simple event handling tasks to guarantee real-time reaction and response to critical events and other BDI-based control components can be used to implement complex goal-based deliberative behaviors with relaxed real-time properties. To facilitate the development of real-time BDI-based distributed control systems, suitable methodologies and tools are needed to develop real-time BDI-based control components and analyze and guarantee their real-time properties. This requires careful design and implementation of a version of agent programming language dedicated to the development of real-time BDI-based components. An example of such work is the commercial C-BDI[3] agent platform. Also a dedicated architecture is required to provide necessary mechanisms for communication between and coordination of distributed BDI-based control components. Such coordination can be performed by a central system clock such as the approached followed by T-REX or performed more asynchronously for example by dynamic prioritization of components similar to the approach followed by ContrACT or by following ideas such as inhibition/stimulation from the behavior-based robotics. There have been already some research recognizing advantages of encapsulating BDI programs into BDI modules (e.g. see [8,15]), however a concrete framework for a distributed BDI control architecture is still missing.

5   Processing Sensory Events

The robot's control component receives streams of sensory events from the functional layer modules, providing information about the robot itself and its environment. Control component uses this information to update the robot's beliefs and goals and to control the execution of the robot's plans. The information provided by functional modules should be processed and maintained to extract the knowledge relevant to the control component operations.

Example 2. To find a requested drink to serve, NAO moves around and scans the kitchen table from different positions using its laser scanner. The object-rec component uses the acquired point cloud data to generate events of identified objects, and their positions with respect to the NAO head coordination frame. In each position that NAO makes a pause to scan the table, base-pos and head-pos components generate events of its body position with respect to the world and its head position with respect to its body coordination frames respectively. Receiving these events asynchronously, the control component should filter them for the position of the specific drink NAO is looking for. To grasp the drink, its position should be computed with respect to the world coordination frame by applying transformations of head-to-body and body-to-world relative positions.

Example 3. When NAO hears, "remember my key is on the desk", it recognizes the commanding user as the last person who has introduced himself or has been appeared in front of its camera. From events of recognized faces and phrases, the control component should maintain the information of the NAO current commander at a time.

Programming an autonomous robot, the processing and the maintenance of sensory events include, but are not limited to, the following event-processing operations.

---

[3] http://www.aosgrp.com/products/c-bdi

- Filtering events based on their contents. E.g. filtering out events of recognized objects for the object NAO is looking for.
- Pattern detection and transformation: E.g. finding the event pattern in which events of the recognition of the requested drink, base position and head position occur at the same time (i.e. finding relative positions of head and body at the time of the scan of the table in which the requested drink has been recognized), computing the position of the drink with respect to the world coordination frame and generating such information as a new event.
- Integrating a domain knowledge. E.g. filtering events of recognized objects for non-alcoholic drinks, based on an ontology of objects and drinks stored as a domain knowledge.
- Maintaining an event history: E.g. maintaining the history of the last person who has introduced himself or has been seen by NAO over time.

The event-processing support provided by current robotic frameworks is limited to low-level filtering mechanisms such as publish-subscribe messaging patterns[4] or processing specific types of sensory events such as position information[5]. On the one hand, robotic frameworks do not provide a general tool for processing sensory events [14]. On the other hand, APLs do not support the processing of events either. Events in APLs are processed as part of the deliberation cycle, preventing event-processing to be performed in a concurrent, parallel and event driven manner. Moreover, they process events using event handling rules which generate plans in response. This brings an extra cost of plan generation and execution. Furthermore, they do not support the programming and efficient implementation of the processing of events. This forces a developer to provide his own choice of tool [7,31] or simply implement event processing operations in an ad-hoc manner using APLs or conventional programming languages such as C++ or Java.

APLs should provide a systematic support for the processing of sensory events to extract relevant information for the robot's control component operations. To this end, APLs should support the development of sensory management components to allow the parallel and concurrent processing of sensory events. This includes the programming language support for the high-level representation of event-processing operations and an efficient implementation of such operations. Event-processing operations should be defined with precise semantics to address problems caused by possible asynchronous and delayed arrival of events. Moreover, the implementation of the interactions between the control component and sensory management components should be supported. This includes the access of the control component to the information processed and maintained by sensory management components both through querying (i.e. active perception) and receiving events (i.e. passive perception). A possible approach to support event-processing in APLs is to integrate and extend existing event-processing languages [9].

---

[4] http://www.ros.org/wiki/Topics
[5] http://www.ros.org/wiki/tf

6   Plan Execution Control

Current APLs provide simple mechanisms for the execution control of a robot's generated plans. Such mechanisms are often a combination of sequence, parallel, atomic, random order (AND), ordered choice (XOR), random choice (OR), conditional choice (IF) and iteration (FOR, WHILE) plan operators. In order to facilitate the programming of autonomous robots, able to achieve complex goals in parallel, different mechanisms are necessary to deal with temporal and functional constraints related to a robot's tasks and its physics, and for a proper parallel use of a robot's resources.

Robotic research has developed many specialized execution languages to represent and execute plans that are generated manually by robotic software developers or automatically by planning systems [38,2,24]. Such languages provide various mechanisms for synchronizing, coordinating and monitoring the executions of plans. This section discusses different plan execution control mechanisms needed by autonomous robots. A check list of such requirements is presented based on generalizing from the analysis of different plan execution control functionalities provided by TDL [36], PLEXIL [37], APEX [11], SMACH [2], RoboGraph [24], SMARTTCL [35], PRS [13] and PRS-lite [25] plan execution languages and programming tools.

6.1   Representation of Complex Plans

To allow the representation of complex plans, plan operators are needed to synchronize the execution of actions/plans in complex arrangements, beyond the simple sequential and parallel settings provided by the existing APLs.

Example 4. To check if there are enough drug A in the box, NAO goes and stays in an specific distance to the box (Location L) and orients its head camera toward the box (Orientation O). Then it takes a picture to analyze if the box is empty or not. To achieve this goal efficiently, NAO performs both Move_To(L) and Orient_Head(O) actions in parallel. The picture needs to be taken only after both Move_To(L) and Orient_Head(O) actions have been successfully performed. Also it might be necessary to wait for a few seconds after maintaining the specified location and orientation, to stabilize the camera before taking the picture. If it is turned out that the box is empty, NAO sends an email to drugstore to order the drug and then waits for the confirmation. If it receives no response in an hour, it informs Mori about the situation.

Programming autonomous robots requires APLs to be enriched with advanced mechanisms to synchronize the execution of actions/plans in order and time. Current robot programming languages support the following mechanisms.

- Hierarchical task decomposition. A complex plan is decomposed into a set of other plans (i.e. sub-plans) in sequence and parallel orderings at different levels of a hierarchy.
- Controllability of the execution of a plan at different levels of its hierarchy.

- Execution of actions in blocking and non-blocking modes.
- Supporting conditional contingencies, loops, temporal constraints and floating contingencies (i.e. event driven task execution) in the task tree decomposition. The execution of sub-plans (i.e. when to start, stop, suspend,
  resume/restart or abort a plan/action) is controlled and monitored by different conditions related to temporal constraints on the absolute time, constraints on execution status of other sub-plans, occurrence of certain events
  and constraints on robot's beliefs. Some conditions should be checked before
  starting/resuming a plan/action, some conditions should be checked con-
  tinuously during a plan/action execution and some should be checked after
  finishing a execution of the plan/action.
- Control on expansion of a sub-plan such as complete expansion before execution or incremental expansion in runtime.

Considering above requirements, the major lack of support in current APLs
is the representation and the coordination of the parallel execution of sub-
plans/actions and the event-driven controlling and monitoring of the sub-plan/
action executions.

Example 5. When Mori says, "NAO, follow the red ball", NAO should run ball-
recognition and search-ball actions in parallel. The ball-recognition action starts
the corresponding image processing task to process camera images for a ball.
The search-ball action starts a behavior to look around. When an event of the
recognition of a ball is received, NAO stops these two actions and starts the
follow-ball action.

6.2   Monitoring and Resource Management

To achieve multiple goals and respond to events in parallel, robot's plans need
to be executed concurrently.

Example 6. When NAO is moving toward the drug box to check if it's empty
or not, it should be at the same time able to respond to Mori if he asks, "NAO,
where is my key?".

The problem in parallel and concurrent execution of robot's plans is that their
execution can be conflicting due to a robot's functional and resource constraints.
Hence, the execution of plans should be coordinated based on plan priorities
and deadlines. Moreover, the failure, suspension or abortion of a plan should be
handled in a proper way to guarantee a safe and an efficient execution of its
tasks.

Example 7. Consider the case that NAO has picked up a piece of trash and going
to throw it into the trash can. Suddenly, NAO hears a user asking for help. To be
able to help the user, NAO should go to the Red_Button and have empty hands
to press it. This has two conflicts with the plan of throwing the trash into the
trash as to execute that plan, NAO needs to walk to the trash can having trash
in its hand. As helping the user is of the highest priority, NAO should leave the
trash and start walking toward the Red_Button immediately.

Example 8. When NAO is carrying a trach to the trash-can, various situations can happen. If Mori orders NAO to pause, NAO should maintain a safe position, and waits for his order to resume its plan. If a guest rings the bell, NAO should put the trash safely on the ground, opens the door and continue its cleaning. If Mori asks for help, NAO should immediately throw away the trash no matter how and go to press the Red_Button.

Programming autonomous robots requires APLs to support the coordination of the parallel execution of plans and handling their failures and preemptions. Current robot programming tools and languages suggest the following as corresponding requirements.

- Representing and determining conflicts between plans (e.g. explicit representation by denoting the resources they require or by providing shared variables and locking mechanisms).
- Resolving plan conflicts based on their priorities and deadlines. This includes dynamic prioritization and preemption.
- Supporting various policies to deal with preempted and failed plans such as stopping, suspending or aborting a preempted plan.
- Recovering from a plan preemption and performing wind-down activities after suspension and before resuming a plan.

To address these requirements, current APLs should be extended to model and resolve plan conflicts. Moreover, current plan failure handling mechanisms should be extended to support the handling of plan preemptions.

7   Conclusion

The paper addresses four basic problems of programming autonomous robots in current APLs, namely, real-time reactivity, sensory data management, plan execution control and integration with robotic software. An application scenario for NAO robot is presented to facilitate research on applying APLs in robotics. The application scenario has been designed in a way to be realizable using current open-source robotic software components with a minimum effort on the development of the robot's low-level sensory data processing and action control capabilities. At the same time, it provides a challenging application for APLs. Guided by the NAO application scenario, and through a study of current autonomous robot programming tools and architectures, the paper presents four general requirements for APLs to support programming autonomous robots.

The first requirement is integration with existing robotic frameworks in general, and in particular with ROS as today's de facto standard robotic framework. APLs should support the component communication mechanisms of current robotic frameworks to ease the programming of the robot's control component interactions with other robot's software components. Integration with robotic frameworks can encourage the use of APLs by robotic community and facilitates their use for rapid prototyping and development of autonomous robots.

The second requirement is supporting the development of sensory management components. Such components should enable a unified representation of heterogeneous events, integrating a domain knowledge, filtering events, detecting complex patterns of events and extracting the information relevant to the control component operations. The information maintained and processed by sensory management components should be accessible by the control component both asynchronously as events and by querying on-demand. APLs should support such sensory management and processing operations by providing a high-level language for the representation of these operations and their efficient implementations.

The third requirement is extending the current plan execution control mechanisms of APLs. Plans should support the representation of hierarchies of actions including concurrent actions. The execution of actions in a plan hierarchy should be governed by sequential and temporal orderings, and based on conditional and floating contingencies. Moreover, APLs should support the representation of conflicts between the parallel execution of plans and resolving such conflicts based on plan priorities and deadlines. Furthermore, the failure, suspension or abortion of a plan should be handled in a proper way to robot operates safe and correct.

The fourth requirement is real-time reactivity to events. The problem of real-time reactivity in BDI architecture is discussed in details and distributed BDI architecture is proposed to approach the reactivity problem for a robot's BDI-based decision layer. In a distributed setting, some BDI-based components are developed to provide bounded reaction and response time to critical events and others are devoted to more deliberative behaviors. To this end, a specific version of an APL is required to be dedicated for the development of real-time control components. The semantics and implementation of such a version should guarantee safe and bounded-time computations to enable analysis and guaranteeing required real-time properties of a control component. Also a dedicated architecture and runtime environment is required to support the real-time coordination and communication of different control components of a robot.

One part of the future work is to address the presented requirements by developing necessary methodologies and set of software libraries and tools for APLs in general and for 2APL in particular. We envision a ROS architecture consisting of a distributed set of control and functional components. Sensory components of a robot process sensory data to various levels of abstraction. Sensory management components manage and process sensory events received from sensory components to extract relevant information for the control component operations. Control components provide different control functionalities (e.g. deliberative, reactive, plan failure handling) and share beliefs and goals. A subset of these components should operate in real-time and guarantee bounded reaction and response time to events. A unified framework guides and facilitates the development of a distributed set of control components and their coordination.

The other part of the future work is developing and exploring the NAO application scenario to further research on applying APLs in robotics. One important subject to address is the APLs requirements for programming multi-robot application scenarios.

References

1. Rao, A.S.: AgentSpeak(L): BDI agents speak out in a logical computable language. In: Van de Velde, W., Perram, J.W. (eds.) MAAMAW 1996. LNCS (LNAI), vol. 1038, pp. 42–55. Springer, Heidelberg (1996)
2. Bohren, J., Cousins, S.: The SMACH high-level executive. Robotics and Automation Magazine (2010)
3. Bollini, M., et al.: Bakebot: Baking cookies with the pr2. In: The PR2 Workshop: Results, Challenges and Lessons Learned in Advancing Robots with a Common Platform, IROS (2011)
4. Bordini, R., Braubach, L., Dastani, M., Fallah, A.E., Gomez-Sanz, J., Leite, J., O'Hare, G., Pokahr, A., Ricci, A.: A survey of programming languages and platforms for multi-agent systems. Informatica 30, 33–44 (2006)
5. Bordini, R.H., Hübner, J.F., Wooldridge, M.: Programming Multi-agent Systems in AgentSpeak Using Jason. Wiley Series in Agent Technology (2007)
6. Brooks, R.A.: Intelligence Without Representation. Artificial Intelligence 47, 139–159 (1991)
7. Buford, J., Jakobson, G., Lewis, L.: Extending BDI Multi-Agent Systems with Situation Management. In: The Ninth International Conference on Information Fusion, Florence, Italy (2006)
8. Cap, M., Dastani, M., Harbers, M.: Belief/Goal Sharing Modules for BDI Languages. In: Proceedings of CSSE 2011, pp. 87–94 (2011)
9. Cugola, G., Margara, A.: Processing Flows of Information: From Data Stream to Complex Event Processing. ACM Computing Surveys Journal (2011)
10. Dastani, M.: 2APL: a practical agent programming language. Autonomous Agents and Multi-Agent Systems 16(3), 214–248 (2008) ISSN:1387-2532
11. Freed, M.: Managing Multiple Tasks in Complex, Dynamic Environments. In: Proceedings of the National Conference on Artificial Intelligence, Madison, WI (1998)
12. Gat, E.: On Three-Layer Architectures, Artificial Intelligence and Mobile Robots. MIT Press (1998)
13. Georgeff, M.P., Lansky, A.L.: Reactive reasoning and planning. In: Proceedings of the Sixth National Conference on Artificial Intelligence (AAAI 1987), Seattle, WA, pp. 677–682 (1987)
14. Heintz, F., Kvarnstrom, J., Doherty, P.: Bridging the sense-reasoning gap: DyKnow-stream-based middleware for knowledge processing. Journal of Advanced Engineering Informatics 24(1), 14–25 (2010)
15. Hindriks, K.V.: Modules as Policy-Based Intentions: Modular Agent Programming in GOAL. In: Dastani, M., El Fallah Seghrouchni, A., Ricci, A., Winikoff, M. (eds.) ProMAS 2007. LNCS (LNAI), vol. 4908, pp. 156–171. Springer, Heidelberg (2008)
16. Inigo-Blasco, P., et al.: Robotics software frameworks for multi-agent robotic systems development. Robotics and Autonomous Systems (2012), doi:10.1016/j.robot.2012.02.004
17. Ingrand, F., Lacroix, S., Lemai-Chenevier, S., Py, F.: Decisional Autonomy of Planetary Rovers. Journal of Field Robotics 24(7), 559–580 (2007)
18. Ingrand, F.F., Coutance, V.: Real-Time Reasoning using Procedural Reasoning. Technical Report 93-104, LAAS/CNRS, Toulouse, France (1993)
19. Kramer, J., Scheutz, M.: Development environments for autonomous mobile robots: A survey. Autonomous Robots 22(2), 101–132 (2007)

20. Verbeek, M.: 3APL as programming language for cognitive robots. Master's thesis, ICS, Utrecht University (2002)
21. Bratman, M.: Intentions, Plans, and Practical Reason. Harvard University Press (1987) 24, 113, 144
22. Estlin, T., et al.: Decision-Making in a Robotic Architecture for Autonomy. In: Proceedings of the International Symposium on AI, Robotics and Automation for Space, Montreal, Canada (2001)
23. Kertesz, C.: Dynamic behavior network. In: IEEE 10th International Symposium on Applied Machine Intelligence and Informatics (SAMI), pp. 207–212 (2012)
24. Lopez, J., Perez, D., Zalama, E.: A framework for building mobile single and multi-robot applications. Robotics and Autonomous Systems 59(3-4), 151–162 (2011)
25. Myers, K.L.: A procedural knowledge approach to task-level control. In: Proceedings of the Third International Conference on AI Planning Systems. AAAI Press (1996)
26. Nilsson, N.J.: Shakey the robot. Technical Report 323, AI Center, SRI International,333 Ravenswood Ave., Menlo Park, CA 94025 (April 1984)
27. Passama, R., Andreu, D.: ContrACT: a software environment for developing control architecture. In: 6th National Conference on Control Architectures of Robots, p. 16 (2011)
28. Proetzsch, M., Luksch, T., Berns, K.: Development of complex robotic systems using the behavior-based control architecture iB2C. Robot. Auton. Syst. 58(1), 46–67 (2010)
29. Rao, A., Georgeff, M.: Modeling rational agents within a BDI architecture. In: Proceedings of Second International Conference on Knowledge Representation and Reasoning (KR 1991), pp. 473–484. Morgan Kaufmann (1991)
30. Rao, A., Georgeff, M.: BDI Agents: From Theory to Practice. In: Proceedings of the First International Conference on Multi-Agent Systems (ICMAS 1995), pp. 312–319 (June 1995)
31. Ranathunga, S., et al.: Identifying events taking place in second life virtual environments. Applied Artificial Intelligence: An International Journal 26(1-2), 137–181 (2012)
32. Rajan, K., Py, F., McGann, C., Ryan, J., O'Reilly, T., Maughan, T., Roman, B.: Onboard Adaptive Control of AUVs using Automated Planning and Execution. In: Intnl. Symposium on Unmanned Untethered Submersible Technology (UUST), Durham, NH (August 2009)
33. Ross, R.J.: MARC - Applying Multi-Agent Systems to Service Robot Control, MSc Thesis, University College Dublin (2003)
34. Quigley, M., et al.: Ros: an open source roboting system. In: ICRA Workshop on Open Source Software (2009)
35. Steck, A., Schlegel, C.: SmartTCL: An Execution Language for Conditional Reactive Task Execution in a Three Layer Architecture for Service Robots. In: Int. Workshop on DYnamic languages for RObotic and Sensors systems (DYROS/SIMPAR), Germany, pp. 274–277 (2010)
36. Simmons, R., Apfelbaum, D.: A Task Description Language for Robot Control. In: IROS (1998)
37. Verma, V., Jonsson, A., Pasareanu, C., Simmons, R., Tso, K.: Plan Execution Interchange Language (PLEXIL) for Executable Plans and Command Sequences. In: Proceedings of the International Symposium on Artificial Intelligence, Robotics and Automation in Space (i-SAIRAS) (2005)

38. Verma, V., Jonsson, A., Simmons, R., Estlin, T., Levinson, R.: Survey of command execution systems for NASA spacecraft and robots. In: Plan Execution: A Reality Check Workshop at the International Conference on Automated Planning and Scheduling (ICAPS) (2005)
39. Vikhorev, K., Alechina, N., Logan, B.: Agent programming with priorities and deadlines. In: Proceedings of the Tenth International Conference on Autonomous Agents and Multiagent Systems (AAMAS 2011), Taipei, Taiwan, pp. 397–404 (May 2011)

An Agent-Based Cognitive Robot Architecture

Changyun Wei and Koen V. Hindriks

Interactive Intelligence, Delft University of Technology, The Netherlands
{C.Wei,K.V.Hindriks}@tudelft.nl

Abstract. We propose a new *cognitive robot control architecture* in which the cognitive layer can be *programmed* by means of the agent programming language GOAL. The architecture exploits the support that agent-oriented programming offers for creating *cognitive robotic agents*, including symbolic knowledge representation, deliberation via modular, high-level action selection, and support for multiple, declarative goals. The benefits of the architecture are that it provides a flexible approach to develop cognitive robots and support for a clean and clear separation of concerns about symbolic reasoning and sub-symbolic processing. We discuss the design of our architecture and discuss the issue of translating sub-symbolic information and behavior control into symbolic representations needed at the cognitive layer. An interactive navigation task is presented as a proof of concept.

1 Introduction

The main motivation for our work is the need for a flexible, generic, high-level control framework that facilitates the development of re-taskable robot systems and provides a feasible alternative to the usual task- and domain-dependent development of high-level robot control. As cognitive robots are supposed to handle complex reasoning problems in dynamic environments [1], we believe that agent-oriented programming offers such an approach as it supports the programming of cognitive agents. Using agent programs to create the cognitive layer in a robot control architecture is natural and provides several benefits. It becomes relatively easy to adapt the control *at the cognitive layer* itself to various domains. This approach is flexible and, if functionality of other layers is generic and can be used in multiple task domains, facilitates reuse. An agent-based approach, moreover, provides support for autonomous, reactive, and proactive behaviors and also endows a robot with the required deliberation mechanism to decide what to do next [2]. Of course, generality may come at a trade-off and does not imply that a generic architecture will always perform better than a dedicated robot control architecture [3].

Designing and developing a *cognitive robot control architecture* poses several challenges. Robots are embedded systems that operate in physical, dynamic environments and need to be capable of operating in real-time. A range of perception and motor control activities need to be integrated into the architecture. This poses a challenge for a cognitive, symbolic architecture as "it can be particularly difficult to generate meaningful symbols for the symbolic components of

M. Dastani, J.F. Hübner, and B. Logan (Eds.): ProMAS 2012, LNAI 7837, pp. 54–71, 2013.
© Springer-Verlag Berlin Heidelberg 2013

cognitive architectures to reason about from (potentially noisy) sensor data or to perform some low-level tasks such as control of motors" [4]. Ideally, moreover, such an architecture should provide support for the integration or exchange of new and different sensors and behaviors when needed. Given the complexity and the number of components needed in a robot control architecture, one also needs to consider how all the processing components in the system communicate and interact with each other [5].

The main focus and contribution of this paper is to provide a simple but also generic and flexible solution to integrate the knowledge representation and reasoning capabilities needed for a cognitive robot [6, 7]. As perception and action need to be tightly coupled for a cognitive robot to be able to operate effectively [1], we also discuss this relationship. We propose an agent-based cognitive robot control architecture that integrates low-level *sub-symbolic* control with high-level *symbolic* control into the robot control framework. We use the agent programming language GOAL [8, 9] for implementing the cognitive layer, whereas low-level execution control and processing of sensor data are delegated to components in other layers in the proposed architecture. GOAL, among others, supports goal-oriented behavior and the decomposition of complex behavior by means of modules that can focus their attention on relevant sub-goals. GOAL has already been successfully applied to control real-time, dynamic environments [10], and here we demonstrate that it also provides a feasible approach for controlling robots. In our approach, the cognitive layer is cleanly separated from the other layers by using the Environment Interface Standard (EIS; [11]). As a proof of concept, we will use a task, in which a robot will navigate in an office environment in order to deliver a message to one of our colleagues, to show how the agent-based cognitive control can be realized in physical robots. The main contribution of our proposed architecture is that it provides:

- a decoupled framework for combining low-level behavioral robot control with high-level cognitive reasoning,
- a generic interface for mapping sensory information to symbolic representations needed at the cognitive layer, and
- a flexible mechanism in the cognitive layer for synchronizing percepts and actions.

The paper is structured as follows. Section 2 briefly discusses some related work. Section 3 presents and discusses the design of the cognitive robot control architecture. Section 4 presents a proof of concept implementation. Section 5 concludes the paper and discusses future work.

2   Related Work

Cognitive robots are *autonomous* and *intelligent* robot systems that can perform tasks in real world environments without any external control, and are able to make decisions and select actions in dynamic environments [12]. It remains a challenge, however, to integrate the symbolic problem solving techniques such as knowledge representation, reasoning, and planning developed within artificial intelligence with sub-symbolic functions such as perception and motor control on a robot [13]. It has been argued, however, that knowledge representation is important to enable robots to reason about its environment [1, 6, 7]. Here we briefly discuss some related work that either explicitly aims at developing a cognitive robot architecture or uses some kind of symbolic representation for controlling a robot.

The work that is most similar in spirit to our own is that of [14] and [15]. In [14] the high-level language Golog is used for controlling a robot. Golog supports writing control programs in a high-level, logical language, and provides an interpreter that, given a logical axiomatization of a domain, will determine a plan. [15] proposes teleo-reactive programming for controlling a robot. A teleo-reactive program consists of multiple, prioritized condition-action rules. However, neither Golog nor teleo-reactive programming provide a BDI perspective on programming agents. Moreover, these papers do not discuss the robot control architecture that allows the symbolic framework to control the robot.

CRAM [2] is a software toolbox designed for controlling the Rosie robot platform developed at the Technische Universität München. It makes use of Prolog and includes a plan language that provides a construct for concurrent actions. The CRAM approach also aims at providing a flexible alternative to pre-programmed robot control programs. [16] proposes to use a common sense ontology for defining predicates for high-level control of a robot that is integrated into the CRAM architecture. One difference between the CRAM and our approach is that the reasoning and planning components are two separate components in CRAM whereas they are integrated into an agent architecture in our robot control framework. Moreover, we propose the use of an explicit interface component for connecting the low-level and high-level control in our architecture that allows for a clean separation of concerns.

It has been argued that building robot systems for environments in which robots need to co-exist and cooperate with humans requires taking a *cognitive stance* [17] . According to [17], translating the key issues that such robot systems have to deal with requires a cognitive robot control architecture. Taking a cognitive stance towards the design and implementation of a robot system means that such a system needs to be designed to perform a range of *cognitive functions*. Various *cognitive architectures*, such as ACT-R [18] and SOAR [19], have been used to control robots. These architectures were not primarily aimed at addressing the robot control problem and in this sense are similar to agent programming languages, the technology that we advocate here for controlling robots. SOAR has been used to control the hexapod HexCrawler and a wheeled robot called the SuperDroid [4]. ADAPT (Adaptive Dynamics and Active Perception for Thought) is a cognitive architecture based on SOAR that is specifically designed for robotics [20]. The SS-RICS (Symbolic and Sub-symbolic Robotic Intelligent Control System) architecture for controlling robots is based on ACT-R; SS-RICS is intended to be a theory of robotic cognition based on human cognition [21, 3]. This work mainly focuses on integrating a broad range of cognitive capabilities into an architecture instead of on more pragmatic issues related to programming cognitive robotics and reuse. Unlike [22], we are not mainly concerned here with the long-term goal of developing robotic systems that have the full range of cognitive abilities of humans based on a cognitive architecture such as SOAR. Our work is oriented towards providing a more pragmatic solution for the robot control problem as discussed above. Still our work may contribute to the larger goal that [22] sets as there appear to be quite a few similarities between BDI-based agents and cognitive architectures such as ACT-R and SOAR).

3   Cognitive Robot Control Architecture

This section introduces our cognitive robot control architecture. We discuss several issues including the processing and mapping of sensory data to a symbolic representation, the translation of high-level decisions into low-level motor control commands, and the interaction of the various architecture components.

3.1   Overall Design of the Architecture

A high-level overview of our layered architecture is shown in Figure 1. The architecture consists of four layers including a symbolic, cognitive layer realized by means of the agent programming language GOAL, a middle layer for controlling robot behavior (written in C++), and a hardware control layer (using URBI[1], a robotic programming language). The Environment Interface Standard (EIS) layer provides the technology we have used to manage the interaction between the symbolic and sub-symbolic layers. We argue here that EIS provides a tool that can be extended to deal with the issue of translating *sub-symbolic* sensory data that consists typically of noisy, incomplete, and quantitative measurements into *symbolic representations* that are needed in the symbolic cognitive layers to support reasoning. Note that the environment layer is not part of the architecture but refers to the physical environment that the robot operates in.

The main functionality for controlling a robot is placed in the behavioral control layer. In addition to the functions such as (object) recognition, navigation, localization, path planning and other common functions, this layer is also responsible for communicating with the higher-level symbolic components, including the interpretation of symbolic messages that represent actions and making the robot perform these actions in its physical environment.

The interface layer acts as a bridge between the behavioral and cognitive control layers. Because these layers use different languages for representing subsymbolic and symbolic information, respectively, we need an interface to translate between these representations. The cognitive control layer acts as a task manager for the robot and provides support for managing the robot's *mental state* which allows the robot to keep track of what is happening while executing a task.

---

[1] http://www.urbiforge.org/

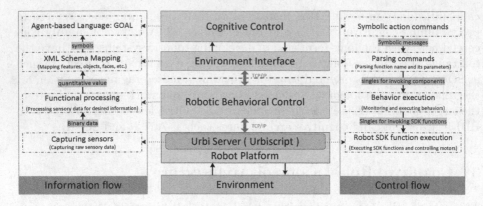

Fig. 1. The overall design of the architecture

3.2   System Architecture and Components

A robot control architecture provides an organizational structure for software components that control a robotic system [23]; such architectures are specialized because of the unique requirements that embedded systems such as robots impose on software. Here we will discuss the detailed architecture shown in Figure 2 that we propose that matches the layered architecture framework of Figure 1.

Robot Platform. The architecture has been implemented on the humanoid NAO robot platform from Aldebaran Robotics.[2] We have used the URBI middleware [24] that provides the *urbiscript* language for interfacing with the robot's hardware. We have chosen URBI instead of the Robot Operating System (ROS[3]) platform because it does not include the orchestration layers present in URBI that provide support for parallel, tag-based, and event-driven programming of behavior scripts. When the application is executed, an urbiscript program, which initializes all API parameters of sensors and motors (e.g., the resolution and frame rate of camera images), is sent to configure the robot platform.

Behavioral Control. The behavioral control layer is written in C++, connecting the robot hardware layer with higher layers via a TCP/IP connection. This layer is mainly responsible for information processing, knowledge processing, communication with the deliberative reasoning layer and external robots, and action and behavior executions. All of these components can operate concurrently. The main functional modules include:

  − **Sensing**, for processing sensory data and receiving messages from other robots. Sensors that have been included are sonar, camera, microphone, an inertial sensor, and all sensors monitoring motors. Because the memory space

[2] http://www.aldebaran-robotics.com/
[3] http://www.ros.org/

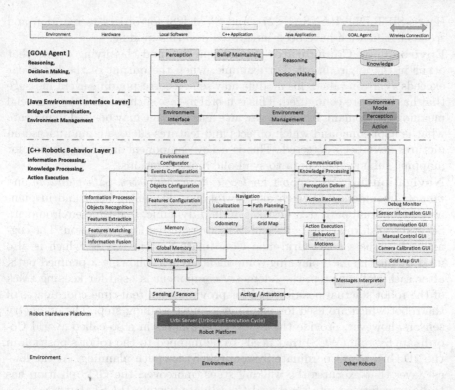

Fig. 2. Overview of the agent-based cognitive robot architecture

required for camera images is significantly bigger than that for other sensors, the transmission of images is realized via a separate communication channel.

– **Memory**, for maintaining the *global memory* and *working memory* for the behavioral layer. In global memory, a map of the environment and properties of objects or features extracted from sensor data are stored. We have used a 2D grid map for representing the environment. This map also keeps track which of the grid cells are occupied and which are available for path planning. The working memory stores temporary sensor data (e.g., images, sonar values) that are used for updating the global memory.

– **Information Processor**, for image processing. This component provides support for object recognition, feature extraction and matching, as well as for information fusion. Information fusion is used to generate more reliable information from the data received from different sensors. For example, the odometry navigation component is only able to provide a rough estimate of the robot's position due to joint backlash and foot slippage. To compensate for this, the robot has also been equipped with the capability to actively re-localize or correct its position by means of predefined landmarks. We have used the OpenCV [25] library to implement algorithms and methods for processing images captured by the camera. Algorithms such as

Harris-SIFT [26], RANSAC [27], and SVM [28] for object recognition and scene classification have been integrated into this module.

- **Environment Configurator**, for interpreting and classifying events that occur in the environment. For example, when the output of the left sonar exceeds a certain value, this module may send a corresponding event message that has been pre-configured. This is useful in case such readings have special meaning in a domain. In such cases, an event message may be used to indicate what is happening and which objects and features such as human faces and pictures have been detected. This is a key component in our approach for mapping sub-symbolic data to symbolic representations.

- **Navigation** includes support for *localization*, *odometry*, *path planning* and *mapping* components, which aid the robot in localizing itself and in planning an optimal path to a destination in a dynamic, real-time environment. Several transformations between layers are required for navigation. The cognitive layer uses a 2D Grid-map Coordinate System (GCS) which is also used by the the path planning component. When following a planned path, after each walking step, the odometry component is used for keeping track of the robot's actual position and for providing the real-time coordinates of the robot which are used for planning its next walking step. The odometry sensors, however, provide the robot's coordinates in a so-called World Coordinate System (WCS) that needs to be mapped to the robot's position in the 2D Grid-map Coordinate System (GCS) for path planning. At the lowest layer that executes the walking steps, moreover, the GCS position has to be transformed into the Local Coordinate System (LCS) that the robot platform uses for actual motor movements.

- **Communication**, which provides outputs from the Environment Configurator to the interface layer and receives action messages from this same layer. The communication component mainly is a technical component that acts as a Server/Client infrastructure and uses the TCP/IP protocol for actual message delivery. The behavior layer in the architecture initiates and starts up a unique server to which a cognitive layer can connect as a client (thus facilitating the swapping of control from one robot to another).

- **Debugger Monitor** provides several GUIs that are useful for debugging robot programs, enabling developers to visualize sensory data and allowing them to set specific function parameters. This component also includes a *Wizard of Oz interface* to conduct human-robot interaction experiments.

- **Action Execution**, for instructing a robot to perform concrete behaviors and actions. The actions include motion movements such as walking and turning around while the behaviors include predefined body gestures such as sitting down, standing up and raising the arms of a humanoid robot.

Environment Interface. The interface layer between the behavior and cognitive layers has been built using a software package called Environment Interface Standard (EIS; [11]). The core components in this layer are an *Environment Model* component that establishes a connection between the cognitive layer with the behavioral control layer, an *Environment Management* component that initializes and manages the interface, and an *Environment Interface* component that provides the actual bridge between the cognitive and behavioral layer.

The benefit of using EIS for implementing the interface layer is that it already provides a well-defined and structured language for representing knowledge, the so-called Environment Interface Language (EIL). Moreover, various agent platforms support EIS which implies that our architecture may be reused to connect languages other than GOAL without much effort to the robot platforms that are supported by the architecture. We thus obtain immediately a clear, simple but sufficiently expressive target language for mapping sub-symbolic data maintained in the behavioral layer to symbolic percepts used in the cognitive layer. Because this language is already supported by GOAL, this allows us moreover to focus completely on the problem of mapping sub-symbolic data to the EIL language. We discuss a generic scheme to do this in Section 3.4 below.

Deliberative Reasoning and Decision Making. Knowledge representation and reasoning is an essential component for a cognitive robot that allows such a robot to keep track of what is happening in its environment and to make rational decisions to change that environment [7, 6]. The cognitive control layer provides support for reasoning and decision making. In our architecture, we employ the GOAL agent programming language for programming the high-level cognitive agent that controls the robot. GOAL is a language for programming logic-based, cognitive agents that use symbolic representations for their beliefs and goals from which they derive their choice of action. Due to space limitations, we do not describe GOAL agent programs in any detail here but refer the interested reader for more information to [8, 9]. In Section 4, we will use a navigation task to illustrate how a GOAL agent program can be used for deliberative reasoning and decision making for controlling a robot.

3.3 Decoupled Architecture Layers

Similar to most layered architectures, we also distinguish reactive and deliberative control in our architecture. In our architecture these layers are loosely coupled and connected through a separate interface layer. We have deliberately chosen for this setup. Alternatively, these layers could have been more tightly coupled. Tight coupling has some benefits such as a more robust integration and a reduced communication overhead which often leads to higher performance than loosely coupled systems [29]. These benefits are obtained by using a memory component that is shared and directly accessible by all other components. This also avoids the need to "duplicate" information at different layers, although one should note that also in a tightly coupled setup mappings between sub-symbolic and symbolic data are needed. The disadvantages of a more tightly coupled approach are an increased complexity of the architecture and a higher interdependence between architecture components. As a consequence, it becomes more difficult to extend such architectures in order to be able to handle a range of different tasks [29].

Our choice to opt for decoupled layers is motivated by our objective to design an architecture that is as flexible as possible. A benefit of decoupling is that it provides for a clean separation of concerns. Moreover, decoupling of these layers facilitates the more or less independent programming of high-level, cognitive agents that control a robot as well as of lower-level behavioral functions. An agent programmer, for example, does not need to spend time handling object recognition. Similarly, a behavior programmer who codes in C++ does not have to consider decision making nor even master the agent programming language used in the cognitive layer. The main challenge that needs to be faced in a decoupled approach is how to translate or transform sub-symbolic data to symbolic representations, an issue to which we turn next.

3.4   Knowledge Acquisition and Representation

We have designed a generic method for transforming sub-symbolic data to symbolic representations that can be used in the cognitive layer. The main function of the interface layer is to perform the actual transformation. The interface layer thus needs to be provided with the functionality to process all sub-symbolic data that is sent to this layer by the behavioral layer. Of course, the type of data that needs to be processed and transformed depends on the robot platform that is used and the sensors available on that platform. In our case, we have listed all the available sensors and associated functionality for processing raw sensor data in the first two columns of Table 1. The key issue is how to interpret and map the sub-symbolic data obtained through sensors to a symbolic representation that is useful for decision making in the cognitive layer. In essence, what we need in order to obtain a transformation is a coding scheme. Such a coding scheme should not only indicate *how* to map data to a particular representation but also allow to specify *when* such a translation should be performed.

The solution that we propose as a generic solution for creating a coding scheme for transforming data into symbols is to use a standard template. To this end, we have used XML to create such a standard message template with the following structure:

```
<?xml version="1.0"?>
<message_percept>
  <descriptor  sensor="sensors" function="name">
      <para1>parameter</para1>
      <para2>parameter</para2>
      <para3>parameter</para3>
      ...
  </descriptor>
</message_percept>
```

Every data item sent from the robotic behavioral layer to the interface layer uses the above XML template, where **sensor** indicates which sensor this data item is produced from, **function** refers to the name of the function used for processing the sensor data, and **para1**, **para2**, **para3**) are parameters of functions that may have various number of parameters.

The XML schema above is used by the interface layer for mapping data items to symbolic representations in a generic and flexible manner. For each sensor and associated functions, an XML schema is stored in a database used by the interface layer. Table 1 shows how to process the data from several sensors and map them to corresponding symbolic representations.

Table 1. Knowledge acquisition and representation

Sensors	Processing	Acquisition and Mapping	Representation
Sonar value	sonarLeftVal	$thr2 \leq para1 < thr1$	obstacle(left)
		$\ldots \leq para1 < thr2$	collision(left)
	sonarRightVal	$thr2 \leq para1 < thr1$	obstacle(right)
		$\ldots \leq para1 < thr2$	collision(right)
Inertial value	placeEstimation	$para1 = x, para2 = y$ $[x, y] \in$ room	in(room)
		$para1 = x, para2 = y$ $[x, y] \in$ room.hallway	inFrontOf(room)
	relativePose	$para1 = x, para2 = y$	position(x,y)
	walkIsActive	$para1 =$ "true"	walking
		$para1 =$ "false"	static
Camera image	featureRecognition	$para1 =$ feature	feature(feature)
	colorDetection	$para1 =$ color	color(color)
	shapeDetection	$para1 =$ shape	shape(shape)
	absolutePose	$para1 = x, para2 = y$	position(x,y)
	sceneClassification	$para1 =$ "true"	doorOpen
		$para1 =$ "false"	doorClosed

As the number of the parameters of processing functions are various in order to convey different messages, we will discuss several conditions with respect to the various parameters, illustrating how to obtain adequate coding schemes using the XML schema proposed.

Functions with Binary Parameter. Some functions, such as `walkIsActive`, `sceneClassification`, only have a binary parameter, namely "true" or "false" value. Suppose the robot needs to figure out if the door in front of it is open or closed. What the deliberative reasoning needs is the symbolic percept: `doorOpen` or `doorClosed`. In order to obtain this percept, the knowledge processing function: `sceneClassification` should analyze the images from the robot's camera. SVM can be chosen as a discriminative classifier for scene classification. As a statistical learning technique, SVM should also handle the uncertainty problem of sensory data, in which the state of the door (i.e., histogram of images) first has to be trained to obtain an appropriate threshold for classification. The The knowledge acquisition and mapping procedure in the interface layer uses the XML schema to examine the contents:

```
<descriptor sensor="Camera image" function="sceneClassification">
    <para1="true"><interpreter>"doorOpen"</interpreter> </para1
    <para1="false"><interpreter>"doorClosed"</interpreter></para1
</descriptor>
```

If the para1 is "true", this data item can be interpreted as doorOpen; likewise, if it is "false", a doorClosed percept can be generated.

Functions with Threshold Parameter. Some functions, such as sonarLeftVal, sonarRightVal, have a threshold parameter. Typically, a parameter will be examined to see if it exceeds a particular threshold or not. But in many practical situation, one parameter should be compared with two or more different thresholds so as to match to corresponding categories. Taking the sonarLeftVal as an example in Table 1, the XML schema in this case can be expressed as:

```
<descriptor sensor="Sonar value" function="sonarLeftVal>
    <thr1=0.8><interpreter>"obstacle(left)"</interpreter> </thr1
    <thr2=0.5><interpreter>"collision(left)"</interpreter></thr2
</descriptor>
```

If the data item intends to represent obstacle(left), the para1 should satisfy: $0.5 \leq para1 < 0.8$; if it intends to represent collision(left) as we have not define the third threshold thr3, the para1 only needs to satisfy: $para1 < 0.5$. Note that this function can have as many as categories if we continually add thresholds and define corresponding interpreters.

Functions with Argument Parameter. The functions, such as relativePose, absolutePose and placeEstimation, have argument parameters, which provide position information of 2D coordinates: x and y. For relativePose and absolutePose, the coordinate data do not need to be mapped to specific symbolic representation, but we still need to add symbolic predicate (i.e., position()) in this percept message so that the cognitive layer can understand what kind of percepts it belongs to.

However, The placeEstimation handles the topological localization problems for place estimation. When a robot knows its 2D coordinate in the world map, the robot can know its topological position (e.g., in room A or in front of room A). The XML database for this condition can be:

```
<descriptor sensor="Camera image" function="placeEstimation">
    <rect x1=0, y1=100, x2=100, y2=0   ><interpreter>"in(roomA)"</interpreter></rect
    <rect x1=0, y1=200, x2=100, y2=100 ><interpreter>"in(roomB)"</interpreter></rect
    <rect x1=0, y1=300, x2=100, y2=200 ><interpreter>"in(roomC)"</interpreter></rect
    ...
    <rect x1=100, y1=100, x2=200, y2=0   ><interpreter>"inFrontOf(roomA)"</interpreter></rect
    <rect x1=100, y1=200, x2=200, y2=100 ><interpreter>"inFrontOf(roomB)"</interpreter></rect
    <rect x1=100, y1=300, x2=200, y2=200 ><interpreter>"inFrontOf(roomC)"</interpreter></rect
    ...
</descriptor>
```

The attribute of the rect describes a rectangle region defined by its upper left and lower right coordinates. If the parameters of the function locate within a defined region, namely $(x1 \leq x \leq x2) \cup (y2 \leq y \leq y1)$. Once the environmental map is known, the topological places can be defined in detail using this XML schema.

Functions with Identification Parameter. Several functions, such as the `featureRecognition`, `colorDetection` and `shapeDetection`, are associated with an identification parameter. The identification is generated from these functions in the robotic behavior layer. For example, as has been discussed the *global memory* stores the properties of features in the robotic behavior layer so as to recognize pictures using Harris-SIFT and RANSAC image processing techniques. We can use the identification of these pictures to match to the correct representation. However, some functions' identification parameter is relatively vague and not clear enough to represent a complete percept, and we need to combine this them in the interface layer. The XML schema in our case for this condition can be:

```
<descriptor sensor="Camera image" function="colorDetection">
    <para1="red"><interpreter>"red"</interpreter> </para1
    <para1="green"><interpreter>"green"</interpreter></para1
    ...
</descriptor>
<descriptor sensor="Camera image" function="shapeDetection">
    <para1="circle"><interpreter>"ball"</interpreter> </para1
    <para1="rectangle"><interpreter>"box"</interpreter></para1
    ...
</descriptor>
```

In the query and matching codes of the interface layer, the `interpreter` should be combined to form a complete percept, such as `redball`, `redbox`, `greenbox` and so forth.

The mechanism for knowledge acquisition and representation in the environment interface layer can support for a flexible, generic mapping approach. When a specific percept (e.g., `in(roomA)`) about the environment needs to be integrated in a task, we can just modify the XML database in the interface layer.

3.5   Information and Control Flow

A key issue in robot control architectures is the information and control flow. Each component in such an architecture needs to have access to the relevant information in order to function effectively. In line with the overall architecture of Figure 1 and layered architectures in general, different types of data are associated with each of the different layers. The information flow follows a strict bottom-up processing scheme whereas the control flow employs a strict top-down scheme. At the lowest level all raw sensory data is captured and then sent to the behavioral layer. The behavioral layer has a diverse set of functions to process the sensory data. By using the quantitative results of these functions, corresponding symbolic representations can be matched based on XML schema in the interface layer. Finally, the cognitive layer can use these symbolic percepts for deliberative reasoning.

Actions are selected for execution by the cognitive layer. These actions are translated by the interface layer into behaviors that can be executed by the behavioral layer which in turn are translated into motor control commands in the lowest layer. Action commands are symbolic messages. For example, the cognitive layer may decide to sent `goto(roomA)`. A message like this needs to be parsed in the EIS interface layer to extract the parameters of the message. Subsequently, the behavioral layer will call the navigation component to actually perform the action. Because such behavior components take time to complete, moreover, it is important to monitor progress. Monitoring may happen at different layers. However, the behavioral layer typically plays a key role here. For example, due to the unreliability of walking (e.g. foot slippage), the path the robot follows needs to be continually re-evaluated and re-planned in real-time. The navigation component monitors and manages this action execution, until the robot arrives at the correct place of the room.

3.6   Synchronization of Perceptions and Actions

An inevitable problem in physical robot control is the synchronization problem of percepts and actions. In general, on the one hand, robots in physical world usually perceive its environment in real-time, and consequently sensors generate duplicated perceptual information that is useless for reasoning. On the other hand, decision making is usually faster than action execution on a robot. Typically, an action command has not been completed before another action command is sent for execution by the cognitive layer. Therefore, we need some means to synchronize the layers. As the functionality we need can be realized by the cognitive layer itself, we discuss some synchronization mechanisms that can be implemented in the cognitive layer.

The interface layer by itself does not guarantee that only those percepts needed by the cognitive layer are provided. In fact, this layer will typically produce a large number of (more or less) the same percepts repeatedly because the behavioral layer and the cognitive layer run in their own thread. For example, assuming the camera image frame rate is 30 fps, and the scene classification algorithm is fast enough, when the robot is standing in front of an open door and intends to figure out the state of the door. In this case, the cognitive layer will receive the same percept **doorOpen** 30 times in 1 second. Because many actions take typically much longer to execute on a robot, the repetition of this percept in such a short period of time does not provide much useful information to the cognitive layer. By sending these percepts nevertheless to the cognitive layer may still affect the reasoning and decision making in various ways. Apart from potential processing overhead, however, GOAL provides various ways to deal with repeated percepts. The following code illustrates how a programmer can handle a stream of percepts in a flexible way:

```
init module{
    knowledge{%can add other items in knowledge base that the robot knows.
        doorOpen:- not(doorClosed).
    }%can define init belief base, goals, and action specifications.
}
event module{
    program{
        if bel(percept(doorOpen), doorClosed) then insert(doorOpen).
        if bel(percept(doorClosed), doorOpen) then delete(doorOpen).
    }%can define the rules of putting percepts in the belief base.
}
```

The rules in the **event module** are also called *event* or *percept* rules. These rules specify how percepts can modify a robot's belief about its environment. In the code snippet above, once a percept **doorOpen** is received, the robot will hold the belief that this door is open. So, other duplicated **doorOpen** percepts coming from the EIS layer will not affect the reasoning and decision making.

Another aspect of the synchronization problem is the actions that are sent from the cognitive layer to the interface layer. Action executions usually have duration and take time to be accomplished. For example, if a robot's is to enters **roomA** and then show an arm raising gesture. When the robot holds a belief that it is **in(roomA)**, it should execute a command **gesture(arm-raising)**. However, showing an arm raising gesture cannot be accomplished immediately. An associated problem might be when the gesture has not been finished, another **gesture(arm-raising)** command will be generated for executing because the robot still holds the belief that when it is in **roomA**, it should perform this gesture. Furthermore, some actions can be run in parallel, but some actions cannot. This problem is very common during many action executions. To cope with it, the cognitive control layer provides a very flexible programming style for synchronizing actions:

```
main module{
    program{
        if bel(in(roomA), static, not(showingGesture))
        then insert(showingGesture) + gesture(arm-raising) + say("Hi, Let's take a coffee break!").
        ... % other rules for reasoning and decision making.
}
```

Only does the robot believe that it is **in(roomA)**, **static** (i.e., not walking), and **not(showingGesture)**, the cognitive layer can generate the **gesture(arm-raising)** command. As the **say()** action can be performed in parallel with the **gesture()** action, such action can be generated so that they can be performed at the same time. We notice that the **showingGesture** will be inserted into the belief base of the robot once the robot begins to show the gesture. As a result, even if the **gesture(arm-raising)** has not been accomplished, and the robot is still **in(roomA)**, the cognitive layer will not generate a duplicated **gesture(arm-raising)** action command. By adding particular **beliefs** in the belief base, we can have a flexible approach achieve the synchronization of actions in the cognitive layer.

4 Navigation Task as an Example

To further illustrate our proposed architecture, we will use a navigation task as an example to explain how the agent-based cognitive control can be used to perform physical robots' tasks. The robot platform is a humanoid robot NAO (See Figure 3(a)) built by Aldebaran Robotics. In this task, the NAO robot acts as a message deliverer which is supposed to enter the destination room (e.g., **roomA**) and deliver a message to the people in the room.

The task is carried out in a domestic corridor environment. A predefined map has been built for the robot to localize itself. The robot begins walking from

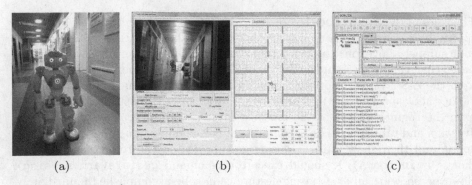

Fig. 3. The navigation task: (a) humanoid robot NAO, (b) the GUI of the robotic behavior layer, (c) the cognitive reasoning in GOAL

a starting place: placeB, and the goal of the robot is to enter the destination roomA, to show an arm-raising gesture, and eventually to deliver a coffee-break message. Figure 3(b) shows the main GUI of the behavioral layer, and Figure 3(c) shows the GUI for the cognitive layer implemented in GOAL.

Figure 4 is the GOAL agent program for reasoning and decision making. The information that the robot knows about its environment consists of the knowledge and of the beliefs. The main differences between the knowledge base and the belief base is that the knowledge base is static and cannot be changed at runtime, whereas the belief base will be updated to keep track of the current state of the environment. Specifically, knowledge defines rules (e.g., static:- not(walking)), which cannot be modified; however, beliefs lists what the robot believes about the current environment (i.e., current belief is in(placeB), but after a while the belief might be in(placeC)). The goals section lists the concrete goals that the robot has to achieve. Action specifications are enumerated in actionspec section. Each action specification also defines the preconditions pre{}: when the action can be performed, and the postconditions post{}: the effects of performing this action. In each reasoning cycle, the event module can modify the robot's belief base based on the percepts from its environment or other robots' messages. In the main module, action rules are defined as strategies or policies for action selection.

Although this navigation task is simple, it shows how the agent-based cognitive control uses the symbolic percepts, generated from uncertain, quantitative sensory data, to keep track of a robot's beliefs about its environment. Based on its beliefs, the robot can infer what actions should execute in order to achieve its goals.

5   Conclusion and Future Work

The navigation task that the robot has performed in the above section demonstrates the feasibility of using a cognitive layer to control physical robots by means of agent-oriented programming. It also demonstrates that the clean separation of sub-symbolic and symbolic layers via the interface layer. Although our

```
1  init module{
2    knowledge{
3      static:- not(walking).
4      doorOpen:- not(doorClosed).
5    }
6    beliefs{
7      in(placeB).
8    }
9    goals{
10     messageDlivered.
11   }
12   actionspec{
13     goto(Place){
14         pre{static}  post{true}
15     }
16     enter(Room){
17         pre{static}  post{true}
18     }
19     gesture(Behavior){
20         pre{static}  post{true}
21     }
22     say(Text){
23         pre{static}  post{true}
24     }
25     % ... add other action functions
26   }
27 }
28 main module{
29   program{
30     if bel(in(placeB), static, not(inFrontOf(roomA))) then adopt(inFrontOf(roomA)).
31     if a-goal(inFrontOf(Room)) then goTo(Room).
32
33     if bel(inFrontOf(roomA), static, not(in(roomA)), doorOpen) then adopt(in(roomA)).
34     if a-goal(in(Room)) then enter(Room).
35
36     if bel(in(roomA), static, not(showingGesture))
37         then insert(showingGesture) + gesture(arm-raising)+ say("Hi, Lets take a coffee break!").
38   }
39 }
40 event module{
41   program{
42     if bel(percept(inFrontOf(Place))) then {
43         if bel(not(inFrontOf(Place))) then insert(inFrontOf(Place)).
44         if bel(inFrontOf(OldPlace)) then insert(not(inFrontOf(OldPlace)), inFrontOf(Place))).
45     }
46     if bel(percept(in(Room))) then {
47         if bel(not(in(Room))) then insert(in(Room)).
48         if bel(in(OldRoom)) then delete(in(OldRoom)) + insert(in(Room)).
49     }
50     if bel(percept(doorOpen), doorClosed) then insert(doorOpen).
51     if bel(percept(doorClosed), doorOpen) then delete(doorOpen).
52
53     if bel(percept(walking), not(walking), static) then insert(walking, not(static)).
54     if bel(percept(static), walking, not(static)) then insert(static, not(walking)).
55
56     % ... add other percepts
57   }
58 }
```

Fig. 4. GOAL agent programming for cognitive control

general architecture is similar to the layered approaches that have been used in many robot projects [30–33], we believe that the use of EIS provides a more principled approach to manage the interaction between sub-symbolic and symbolic processors. Of course, it is important that the cognitive layer (agent program) needs adequate perceptions to make rational decisions given its specific environment. Our architecture provides sufficient support from various components dealing with perception, knowledge processing, and communication to ensure this. Especially, it provides a generic, flexible interface to map sensory data into symbolic knowledge for the cognitive layer.

Future work will concentrate on applying our proposed architecture for multi-robot teamwork in the Block World for Teams environment [34], in which each robot can exchange their perceptions and share their mental states in the cognitive layer so as to coordinate their actions.

References

1. Levesque, H., Lakemeyer, G.: Cognitive robotics. Handbook of Knowledge Representation, 869 (2008)
2. Beetz, M., Mosenlechner, L., Tenorth, M.: CRAM - A Cognitive Robot Abstract Machine for Everyday Manipulation in Human Environments, pp. 1012–1017. IEEE (2010)
3. Kelley, T.D.: Developing a psychologically inspired cognitive architecture for robotic control: The symbolic and subsymbolic robotic intelligence control system. Advanced Robotic 3, 219–222 (2006)
4. Hanford, S.D., Janrathitikarn, O., Long, L.N.: Control of mobile robots using the soar cognitive architecture. Journal of Aerospace Computing Information and Communication 5, 1–47 (2009)
5. Hawes, N., Sloman, A., Wyatt, J., Zillich, M., Jacobsson, H., Kruijff, G., Brenner, M., Berginc, G., Skocaj, D.: Towards an Integrated Robot with Multiple Cognitive Functions, vol. 22, pp. 1548–1553. AAAI Press, MIT Press, Menlo Park, Cambridge (1999/2007)
6. Tenorth, M., Jain, D., Beetz, M.: Knowledge processing for cognitive robots. KI-Künstliche Intelligenz 24, 233–240 (2010)
7. Tenorth, M., Beetz, M.: Knowrob - knowledge processing for autonomous personal robots. In: IEEE/RSJ International Conference on Intelligent Robots and Systems, IROS 2009, pp. 4261–4266. IEEE (2009)
8. Hindriks, K.: Programming rational agents in goal. In: Multi-Agent Programming: Languages, Tools and Applications, pp. 119–157. Springer US (2009)
9. http://ii.tudelft.nl/trac/goal (2012)
10. Hindriks, K.V., van Riemsdijk, M.B., Behrens, T.M., Korstanje, R., Kraaijenbrink, N., Pasman, W., de Rijk, L.: Unreal goal agents. In: AGS 2010 (2010)
11. Behrens, T., Hindriks, K., Dix, J.: Towards an environment interface standard for agent platforms. Annals of Mathematics and Artificial Intelligence, 1–35 (2010)
12. Shanahan, M., Witkowski, M.: High-level robot control through logic. Event London, 104–121 (2000)
13. Duch, W., Oentaryo, R., Pasquier, M.: Cognitive architectures: Where do we go from here? In: Proceeding of the 2008 Conference on Artificial General Intelligence, pp. 122–136 (2008)
14. Soutchanski, M.: High-level Robot Programming and Program Execution (2003)

15. Coffey, S., Clark, K.: A Hybrid, Teleo-Reactive Architecture for Robot Control (2006)
16. Lemaignan, S., Ros, R., Mösenlechner, L., Alami, R., Beetz, M.: Oro, a knowledge management platform for cognitive architectures in robotics. In: IEEE/RSJ International Conference on Intelligent Robots and Systems (2010)
17. Burghart, C., Mikut, R., Stiefelhagen, R., Asfour, T., Holzapfel, H., Steinhaus, P., Dillmann, R.: A cognitive architecture for a humanoid robot: a first approach. Architecture, 357–362 (2005)
18. Anderson, J.R., Lebiere, C.: The atomic components of thought, vol. 3. Erlbaum (1998)
19. Laird, J.E., Newell, A., Rosenbloom, P.S.: Soar: An architecture for general intelligence. Artificial Intelligence 33, 1–64 (1987)
20. Benjamin, P., Lyons, D., Lonsdale, D.: Designing a robot cognitive architecture with concurrency and active perception. In: Proceedings of the AAAI Fall Symposium on the Intersection of Cognitive Science and Robotics (2004)
21. Avery, E., Kelley, T., Davani, D.: Using cognitive architectures to improve robot control: Integrating production systems, semantic networks, and sub-symbolic processing. System 77 (1990)
22. Laird, J.E.: Toward cognitive robotics. In: Proceedings of SPIE, vol. 7332, pp. 73320Z–73320Z–11 (2009)
23. Bekey, G.A.: Autonomous Robots: From Biological Inspiration to Implementation and Control. The MIT Press (2005)
24. Baillie, J.C.: Urbi: Towards a universal robotic low-level programming language. In: 2005 IEEE RSJ International Conference on Intelligent Robots and Systems, pp. 820–825 (2005)
25. Bradski, G.: The OpenCV Library. Dr. Dobb's Journal of Software Tools (2000)
26. Azad, P., Asfour, T., Dillmann, R.: Combining Harris interest points and the SIFT descriptor for fast scale-invariant object recognition. In: 2009 IEEE/RSJ International Conference on Intelligent Robots and Systems, pp. 4275–4280. IEEE (2009)
27. Fischler, M.A., Bolles, R.C.: Random sample consensus: a paradigm for model fitting with applications to image analysis and automated cartography. Communications of the ACM 24, 381–395 (1981)
28. Mika, S., Schaefer, C., Laskov, P., Tax, D., Müller, K.R.: Support vector machines, vol. 1, pp. 1–33. Springer (2004)
29. Kurfess, F.: Integrating symbol-oriented and subsymbolic reasoning methods into hybrid systems. In: From Synapses to Rules-Discovering Symbolic Rules from Neural Processed Data, pp. 275–292. Kluwer Academic Publishers (2002)
30. Qureshi, F., Terzopoulos, D., Gillett, R.: The cognitive controller: A hybrid, deliberative/reactive control architecture for autonomous robots. In: Orchard, B., Yang, C., Ali, M. (eds.) IEA/AIE 2004. LNCS (LNAI), vol. 3029, pp. 1102–1111. Springer, Heidelberg (2004)
31. Arkin, R.C.: Integrating behavioral, perceptual, and world knowledge in reactive navigation. Robotics and Autonomous Systems 6, 105–122 (1990)
32. Connell, J.H.: SSS: a hybrid architecture applied to robot navigation, vol. 3, pp. 2719–2724. IEEE Comput. Soc. Press (1992)
33. Gat, E.: Integrating Planning and Reacting in a Heterogeneous Asynchronous Architecture for Controlling Real-World Mobile Robots, pp. 809–815. Citeseer (1992)
34. Johnson, M., Jonker, C., van Riemsdijk, B., Feltovich, P.J., Bradshaw, J.M.: Joint activity testbed: Blocks world for teams (BW4T). In: Aldewereld, H., Dignum, V., Picard, G. (eds.) ESAW 2009. LNCS, vol. 5881, pp. 254–256. Springer, Heidelberg (2009)

A Programming Framework for Multi-agent Coordination of Robotic Ecologies

M. Dragone[1], S. Abdel-Naby[1], D. Swords[1], G.M.P. O'Hare[1], and M. Broxvall[2]

[1] University College Dublin, Dublin (UCD), Ireland
mauro.dragone@ucd.ie
[2] Örebro University, Fakultetsgatan 1, SE-70182, Örebro, Sweden

Abstract. Building smart environments with Robotic ecologies, comprising of distributed sensors, actuators and mobile robot devices facilitates and extends the nature and form of smart environments that can be developed, and reduces the complexity and cost of such solutions. While the potentials of such an approach makes robotic ecologies increasingly popular, many fundamental research questions remain open. One such question is how to make a robotic ecology self-adaptive, so as to adapt to changing conditions and evolving requirements, and consequently reduce the amount of preparation and pre-programming required for their deployment in real world applications. This paper presents a framework for the specification and the programming of robotic ecologies. The framework extends an existing agent system and integrates it with the pre-existing and dominant traditional robotic and middleware approach to the development of robotic ecologies. We illustrate how these technologies complement each other and offer a candidate technology to pursue adaptive robotic ecologies.

1 Introduction

This paper presents a framework for the specification and the programming of robotic ecologies. The framework extends an existing agent system and integrates it with the pre-existing and dominant traditional robotic and middleware approach to the development of robotic ecologies.

Robotic ecologies constitute an emerging paradigm, which transcends traditional borders between the fields of robotics, sensor networks, and ambient intelligence (AmI). Central to the robotic ecology concept is that complex tasks are not performed by a single, very capable robot (e.g., a humanoid robot butler), instead they are performed through the collaboration and cooperation of many networked robotic devices (including mobile robots, static sensors or actuators, and automated home appliances) performing several steps in a coordinated and goal oriented fashion.

One of the key strengths of such an approach is the possibility of using alternative mechanisms by which to accomplish application goals when multiple courses of actions are available. For instance, a robot seeking to reach the user in another room may decide to localize itself with its on-board sensors, or to

M. Dastani, J.F. Hübner, and B. Logan (Eds.): ProMAS 2012, LNAI 7837, pp. 72–89, 2013.
© Springer-Verlag Berlin Heidelberg 2013

avail itself of the more accurate location information from a localization system. However, while having multiple options is a potential source of robustness and adaptability, the combinatorial growth of possible execution traces compromises scalabiliy. Adapting, within tractable time frames, to dynamically changing goals and environmental conditions is made more challenging when these conditions fall outside those envisioned by the system designer.

In the EU FP7 project RUBICON (Robotic UBIquitous COgnitive Network) [1][2] we tackle these challenges by seeking to develop goal-oriented robotic ecologies that exhibit a tightly coupled, self-sustaining learning interaction among all of their participants. Specifically, we investigate how all the participants in the RUBICON ecology can cooperate in using their past experience to improve their performance by autonomously and proactively adjusting their behaviour and perception capabilities in response to a changing environment and user needs.

An important pre-requisite of such an endeavour, which is addressed in this paper, is the necessary software infrastructure underpinning the specification, integration, and the distributed management of the operations of robotic ecologies. Specifically, this work builds upon the *Self*-OSGi [3] [4], a modular and lightweight agent system built over Java technology from the Open Service Gateway Initiative (OSGi) [5], and (i) extends it to operate across distributed platforms, and (ii) integrates it with the PEIS middleware, previously developed as part of the *Ecologies of Physically Embedded Intelligent Systems* project [6].

The remainder of the paper is organized in the following manner: Section 2 provides an overview of the state of the art techniques for the coordination of robotic ecologies, with an emphasis on those pursued within the PEIS initiative - the starting point for the control of RUBICON robotic ecologies. Section 3 presents the *Self*-OSGi component & service-based agent framework, and the way it has been recently extended and integrated with PEIS. Section 4 illustrates the use of the resulting multi-agent framework with two robotic ecology experiments. Finally, Section 5 summarizes the contributions of this paper and points to some directions to be explored in future research.

2   PEIS

The PEIS kernel [7] and related middleware tools represent a suite of software, previously developed as part of the PEIS project [6] in order to enable communication and collaboration between heterogeneous robotic devices.

The PEIS kernel is written in pure C (with binding for Java and other languages) and with as few library and RAM/processing dependencies as possible to maximize compatibility with heterogeneous devices.

PEIS includes a decentralized mechanism for collaboration between separate processes running on separate devices which allows for automatic discovery, high-level communication and collaboration through subscription based connections. It also offers a shared, tuple space blackboard that allows for high level collaboration and dynamic self-configuration between different devices through the exchange and storage of tuples (key-value pairs) used in associating any piece of data (and related meta-information, such as timestamps and MIME types), to a logical key.

2.1   Tuples and Meta-tuples

A tuple's key in PEIS consists of two parts: *(name, owner)* where *name* is a string key for the tuple, and *owner* is the address (id) of a PEIS responsible for the tuple.

In the most simple scenario for executing a collaboration between components, producers create data in their own tuple space and consumers establish subscriptions to these tuples to access the data that is to be used.

However, consuming components cannot know in advance from where to read the data to be used. Meta tuples offer a mechanism to address this problem. By using these as inputs it is possible for consumers to read hard coded meta tuples from their own tuplespace. This corresponds to meta tuples acting as named input ports in other middleware.

To configure such a consumer, a configuration writes the id and key of tuples produced by any producer. The consumer will then automatically subscribe to, and read the data from, the producer. From the developers' point of view this makes programming configurable components very simple since *input* tuples then can be read with a simple API call and the kernel automatically handles the setting up and removing of new subscriptions as the configuration is changed. This is in the following (pseudo-code) example.

```
Producer 42:
  while (true):
    setTuple "temperature" <= sensorReading()

Consumer 22:
  subscribeIndirectTuple(peisId(), "heat")
  while true:
    T = findIndirectTuple("heat")
    ... do something with T ...

Configurator:
    setTuple "22.heat" <= "META 42 temperature"
```

2.2   PEIS-Init

PEIS relies on a program called PEIS-Init to act as central location on each host to start or stop and monitor the execution of functional components. To this end, PEIS-init component relies on a set of component files on the local machine to determine which component can run on it and what their semantic descriptions are. For each possible component, PEIS-init subscribes to tuples to set the start, stop or restart state of the components. It forks and executes the corresponding software components if the components are requested to be run (i.e. when their *reqState* tuples are set to value *on*), monitors their inputs, outputs and execution states (restarting them if necessary) and stops the components when they are no longer needed (when their *reqState* tuple is set to *off*). Noticeably, PEIS is agnostic to the type of semantic used to describe the components. The responsibility of managing and using components' semantic description is delegated to external coordinator components, as discussed in the next section.

2.3 Action Coordination and Configuration for Robotic Ecologies

Computing which actions are to be performed by individual devices has been traditionally solved in a centralized manner by using an action planner that reasons about the possible outcomes of different actions on a given model of the environment [8].

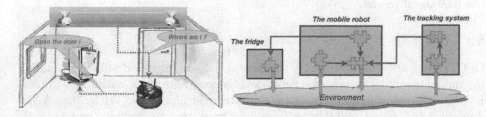

Fig. 1. A simple PEIS-Ecology (taken from [6]). Left: The ceiling cameras provide global positioning to the robot. The robot performs the door opening action by asking the refrigerator to do it. Right: Corresponding functional configuration of the devices involved

We call the set of devices that are actively exchanging data in a collaborative fashion at any given time the *configuration* of the ecology. The task of computing the configuration to be used at any given time in order to accomplish the actions generated by an action coordinator can also be modeled explicitly as a search problem and solved, either, in a dedicated configuration planner or as an integral step of the action planning process.

This is illustrated in Figure 2 where a configuration plans for a subset of the available devices to perform specific localization tasks in order to assist the robot Astrid to navigate and open a refrigerator door.

In our work we propose to distribute certain aspects of these tasks over a number of agents with varying responsibilities and functionalities in order to lead to better scalability, robustness and fault tolerance.

Agent and Multi Agent Systems (MASs) are regarded as a general-purpose paradigm by which to facilitate the co-ordination of complex systems built in terms of loosely-coupled, situated, autonomous and social components (the *agents*). In particular, the Belief Desire Intention (BDI) agent model, used in the *Self*-OSGi framework discussed in the following section, provides a simple, yet, extensible model of agency that explicitly addresses the production of rational and autonomous behaviour by agents with limited computational resources.

3   *Self*-OSGi

Self-OSGi [3] [4] is a BDI agent framework built on OSGi Java technology and purposefully designed to support the type of collaboration envisaged within the ubiquitous and embedded systems targeted by RUBICON.

The component & service orientation used in the design of *Self*-OSGi is an highly popular, mainstream approach used to build modular software systems. Component & service frameworks operate by posing clear boundaries (in terms of provided and required service interfaces) between software components and by guiding the developers in re-using and assembling these components into applications. *Self*-OSGi addresses the lack of common adaptation mechanisms in these frameworks by leveraging their previously unexploited similarities with the BDI agent model.

3.1   OSGi

OSGi specification [5] is currently the most widely adopted technology for building modular control systems for networked home applications, with many implementations targeting computationally constrained platforms. Within the AAL domain, OSGi-based middleware have long been used to provide the technical basis for integrating network devices and services, e.g. in EU projects such as Amigo, OASIS, SOPRANO, and their recent consolidation in the UniversAAL platform.

OSGi defines a standardised component model and a lightweight container framework, built above the JVM, which is used as a shared platform for network-provisioned services and components specified through Java interfaces and Java classes. Each OSGi platform facilitates the dynamic installation and management of units of deployment, called *bundles*, by acting as a host environment whereby various applications can be executed and managed in a secured and modularised environment. An OSGi bundle is packaged in a Jar file and organises the frameworks internal state and manages its core functionalities. These include both container and life cycle operations to install, start, stop and remove components as well as checking dependencies.

The separation between services and their actual implementations is the key to enable system adaptation. With OSGi, in addition to syntactic matching of service interfaces, developers can also associate lists of name/value attributes to describe the semantic of each service, and use the LDAP filter syntax to search the services that match given search criteria. Furthermore, *Declarative Services* (DS) for OSGi offers a declarative model for managing multiple components within each bundle and also for automatically publishing, finding and binding their required/provided services, based on XML component definitions. However, DS only matches pre-defined filters with pre-defined services attributes of already active components, but does not consider the automatic instantiation of new components, the context-sensitive selection of their services, or the automatic recovery from their failure - all necessary features for the construction of context-aware, adaptive systems.

3.2   Component and Service Based Agent Model

Self-OSGi addresses the issues outlined in the previous section by translating the BDI agent model [9] into general component & service concepts. In particular, the separation between the services interface and the services implementation is the basis for implementing both the declarative and the procedural components of BDI-like agents, and also for handling dynamic environments, by replicating their ability to search for alternative applicable plans when a goal is first posted or when a previously attempted plan has failed.

Belief Model: As in the Jadex agent language [10], *Self*-OSGi represents beliefs as simple Java objects. Compared to agent toolkits where beliefs are stored as logic predicates, objects have the advantage of providing a strong typed definition of agent's beliefs. In addition, within *Self*-OSGi, a belief set is implemented as a *Belief Set* component with clearly defined interfaces, which are used to access any data that may affect the value of its beliefs.

Service Goal Model: Goals, describing the desires that the agent may possibly intend, are represented in *Self*-OSGi by the (Java) interfaces of the services that may be used to achieve them, or *service goals*.

Service goals may represent either: (i) **performative** sub-goals defining the desired conditions to bring about in the world and/or in the systems state - for instance, the method *"(void) beAt(X, Y)"* in the goal service *GoalNavigation* may be used by a robotic agent to represent the goal of being at a given location - and (ii) **knowledge** sub-goals subtending the exchange of information. For instance, the method *"Image getImage()"* in the *GoalImage* service goal may be used to express the goal of retrieving the last video frame captured by one camera. In addition, service goals attributes may be used to further characterise each service goal, e.g. the characteristic of the information requested/granted, as well as important non-functional parameters. In particular, attributes may be used to identify the entity (a specific robot agent or part of it) responsible of some perceptual and/or acting process. For instance, the attribute *Agent* may be used to represent the name of the robot providing video frames, while the attribute *Side* may be used to specify to which one of the robotic cameras (left or right eye) the video corresponds to.

Component Plan Model: A plan, describing the means to achieve a goal (its post-condition), is represented by the component - *component plan* - implementing (providing) it. A component plan may require a number of service goals in order.to post sub-goals, to perform actions, and also to acquire the information it needs to achieve its post-condition. For instance, a *Navigator* component plan may process the images from a robots camera and control the velocity and the direction of the robot to drive it safely toward a given location. The same component plan may subscribe to range data from a laser sensor, to account for the presence of obstacles on its path.

Semantic Descriptions: *Self*-OSGi re-uses the OSGi XML component descriptions and enriches them with properties guiding its agent-like management of components' dependencies and components' instantiation.

As a way of example, the following is part of the XML documents describing a *Navigation*, a *CameraLocalization* and a *LaserLocalization* component plans.

In order to clarify its correspondence with the BDI model it represents, each XML is preceded with a comment in the form $e : \Psi \leftarrow P$ where P is the body of the plan, e is the event that triggers the plan (the plan's post-conditions), and Ψ is the context for which the plan can be applied (which corresponds to the preconditions of the plan).

$$GoalNavigation(?Agent) : true \leftarrow \{achieve(GoalLocalization(?Agent)); ...\}$$

```
<scr:component ... factory="Navigation" name="Navigator">
<implementation class= "Navigator"/>
<property name="?Agent" type="String" value="The name of the robot supposed to move">
<service>
        <provide interface="GoalNavigation"/>
</service>
<reference cardinality="0..1" interface= "GoalLocalization" policy="dynamic"
target="(Agent=?Agent)>
</scr:component>
```

$$GoalLocalization(?Agent) : (light > 30) \leftarrow \{achieve(GoalVideo(?Agent)); ...\}$$

```
<scr:component ... factory="CameraLocalization" name="CameraLocalization">
<implementation class= "CameraLocalization"/>
<property name="?Agent" type="String" value="The name of the robot to be localized">
<service>
        <provide interface="GoalLocalization"/>
</service>
<reference cardinality="0..1" interface= "GoalVideo" name="Video" target="(Agent=?Agent)"/>
<property name="self.osgi.precondition.LDAP" value="(light>30)"/>
</scr:component>
```

$$GoalLocalization(?Agent) : true \leftarrow \{achieve(GoalLaser(?Agent)); ...\}$$

```
<scr:component ... factory="LaserLocalization" name="CameraLocalization">
<implementation class= "LaserLocalization"/>
<property name="?Agent" type="String" value="The name of the robot to be localized">
<service>
        <provide interface="GoalLocalization"/>
</service>
<reference cardinality="0..1" interface= "GoalLaser" name="Laser" target="(Agent=?Agent)"/>
</scr:component>
```

Post-Conditions: The post-conditions of both component plans are specified with the OSGi XML *service* element. The *Navigation* component plan implements a move-to navigation behaviour in order to provide the service goal *GoalNavigation*, while both the *CameraLocalization* and the *LaserLocalization* component plans implement localization methods in order to provide localization updates through the service goal *GoalLocalization*, that is:

```
interface GoalNavigation {
      void beAt (Location location);
}
```

```
interface GoalLocalization {
   Location getLocation();
}
```

Service Goal Requirements: Service goal requirements are declared using OSGi XML *reference* elements. The definition of *Navigator* declares its requirement of localization information as *dynamic*, in order to allow OSGi to activate it even when the reference to the *Localization* service goal is not resolved, thus avoiding to having to commit to a specific localization mechanism before the behaviour is started.

Noticeably, the definition of *CameraLocalization* includes *Self*-OSGi-specific property fields, *self.osgi.precondition.LDAP*, whose value may be used to characterise the context when the component plan is applicable. In the example, the LDAP pre-condition describes how *CameraLocalization* can only be used when the intensity of the ambient light, e.g. sensed by a light sensor component, is believed to be above a given threshold.

Variables: In order to link post-conditions with pre-conditions and service goal requirements, *Self*-OSGi allows the use of variable attributes whose name starts with the special character "?". Variables may be used as names of the property associated to a component plan in order to specify that the component plan can be instantiated with any value for that property. In such a case, the value of the variable is used as default value of the property. For instance, both the *Navigator* and the *CameraLocalization* component plans declare the property *Agent* to specify that they can be used by any agent to achieve, respectively, the *GoalNavigation* and the *GoalLocalization* service goals. Once the respective component plans have been instantiated for a specific robot agent, i.e. *TurtleBot*, the services they provide will have an *Agent* attribute with value *TurtleBot*. However, in order for the same services to work, they must receive updates, respectively, of location and video data related to the same robot agent. Both XML descriptions specify this dependency by repeating the attribute *?Agent* in the reference elements describing their required service goals. It is the responsibility of *Self*-OSGi to propagate the value of these variable properties from the post-condition/service side to the requirement/reference side, for instance, to wire a *Navigator* component activated in the *TurtleBot* robot agent, with a *LaserLocalization* activated for the same robot agent, rather than using the pure syntactic match (which could be satisfied by any localization data, e.g. related to other robots or used to represent the location of a human user).

3.3 Core Implementation

The interested reader is refered to Dragone [3], for more detailed information on the internal architecture of each *Self*-OSGi platform.

The main difference from traditional agent platforms, such as the Agent Factory (AF) platform developed in UCD [11], is that agent container functionalities are built directly over the OSGi bundle and component container. In addition, rather than employing logic-based agent languages, *Self*-OSGi's goals and plans are directly specified in Java, as discussed in the previous sections.

As a way of example, the following code is used to send a robot to a given location by initializing a standard OSGi *ServiceTracker* object to request the *GoalNavigation* service goal, before invoking it by passing the location coordinates. The special attribute *selfosgi=true* is used to demand the *Self*-OSGi management of the call. Noticeably, no other modifications are required to standard OSGi programming.

```
ServiceTracker tracker = new ServiceTracker(...,
context.createFilter("(\&(objectClass="+GoalNavigation.class.getName()+") (selfosgi=true)").open();
(GoalNavigation)(tracker.waitForService(0)).beAt (100, 200);
```

The service goal request is intercepted by *Self*-OSGi, which queries the OSGi DS for the list of all the components able to provide the requested service (i.e. *LaserLocalization* and *CameraLocalization* in the example). After that, *Self*-OSGi implements the BDI cycle by (i) finding all the component plans (installed in the same OSGi platform) with satisfied pre-conditions (i.e. which hold against the current content of the belief set), and (ii) instantiating (loading) and activating the most suitable one by using user-provided ranking components. Finally, *Self*-OSGi installs a proxy between the client that has originally requested a service goal, and the component activated to provide it. It is thanks to this mediation, that *Self*-OSGi can catch failures in the instantiated services activation, and trigger the selection of alternative component plans.

In the localization example, these features are used to make the robot reach its destination while opportunistically exploiting any suitable localization mechanism, for instance, starting with the *CameraLocalization* and then switching to the *LaserLocalization* if the first fails when the ambient light drops below the given threshold.

4   Distributed *Self*-OSGi and PEIS Integration

While the *Self*-OSGi system described in [3] [4] and summarised in the previous section was limited to components and services running on a single platform and single JVM, the latest *Self*-OSGi version described in this paper has been fitted with extension mechanisms in order to provide seamless system distribution.

By default, such mechanisms leverage the R-OSGi distributed extension of OSGi to support service goal invocation across remote platforms. The other distributed extension of OSGi, D-OSGi, specifically targets Web Services technology and poses a much bigger overhead - 10MB - compared to the 230KB of R-OSGi footprint. R-OSGi can be deployed in minimal OSGi implementations and uses a very efficient network protocol. This makes it ideal for small and embedded devices with limited memory and network bandwidth.

Both R-OSGi and D-OSGi allows programs to bind and invoke remote services through port and proxy mechanisms. To this end, application components must register their services for remote access. Subsequently, other peers must connect to the R-OSGi registry of their peers to get access to their remote services.

Within *Self*-OSGi, the framework automatically manages these steps so that distribution becomes totally transparent to the application developer. In addition, *Self*-OSGi extends its automatic instantiation and selection of component plans to multiple platforms by integrating agent-based negotiation protocols within the standalone *Self*-OSGi system.

In the example depicted in Figure 2, a model bundle containing the specifications of three service goals (their Java interfaces) is equally shared by four platforms (A, B, C, D). However, the implementation of these service goals is distributed across the system. Specifically, platform A hosts two component plans implementing two of the service goals while platform D hosts one implementation of the service goal missing in platform A.

Developers can install a number of protocol components to handle the distribution of service goal requests. Thanks to OSGi DS, the fitting of a distribution protocol is done completely transparently from the application components, which do not need to be aware of their distribution across platforms.

Distribution protocols can range from simple delegation mechanism, which routes the service goal requests to specific platforms in the network, to more complex agent-style negotiation protocols, such as the contract net protocol (CNP) depicted in Figure 2. The latter can be used to query a group of platforms - which can be discovered via any network discovery solution - through a *call for proposal* (CFP) message. Upon reception of such a message, each platform will lookup their XML component repository and - in the case they can satisfy the request - reply with a bid message reporting the details of the component plan they consider most suitable to satisfy it. At this point, the original requester (platform A in the example) can evaluate all bids, including its own, before sending a message (to platform D in the example) to accept the best bid. Upon reception of the *accept* message, the chosen platform will instantiate the selected component plan and automatically register with R-OSGi the service goal it provides. The initiating platform will then retrieve the reference to the service goal from the remote platform, create a proxy, and export it to the local OSGi registry.

Within the RUBICON Control Architecture, the distributed extension of *Self*-OSGi has the following roles:

- provide a semantic vocabulary for expressing the capabilities and the requirements of all available devices and software components in the ecology, in order to support self-organization capabilities and the modular specification of the behaviour of the robotic ecology.
- enhance system's scalability by framing it as a multi-agent system in order to leverage agent communication languages (ACLs) and multi-agent system (MAS) coordination & negotiation protocols.
- reduce the gap between the mainstream software solutions traditionally used in AmI/AAL domains and the state of the art techniques used in agent-oriented software engineering and in the control of robotic ecologies.

The final element to allow the use of the same mechanisms for the coordination of robotic ecologies is the interface between *Self*-OSGi and the PEIS middleware discussed in Section 2.

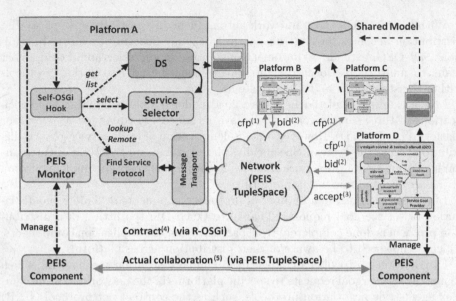

Fig. 2. Automatic distribution of *Self*-OSGi Systems

Specifically, the PEIS tuplespace is used to:

1. serve as platform discovery mechanism, by leveraging its peer-to-peer communication functionalities to re-create on each platform the directory of all the platforms available over the network. *Self*-OSGi uses these directories to find out the url of remote instances of *Self*-OSGi, before using R-OSGi to contact them by sending service goal requests and conducting auction-based negotiation protocols.

2. communicate with the PEIS-Init components installed on each platform, in order to manage PEIS components running outside the JVM, such as robotic behaviour components implemented in native C/C++ languages. In these cases, component plans in *Self*-OSGi acts as proxies of the underlying PEIS components they manage. A basic implementation - *PEIS Component Monitor* - provides generic functionalities to start/stop/configure peis components by setting the value of special tuples used to propagate these instructions via the tuplespace.

5   Testing Tools and Examples

For the purpose of testing and demonstrating the overall implementation of the multi-agent framework presented in this paper, we have developed a set of PEIS tools capable of visualizing and even simulating each component of a robotic ecology. These tools are intended to simplify the development and debugging of the agent based tools and their interaction with the robotic ecology, and facilitate their adoption in real world situations.

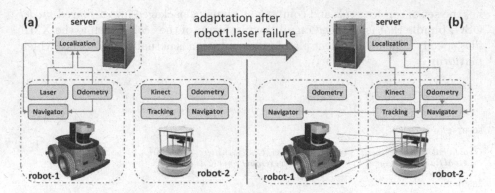

Fig. 3. Test scenario: before and after self-configuration

5.1   Configuration Example

The first example illustrated in this section shows the ability of our framework to automatically generate a sequence of configurations to perform a given task in the current context (state). The test has been performed in a low-fidelity simulator emulating the behaviour of real devices distributed over three platforms:

1. a robot (*robot-1*) equipped with a laser ranging sensor, an odometry sensors, and a navigation component plan.
2. a robot (*robot-2*) equipped with a 3D ranging camera, an odometry sensors, a navigation and a tracking component plan.
3. a server (*server*) with an installation of a simultaneous localization and mapping (SLAM) component plan.

Simulated components allow us to while running the full framework for specification, introspection, deployment, communication and configuration

Scenario: In order to drive the robots, both navigation component plans must rely on odometry and localization information (their service goal requirement). However, none of the robot platforms have enough computational power to run a localization component plan locally. Fortunately, an instance of the *SLAM* component plan - running on the server - can provide location updates, as long as it receives data from both one ranging sensor and from the odometry of the robot. In addition, *robot-2* can use its 3D ranging camera to observe the scene from an external point of view, and compute its position relative to *robot-1*. *Robot-2* can use this information and the knowledge of its own location, to provide an estimate of the absolute location of *robot-1*, which may then be used by *robot-1* as an alternative to the location updates sent by the server.

These two alternative configurations, illustrated in Figure 3, can be easily deduced from the following dependencies (expressed in BDI-style notation here for simplicity in place of their actual XML form) between the localization, odometry, navigation and tracking service goals. The definition of these dependencies,

i.e. the set of service goals and component plans, is packaged into a shared *model*
OSGi bundle that is installed on all the platforms of the ecology, while the XML
files specify which component plan implementation is actually available to which
platform.

SERVER:

$GoalNavigation(?Agent) : true \leftarrow \{achieve(GoalLocalization(?Agent)\&GoalOdometry(?Agent)); \}$

ROBOT-1:

$GoalLocalization(?Agent) : true \leftarrow \{achieve(GoalRanging(?Agent)); ...\}$
$\quad GoalRanging(?Agent) : true \leftarrow \{achieve(GoalLaser(?Agent)); \}$

ROBOT-2:

$GoalLocalization(?Agent) : true \leftarrow \{achieve(GoalRanging(?Agent)); \}$
$\quad GoalRanging(?Agent) : true \leftarrow \{achieve(GoalKinect(?Agent)); \}$

$\quad GoalLocalization(?Agent1) : true \leftarrow \{achieve(GoalKinect(?Agent2)\&GoalLocalization(?Agent2)); \}$

Finally, figure 4 and 5 show the outputs of the PEIS visualization tools, respectively showing the timeline and the connectivity graph of the wiring of the
component plans in the ecology during the different phases of the experiment.
In particular, the diagrams illustrate the status of the robotic ecology (1) after
robot-1 was tasked to move to a given location, (2) after its laser was (artificially)
disconnected to simulate a component failure, and (3) after the system had recovered from failure. The whole process can be summarised with the following
steps:

1. *robot-1* issues a *Localization(robot-1)* service goal request , before assigning
   it to *server*, which is randomly preferred to the *robot-2* (the other bidder,
   as the post-condition of its tracking component plan also matches with the
   requested service goal).
2. *server* instantiates a *SLAM* component plan and issues two service goal requests to satisfy its service goal requirements, respectively for *Ranging(robot-
   1)* and *Odometry(robot-1)*, before assigning both of them to *robot-1* (the only
   bidder).
3. upon failure of the *robot-1*'s laser, the *SLAM* component plan on server also
   fails and *robot-1* re-issues a *Localization(robot-1)* request. However, since the
   last time the *SLAM* component plan has failed, this time the service goal is
   assigned to *robot-2*.
4. *robot-2* instantiates a *tracking(robot-1)* component plan, causing the issuing
   of requests for *Localization(robot-2)* and the successive wiring between its
   sensors and a new *SLAM* component plan on the server.

5.2 Task Allocation Example

This section illustrates a second example showing the ability of our framework
to manage task allocation for a multi-robot system. The example consists of two
robots (Figure 6.a) and a server. Both robots have identical functionality and are
running the Robotic Operating System (ROS) framework [12]. In addition, both

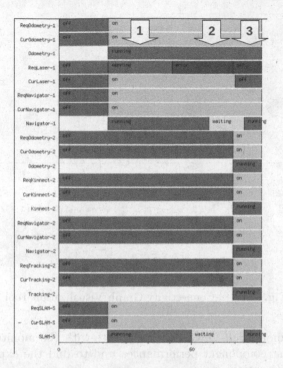

Fig. 4. PEIS Timeline Visualization Tool

robots and the server run instances of *Self*-OSGi and the PEIS middleware. PEIS *Navigation* components are running on both robots. The PEIS *Navigation* components accept goal tuples describing navigation way-points, and submit those goals to the underlying ROS navigation stack, which then performs localization and path-finding functionality. The PEIS *Navigation* components provide progress updates via a progress tuple. Progress is described by the estimated distance from the goal. The server runs a *Navigation Monitor* component also offering the *GoalNavigation* service. However, rather than actually implementing this service, that component is used to monitor the performance of the actual navigator component running on the robot, as shown in (Figure 6.b), by subscribing and reading its output tuple in order to monitor its progress toward its goal. In this manner, when a *GoalNavigation* service is first posted to *Self*-OSGi, this will first activate a monitor component on the server and then wire it to the navigator component of one of the two available robots. In the case that the first selected robot fails, e.g. due either to an hardware, physical or software problem, the monitor component will notice either the interruption of the progress feedback, or a problem in its values. *Self*-OSGi will then search for another component able to provide the *GoalNavigation* service to recover from the failure. Since another *Navigator* component is available on the second robot, that robot is then allocated the original goal. Noticeably, this last step is performed by using the same auction-based schema described in the previous

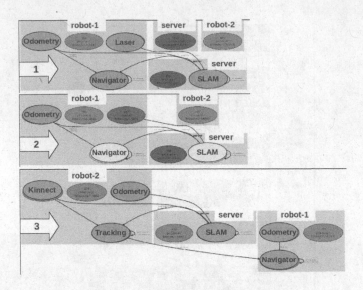

Fig. 5. PEIS Connectivity Graph Visualization Tool

section. Furthermore, *Self*-OSGi may cooperate with the monitor components to remember past component performances and to find the expected value of each configuration option.

In this manner, *Self*-OSGi's re-configuration can be used as a basis for task allocation, with the added advantage that monitor components help further grounding the semantic of functional components (which is described by their XML component representations) by linking them with the operative description of what the components must achieve once activated.

6   Related Work

The general problem of self-configuration of a distributed system is addressed in several fields, including ambient intelligence [13][14], web service composition [15], distributed middleware [16], and autonomic computing [17]. These works, however, do not address the same type of problem considered here: functional coordination of a robotic ecology, in which the components of the system exchange continuous streams of data and can interact with the physical world.

Classical AI planning such as STRIPS based operators can easily be extended to take the role of high-level coordinators for robotic ecologies [8]. However, these planning methods suffer from a number of challenges that make them less than ideal. The first of these challenges is due to the demands on robustness combined with a demand of combinatorial generality where the possible combinations of devices should be able to provide functionalities to assist other devices is expected to grow superlinearly as more devices are added to the ecology. Secondly, as the environments become increasingly complex and unstructured, these planning methods tend to increase in complexity and to become intractable.

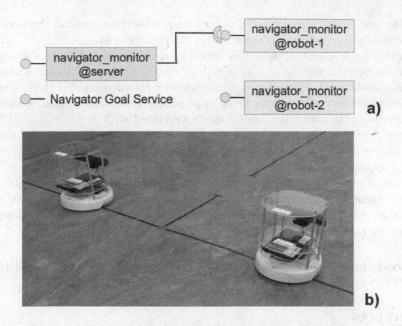

Fig. 6. Task Allocation Experiment: a) wiring, b) robots performing the experiment

Purely reactive configuration of robotic ecologies have also been explored within the PEIS project [18]. Such an approach creates its configurations by instantiating plan-based task operators used to represent components and their operative dependencies. As in *Self*-OSGi, searching for suitable configuration is done in a reactive (one-step look-ahead) manner. Most noticeably on the multi-robot front, [19] [20] presents a distributed reasoning system, called ASyMTRe-D, which enables a team of robots to form coalitions to accomplish a multi-robot task through tightly-coupled sensor sharing. Such an approach represents competences using biologically-inspired schema abstractions grounded in the information theoretical work of Donald, et al. [21], and which share many similarities with the XML component semantic descriptions described used in *Self*-OSGi. Specifically, both representations can be used to explicitly model the conversion among information types that are specified with referent entities. However, compared to those approaches, our work with *Self*-OSGi is concerned with extending this type of component representations and incorporating them into mainstream, agent & component-based programming frameworks to be used for the specification and programming robotic ecologies.

7   Conclusions and Future Work

This paper has described the distributed extension of the *Self*-OSGi agent framework and its integration with pre-existing middleware employed for the control of robotic ecologies. The resulting framework provides re-usable, lightweight, modular end extensible mechanisms for the specification and the development of decentralized coordination mechanisms for robotic ecologies.

While a multi-agent approach is often adopted for robot system design, a key and original result of our approach is that both system distribution and system adaptation become orthogonal concerns thus freeing the developers to tackle application requirements. Once application components are implemented, and their semantic and inter-dependencies described with *Self*-OSGi XML files, they can be freely distributed over the network, and thereafter the distributed *Self*-OSGi will automatically manage their instantiation and configuration to achieve application's objectives.

Future work will test the framework with larger scale problems and also seek to adapt agent/planning integration and agent learning techniques to tackle some of the main limitations of our architecture, such as its lack of look-ahead and its reliance on hard-coded pre-conditions of component plans.

Acknowledgment. This work has been supported by the EU FP7 RUBICON project (contract n. 269914).

References

1. Amato, G., Broxvall, M., Chessa, S., Dragone, M., Gennaro, C., López, R., Maguire, L., Mcginnity, T.M., Micheli, A., Renteria, A., O'Hare, G.P., Pecora, F.: Robotic UBIquitous COgnitive network. In: Novais, P., Hallenborg, K., Tapia, D.I., Rodríguez, J.M.C. (eds.) Ambient Intelligence - Software and Applications. AISC, vol. 153, pp. 191–195. Springer, Heidelberg (2012)
2. Robotic UBIquitous COgnitive Network, http://fp7rubicon.eu
3. Dragone, M.: Component & Service-based Agent Systems: Self-OSGi. In: ICAART (1), pp. 200–210 (2012)
4. Dragone, M.: A BDI Model for Component and Service-Based Systems: Self-OSGi. In: PAAMS, pp. 67–72 (2012)
5. Alliance, O.: OSGi Service Platform: The OSGi Alliance. IOS Press, US (2007)
6. Saffiotti, A., Broxvall, M., Gritti, M., LeBlanc, K., Lundh, R., Rashid, M.J., Seo, B., Cho, Y.J.: The PEIS-Ecology Project: Vision and results. In: IROS, pp. 2329–2335 (2008)
7. Broxvall, M.: The PEIS Kernel: A Middleware for Ubiquitous Robotics. In: Proc. of the IROS 2007 Workshop on Ubiquitous Robotic Space Design and Applications (2007)
8. Lundh, R., Karlsson, L., Saffiotti, A.: Plan-Based Configuration of an Ecology of Robots. In: ICRA, pp. 64–70 (2007)
9. Kinny, D., Georgeff, M., Rao, A.: A Methodology and Modelling Technique for Systems of BDI Agents (1996)
10. Pokahr, A., Braubach, L., Lamersdorf, W.: A Goal Deliberation Strategy for BDI Agent Systems. In: Eymann, T., Klügl, F., Lamersdorf, W., Klusch, M., Huhns, M.N. (eds.) MATES 2005. LNCS (LNAI), vol. 3550, pp. 82–93. Springer, Heidelberg (2005)
11. Ross, R., Collier, R., O'Hare, G.M.P.: AF-APL: Bridging Principles & Practices in Agent Oriented Languages. In: Bordini, R.H., Dastani, M., Dix, J., El Fallah Seghrouchni, A. (eds.) PROMAS 2004. LNCS (LNAI), vol. 3346, pp. 66–88. Springer, Heidelberg (2005)

12. Quigley, M., Conley, K., Gerkey, B., Faust, J., Foote, T.B., Leibs, J., Wheeler, R., Ng, A.Y.: ROS: An open-source robot operating system. In: ICRA Workshop on Open Source Software, Anchorage, USA (2009)
13. Kaminsky, A.: Infrastructure for Distributed Applications in Ad Hoc Networks of Small Mobile Wireless Devices. Tech. rep., Rochester Institute of Technology, IT Lab (2001)
14. Hellenschmidt, M., Kirste, T.: Self-organization for Multicomponent Multimedia Environments. In: Proc. of the UniComp Workshop on Ubiquitous Display Environments (2004)
15. Rao, J., Su, X.: A Survey of Automated Web Service Composition Methods. In: Cardoso, J., Sheth, A.P. (eds.) SWSWPC 2004. LNCS, vol. 3387, pp. 43–54. Springer, Heidelberg (2005)
16. Oaks, S., Traversat, B., Gong, L.: JXTA in a Nutshell. O'Reilly, Sebastopol (2002)
17. Tesauro, G., Chess, D.M., Walsh, W.E., Das, R., Segal, A., Whalley, I., Kephart, J.O., White, S.R.: A Multi-Agent Systems Approach to Autonomic Computing. In: AAMAS, pp. 464–471 (2004)
18. Gritti, M., Broxvall, M., Saffiotti, A.: Reactive Self-Configuration of an Ecology of Robots. In: Proc. of the ICRA 2007 Workshop on Network Robot Systems, Rome, Italy, pp. 49–56 (2007)
19. Parker, L.E., Tang, F.: Distributed multi-robot coalitions through asymtre-d. In: Proc. of IEEE International Conference on Intelligent Robots and Systems, Edmonton, Canada (2005)
20. Zhang, Y., Parker, L.E.: Iq-asymtre: Synthesizing coalition formation and execution for tightly-coupled multirobot tasks. In: Proc. of IEEE International Conference on Intelligent Robots and Systems, Taipai, Taiwan (2010)
21. Donald, B.R., Jennings, J., Rus, D.: Towards a theory of information invariants for cooperating autonomous mobile robots. Technical report, Ithaca, NY, USA (1993)

Evaluation of a Conversation Management Toolkit for Multi Agent Programming

David Lillis, Rem W. Collier, and Howell R. Jordan

School of Computer Science and Informatics
University College Dublin
{david.lillis,rem.collier}@ucd.ie,
howell.jordan@lero.ie

Abstract. The Agent Conversation Reasoning Engine (ACRE) is intended to aid agent developers to improve the management and reliability of agent communication. To evaluate its effectiveness, a problem scenario was created that could be used to compare code written with and without the use of ACRE by groups of test subjects.

This paper describes the requirements that the evaluation scenario was intended to meet and how these motivated the design of the problem. Two experiments were conducted with two separate sets of students and their solutions were analysed using a combination of simple objective metrics and subjective analysis. The analysis suggested that ACRE by default prevents some common problems arising that would limit the reliability and extensibility of conversation-handling code.

As ACRE has to date been integrated only with the Agent Factory multi agent framework, it was necessary to verify that the problems identified are not unique to that platform. Thus a comparison was made with best practice communication code written for the Jason platform, in order to demonstrate the wider applicability of a system such as ACRE.

1 Introduction

The Agent Conversation Reasoning Engine (ACRE) is a suite of components and tools to aid the developers of agent oriented software systems to handle inter-agent communication in a more structured and reliable manner [1]. To date, ACRE has been integrated into the Agent Factory multi-agent framework [2] and is available for use with any of the agent programming languages supported by Agent Factory's Common Language Framework [3]. Related work is presented in Section 2, followed by an overview of ACRE itself in Section 3.

The principal focus of this paper is to describe an experiment that was conducted to evaluate the benefits that ACRE can provide in a communication-heavy Multi Agent System (MAS). Section 4 outlines the motivations underpinning the design of the experiment and discusses how a scenario was designed with these in mind. In particular, we identified a number of variables that should be eliminated so as to ensure that comparisons of ACRE and non-ACRE code would be fair. This scenario was given separately to two classes of students:

M. Dastani, J.F. Hübner, and B. Logan (Eds.): ProMAS 2012, LNAI 7837, pp. 90–107, 2013.
© Springer-Verlag Berlin Heidelberg 2013

one undergraduate and one postgraduate. The students were required to develop agents that could interact with a number of provided agents in order to trade virtual stocks and properties for profit. For each class, the subjects were divided into two groups: one using ACRE and one working without.

The code was analysed both objectively and subjectively and comparisons were made between ACRE and non-ACRE code. This analysis is presented for each of the two classes in Sections 5 and 6 respectively. We then examined some conversation handling code written for the Jason multi agent platform [4] to draw some conclusions about the wider applicability of this work in Section 7. Conclusions and ideas for future work are contained in Section 8.

2   Related Work

Although many well-known agent frameworks and languages have support for some Agent Communication Language (ACL), less attention has been paid to conversations between agents, where two or more agents will exchange multiple messages that are related to the same topic or subject, following a pre-defined protocol. The JADE toolkit provides specific implementations of a number of the FIPA interaction protocols [5]. It also provides a Finite State Machine (FSM) behaviour to allow custom interaction protocols to be defined in terms of how they are handled by the agents. Jason includes native support for communicative acts, but does not provide specific tools for the development of agent conversations using interaction protocols [4]. A similar level of support has previously been present within the Agent Factory framework prior to the adoption of ACRE.

Agent toolkits with support for conversations include COOL [6], Jackal [7] and KaOS [8]. Other than FSMs, alternative representations for protocols include Coloured Petri Nets [9] and Global Session Types [10].

The comparative evaluation of programming toolkits, paradigms and languages is a matter of some debate within the software engineering community. One popular approach is to divide subjects into two groups with each asked to perform the same task [11–13]. To the greatest extent possible, objective quantitative measures are used to draw comparisons between the two groups. A common concept to evaluate is that of *programmer effort*, which has been measured in numerous different ways including development time [11, 12], non-comment line count [12] and non-commented source code statements [14]. These measures are used to ensure that a new approach does not result in a greater workload being placed on developers using it.

3   ACRE

ACRE is a framework that aims to give agent programmers greater control over the management of conversations within their MASs. It is motivated by the fact that many widely-used Agent Oriented Programming (AOP) languages and frameworks require communication to be handled on a message-by-message basis, with no explicit link between related messages. It frequently tends to be left as an exercise for the developer to ensure that messages that form part of the same conversation[1] are interpreted as such. This section provides a brief overview of ACRE's capabilities. For further information, it is presented in some detail in [1].

The principal components of ACRE are as follows:

- *Protocol Manager (PM):* The PM is shared amongst all agents residing on the same agent platform. It accesses online protocol repositories and downloads protocol definitions at the request of agents.
- *Conversation Manager (CM):* Each agent has its own CM, which is responsible for monitoring all its communication so as to group individual messages into conversations. Messages are compared to known protocol definitions and existing conversations to ensure that they are consistent with the available descriptions of how communication should be structured.
- *ACRE/Agent Interface (AAI):* Unlike the PM and CM, the AAI is not platform-independent, with its implementation dependent on the framework and/or AOP language being employed. The AAI serves as the API to the CM and PM: agents can perceive and act upon the ACRE components.

Additionally, the wider ACRE ecosystem provides an XML format for defining custom interaction protocols, a standard for the organisation of online protocol repositories and a suite of tools to aid developers in communication handling. These tools include a graphical protocol designer, a runtime conversation debugger, a GUI to manage and explore protocol repositories and a runtime protocol view to show what protocols have been loaded on an agent platform.

ACRE's representation of protocols uses FSMs where transitions between states are activated by the sending and receiving of messages. An example of this can be seen in Figure 1. Here, the conversation is begun by a message being sent that matches any of the transitions emanating from the initial "Start" state. When this occurs, the variables (prefixed by the ? character) are bound to the values contained in the message itself. This will, for example, fix the name of the conversation initiator (bound to the `?player` variable) and the other participant (`?broker`) so that subsequent messages must be sent to and from those agents.

If a message fails to match the specification of the relevant protocol, the CM will raise an error to make the agent aware of this. This feature is not readily available in existing AOP languages, as these typically depend on event triggers to positively match an expected message, with unrecognised or malformed messages being silently ignored if they match no rule.

From an AOP developer's point-of-view, ACRE facilitates the implementation of interaction protocols by automatically checking messages against known protocols and conversations, providing information about the state of conversations as well as making available a set of actions that operate on them. The information available includes the participants in a conversation, the conversation state,

---

[1] In this work we draw a distinction between *protocols*, which define how a series of related messages should be structured and *conversations*, which are individual instances of agents following a protocol.

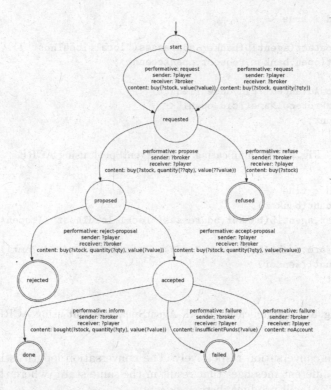

Fig. 1. An ACRE protocol

the messages that make up the conversation history and the protocol a conversation follows. Additionally, the agent is made aware of conversation events such as the conversation being advanced, cancellation, timeouts and errors (such as messages failing to match a transition in a defined protocol). Available actions include creating or advancing a conversation, cancelling existing conversations or communicating protocol errors to other participants.

Figures 2 and 3 show short code samples, written in AF-AgentSpeak (an adaptation of Rao's AgentSpeak(L) [15] that is inspired by Jason [4]), showing how a simple interaction could be carried out with and without ACRE respectively. From these samples, the difference in approach may be seen.

The ACRE code adds the contact details of another agent only once, referring thereafter only to its name ("banker" in this example). Additionally, the events, beliefs and actions refer to details of a conversation (identified by a unique conversation identifier, ?cid). The second rule reacts to a conversationAdvanced event, which indicates that a conversation has been advanced by the communication of a message to a state named "done". This state name is taken from the definition of the protocol that the conversation is following. The variables ?cid and ?length will be matched to the unique identifier of the conversation and the

```
+initialized : true <-
  acre.init,
  acre.addContact(agentID(banker,addresses("local:localhost"))),
  acre.start(open,banker,request,openAccount);

+conversationAdvanced(?cid,done,?length) :
conversationProtocolName(?cid,open) <-
  +bankAccount;
```

Fig. 2. Communicating in AF-AgentSpeak using ACRE

```
+initialized : true <-
+openingAccount(banker),
.send(request,agentID(banker,addresses("local:localhost")),openAccount);

+message(inform,agentID(?sender,?addr), openedAccount(?id,?amt)) :
openingAccount(?sender) <-
+bankAccount;
```

Fig. 3. Communicating in AF-AgentSpeak without using ACRE

length of the conversation respectively. The conversation length is included to ensure that different messages that result in the same state (where the protocol contains a loop) will produce distinct events.

Without ACRE, messages are dealt with individually, with conversation handling left to the developer (in this example, the openingAccount(banker) belief records that the Player is engaging with the Banker agent to open a bank account). In addition, the name and address of the other agent must be provided each time a message is sent, and matched for every incoming message.

4   Evaluation Experiment

In order to evaluate the usefulness of ACRE, an experiment was designed whereby two groups of participants would write AOP code to tackle a particular problem. One group was required to write their code using the capabilities of ACRE whereas the other worked without ACRE. Before describing the experiment that was conducted, it is important to outline the motivations involved in its creation.

4.1   Motivations

The design of the problem was guided by the desire for the scenario to be *communication-focused*, *accessible* and *reproducible*, with a *clearly defined implementation sequence* and a clear *reward for active agents*, so that is it not possible for an agent to benefit by being inactive. Some of these motivations are specific to this particular experiment but many are desirable properties of any experiment where programming languages, paradigms or tools are being evaluated comparatively. These motivations are discussed in more detail below.

- *Focus on Communication:* The aim of the evaluation was to engage in a scenario that was communication-heavy. To facilitate this, it was decided that the problem should require developers to create a single agent, so that they would not be distracted from the core focus by having to deal with issues such as co-ordination and co-operation. A group of "core agents" would be provided with accompanying protocols, with which the participant's agent must interact. Communicating with the core agents should be required from the beginning, with no progress being possible without communication.
- *Accessibility:* As the primary focus of the scenario is communication, little complex reasoning should be required to build a basic implementation that can perform well.
- *Reproducibility:* Every non-deterministic environment state change and core agent decision should be recorded, so that the experiment can be exactly replicated. Given a deterministic player agent, each replication should yield identical results.
- *Clearly defined goal:* From the point of view of participants, the assigned tasks, time allowed and scoring criteria should be clear.
- *Clearly defined implementation sequence:* Participants should not be able to gain a better score merely by implementing parts of their solution in a different order. The easiest way to ensure this is to fix the task order. In the context of a communication-heavy experiment, task ordering may be enforced by making later protocols dependent on others, thus avoiding the need to monitor participants directly.
- *Rewards for Active Agents:* There should be no features of the experiment where an agent implementing that feature is at a disadvantage when compared to an agent that does not implement it.

4.2   Scenario

The scenario chosen for the experiment was a simple asset trading game. Each participant was asked to develop an agent named *Player*. This agent was required to interact with a number of provided core agents in order to buy and sell virtual stocks and properties so as to increase the amount of money they had. The core agents were as follows:

- *Banker:* The Banker agent maintains a Player's bank account. The first task of each agent is to interact with the Banker to open an account, in which an initial amount of virtual currency is placed.
- *Stockbroker:* This agent is responsible for buying and selling stocks. Players earn money by buying from the Stockbroker and selling later at a profit.
- *Guru:* The Guru agent is aware of how the market operates and can provide tips on which stocks will rise quickly in price and which should be avoided.

– *Auctioneer:* Properties can be bought from the Auctioneer agent. The value of properties rises quickly so they offer a method of making greater profits than on the stock market alone.
– *Bidder:* Bidders will participate in auctions organised by the Player to buy properties that the Player has previously purchased from the Auctioneer.

A number of features of the game were created with the motivations outlined above in mind. The *focus on communication* is maintained by providing a number of protocols that the core agents are capable of following. Each protocol is based on one or more of the FIPA interaction protocols. These are summarised in Table 1. An illustration of one of these protocols is shown in Figure 1, namely the protocol invoked to buy stock from the Stockbroker agent. Similar illustrations were available for all protocols.

Table 1. Core Agent Protocols

Agent	Protocol	Based On	Purpose
Banker	open	request	Open a bank account
	enquiry	query	Query your bank balance
Stock Broker	listing	query	Get a list of available stocks
	price	query	Query the price of a particular stock
	portfolio	query	Query details of stocks currently owned
	buy	request	Buy a quantity/value of a particular stock
	sell	request	Sell a quantity/value of a particular stock
Guru	subscribe	subscribe	Subscribe to the guru agent's stock tips
Auctioneer	subscribe	subscribe, english-auction	Subscribe to details of new auctions and participate in these auctions.
Bidder	sell	contract-net	Sell a property

The *clearly defined goal* of the task is maximise capital. Thus participants are aware of what they need to do in order to be successful.

As a result of the *accessibility* motivation, the scenario is designed so that a Player can be successful using a simple strategy, without requiring advanced reasoning. This is important when experiment participants are time-constrained.

By default, the movement of stock prices is determined randomly. An internal clock is used to track the time of the experiment: stock prices may change on every "tick" of the clock. A *reproducible* experiment may be conducted by loading pre-prepared stock prices at the beginning of the experiment, thus ensuring that the price movements are repeated across multiple experiments.

The ordering of the core agents in the list above reflects the order in which they should be interacted with, thus creating a *clearly defined implementation sequence*. The tasks are designed so that successfully completing a task will be dependent on previous tasks being completed first. Although there are no technical restrictions on the order in which participants may choose to implement the tasks, these dependencies discourage them from writing their implementations in a different order. For example, selling items to bidders is impossible before interacting with the Auctioneer to buy properties. However, these cannot be bought prior to interacting with the stock market, as the minimum property price is deliberately set to be higher than the Player's initial capital. Similarly, the advice of the Guru is useless unless an agent can use it when interacting with the Stockbroker, and it is impossible to buy or sell stocks without having previously opened an account with the banker.

To *reward active agents*, the stock price calculation mechanism is intentionally artificial, in that the price of stocks always rises. This rewards developers for implementing features, to the detriment of idle agents. If stock prices can fall, an agent that does not participate in the market may end with more money than one that has interacted with a Stockbroker but that has lost money in doing so.

5   First Experiment

The experiment was first conducted with a final year undergraduate class in Fudan University, Shanghai, China. The evaluation was conducted as part of a module on Agent Oriented Programming. None of the participants had previous experience in developing MASs or in using an AOP language.

For consistency, all participants were required to write their code in AF-AgentSpeak so as to run within the Agent Factory framework. This removes any bias associated with the use of different AOP languages or frameworks.

Students were allowed three hours in a supervised laboratory setting in which to create their solutions. The fixed time period allows quantitative comparisons to be done with regard to the number of protocols each student implemented. The choice of a supervised in-class test ensured that each student submitted their own work. Subjects were permitted to access lecture notes and refer to manuals and user guides relating to Agent Factory, AF-AgentSpeak and ACRE.

The participants were divided into two groups of equal size using a random assignment: one group was requested to implement their solution using the extensions provided by ACRE whereas the other group was requested to implement their solution using the existing Agent Factory message-passing capabilities. In preparation for the experiment, a practical session was conducted so the participants had the opportunity to gain familiarity with both forms of message handling. This occurred a week prior to the evaluation so as to afford the students sufficient time to get accustomed to agent communication. Previous practical sessions held as part of the module exposed the participants to other aspects of AF-AgentSpeak and AOP programming in general.

The class consisted of 46 students in total, therefore 23 were asked to implement each type of solution. One student from the non-ACRE group did not attend the evaluation, leaving 45 submissions. Additionally one other student from the non-ACRE group instead submitted a solution that did use ACRE.

Of the remaining 21 students in the non-ACRE group, one submission was not included in this research as only one protocol had been attempted and this attempt had not been successful, leaving a total of 20 non-ACRE submissions.

24 submissions were received that had used ACRE. Again, one of these has not been included in this analysis, as the agent submitted did not successfully interact with any core agent. This left a total of 23 submissions using ACRE.

The submissions were evaluated using both objective and subjective measures. Initially, some simple objective measures were employed to measure programmer effort (following the examples outlined in Section 2). Following this, the implementations were examined to identify any issues that the implementations may have failed to address.

5.1   Objective Measures

The principal aim of ACRE is to help developers to deal with complex communication more easily. As such, it is important to ensure that the use of ACRE does not add to the effort required to develop MASs. Objective measures are required to attempt to quantify programmer effort. Two simple metrics were employed for this purpose: 1) the number of protocols implemented within a specified time period and 2) the number of non-comment lines of code per protocol.

The first of these can be used to compare the two participant groups in terms of the time taken to implement protocols. Because of the ordering of the tasks, participants are encouraged to implement the protocols in the same order as one another. For example, it is not productive for a participant to begin by implementing the complex auctioneer protocols while others are implementing the simple protocol required to open a bank account. This helps to prevent the metric being skewed by certain subjects being delayed by the order in which they chose to implement their system.

Because there is variation in the number of protocols successfully implemented by each participant, the count of code lines is averaged for the number of protocols implemented. Again, the clear implementation sequence means that this is to the greatest extent possible measuring like-with-like.

Table 2. Objective measures of programmer effort for the first experiment

	Protocols Implemented	Lines per Protocol
ACRE	5.43	18.35
Non-ACRE	5.85	27.06

Table 2 shows the average number of protocols implemented by each group, along with the average number of non-comment lines of code present per protocol implemented. For the number of protocols implemented, the difference is not statistically significant using an unpaired t-test for $p = 0.05$. There is, however, a statistically significant difference in lines per protocol using the same test.

It can be seen that participants in the ACRE group implemented marginally fewer protocols on average within the three-hour period. However, as this difference is not significant, it indicates that the speed of development is comparable whether ACRE is being used or not. This suggests that ACRE does not impose a steep learning curve compared to traditional methods of conversation handling.

It is interesting that the ACRE implementations did tend to have significantly fewer lines of code per protocol. Although this is a somewhat crude metric, it does suggest that the automated conversation handling of ACRE may reduce the amount of code that is required in order to successfully implement protocols.

Although objective measures are desirable in any evaluation, it is important to take a subjective view of the code also. While no significant difference in the amount of programmer effort required was observed, these metrics do not capture the quality of the implementations. The next section presents subjective analysis of the code submitted that attempts to identify this quality.

5.2   Subjective Assessment

The adoption of ACRE will be most beneficial if it improves code quality. To gauge this, the code was examined and a number of issues were found to be prevalent in the non-ACRE code. These issues meant that the solutions that were submitted were very closely tied to the scenario as presented, and would have required much more additional work to be done for an extended MAS.

By its nature, AF-AgentSpeak reacts to the receipt of messages using rules that have a *triggering event* and a *context*. The triggering event is a some event that has occurred (i.e. a change in the belief base) whereas the context is a set of beliefs that should be present for the rule to be relevant. When writing non-ACRE code in AF-AgentSpeak, the event that triggers the rule is the receipt of an incoming message and the context consists of beliefs about the state of the conversation (checking the sender, ensuring that the message follows the correct preceding message etc.). This can be seen in Figure 3. For the issues that were identified, the context of the rules were not written in the best way possible.

Identification of Issues. The particular issues that were identified are as follows. Words in parentheses are short descriptions that are used to refer to each issue in the ensuing analysis:

- *No Checking of Message Senders (Sender):* Incoming messages were matched only using their performative and content, with no checks in place to ensure they were sent by the correct agent.
- *No Checking of Conversation Progress (Progress):* As the messages followed particular protocols, they were exchanged in a clearly-defined sequence. Many programmers did not attempt to check the context of messages that were received, treating them as individual messages.
- *Hard-coded name checking (Name):* When the message sender was checked, it was frequently the case that the name of the sender was hard-coded.
- *Checking addresses (Address):* Agent's addresses were also hard-coded.

While a solution that includes these issues is capable of successfully participating in the trading scenario, their presence means that additional effort would be required to adapt the solution for a more open agent system or if the scenario were to be extended with additional protocols and/or agents.

When an agent fails to check the identity of the sender, this may have unintended consequences. For example, a Player agent would normally react to a recommendation from the Guru to buy a particular stock by following that recommendation. In a more open MAS, a malicious agent may send recommendations that cause other players to buy stocks that will not perform well. All that would be required is to send a message with the same performative and content as the Player would expect from the Guru.

Similarly, a Player that does not record the state of conversations is also susceptible to exploitation. For example, the protocol for buying stock (shown in Figure 1) insists that the Player must have accepted a proposal to buy stock before the purchase proceeds. However, without a notion of conversation, a Player may be persuaded that it has bought some quantity of a stock without it being involved in the process. If this is combined with the message sender not being checked, an agent other than a Stockbroker may trick a Player into buying stocks it had no intention to buy. As an aside, it is interesting to note that those agents that did record the progress of a conversation tended to use the state names provided in the ACRE FSM diagrams, suggesting that even for developers who do not use ACRE (or lack ACRE support in their AOP platform of choice), the availability of protocols defined in this way is useful for visualising and reasoning about conversations.

The two other issues relate to the difficulty in re-using the code for an extended scenario where conversations are conducted with different agents and/or multiple platforms. Even where the sender of a message was checked, it was frequently the case that this was hard-coded into the context of every rule. As such, the code was capable of conducting a conversation only with an agent of a specific name. If the scenario were to be extended so that multiple agents were capable of engaging in the same protocols (e.g. two Stockbroker agents that handled a different set of stocks) then these rules would all require re-writing to allow for additional agents. Similarly, hard-coding the addresses in the context of each rule limits the code to single platform MASs. Adding agents on another platform will also require all rules to be rewritten.

Because ACRE's Conversation Manager automatically performs checking of this type, such issues cannot arise within ACRE code. As illustrated in the code from Figure 2, the triggering event is typically that a conversation has advanced, with the context being used to check other details about the conversation. Conversation participants need only be named when the conversation is initiated.

Assuming a pre-existing conversation, a `conversationAdvanced` event can only be triggered by a message that has been sent by the existing participant to the conversation and has a performative and content that match the next expected message in the protocol. If a message is sent by a different agent, an `unmatchedMessage` event is raised to indicate that the message does not belong to any particular conversation. This means that it is not necessary to check the message sender for each rule relating to communication, as the event cannot be triggered by the wrong agent.[2]

This automatic checking also guards against out-of-sequence messages. In the example of the buying protocol shown in Figure 1, the Conversation Manager insists that the messages be communicated in the specified sequence, so the Stockbroker cannot inform the Player of a successful purchase unless the Player has previously agreed to that purchase (again, an unmatchedMessage event would be triggered).

Thus the use of ACRE automatically protects against these issues, meaning that were the MAS be more open or the scenario extended, far less effort would be required to adapt the existing ACRE code to the altered circumstances. ACRE can be seen to prevent certain coding styles that would restrict the extensibility and reusability of communication-handling code. Although subjects were not explicitly instructed to create generic code with wider applicability, we believe that ACRE's prevention, by default, of these type of problems is a strong argument in its favour.

Prevalence of Issues. For each of the issues outlined in the previous section, it is necessary to measure how prevalent they are amongst the implementations that were submitted. Each implementation was given one of three classifications with regard to each of the four issues identified:

- *Not susceptible:* The issue was not present for any rule in the implementation.
- *Totally susceptible:* The issue in question was present in every rule where it was relevant.
- *Somewhat susceptible:* The issue was present for some relevant rules but not all. This ranges from those implementations where a check was omitted only once to those where the check was only performed for one rule.

In relation to hard-coded name and address checking, these issues could not be present in agents that were totally susceptible to the issue of checking message senders. For those agents that did not check message senders at all, it is not possible for these other issues to arise. For this reason, in the following analysis, the figures shown for these two issues are displayed as a percentage of those agents in which is was possible for them to arise.

Table 3 shows the prevalence of the issues amongst the non-ACRE submissions. Figures in parentheses are the absolute number of subjects each percentage relates to. Agents that were totally susceptible to the *Sender* issue are not included in the calculations for *Name* or *Address*, as these are only based on the number of agents that attempted to check the message sender.

From these, it can be seen that the issues raised were widespread amongst non-ACRE developers. The hard-coding of agents' addresses is the only issue that was found in less than half of relevant agents.

---

[2] ACRE does not protect against messages sent by an agent other than that identified in the message's sender field. This type of secure communication is considered to be a task for the underlying Message Transport Service.

Table 3. Issues present in non-ACRE code for the first experiment

	Sender	Progress	Name	Address
Totally Susceptible	40% (8)	55% (11)	67% (8)	25% (3)
Somewhat Susceptible	30% (6)	30% (6)	0% (0)	17% (2)
Not Susceptible	30% (6)	15% (3)	33% (4)	58% (7)

Over two thirds of agents would react to messages sent by the wrong agent at least some of the time, with 40% failing to ever check the identity of a message sender. Of those that did check, two thirds hard-coded the name of the sender, which would require every rule to be re-written if the scenario was to be altered.

Just three participants (15%) always checked that messages were in the correct order. On further analysis, all of these implementations were somewhat suscep-tible to the Sender issue, which meant that there were no submissions where no issues were found.

The following Section describes a second run of the same experiment using different participants. The results of this can be compared to those presented above to further demonstrate the extent to which the issues identified here appear in code written by more experienced programmers.

6   Second Experiment

The same experiment was repeated later with a different set of participants. On this occasion, the subjects were part of a part-time Masters-level Agent Ori-ented Software Engineering module in University College Dublin, Ireland. These students are experienced professional software developers working in industry, although none had prior experience with AOP.

For this group, classes were conducted daily for five days. This included prac-tical work each afternoon to allow students to become familiar with AOP. Com-munication handling and ACRE were introduced on the fourth day and the evaluation occurred on the fifth day. Thus these students had less preparation time than those in the first experiment.

Students were again divided into two groups by random assignment. In a class of 19 students, 10 submitted ACRE-based solutions while the remaining 9 students created non-ACRE agents. The scenario was conducted in exactly the same way as for the first experiment.

6.1   Objective Measures

The objective metrics employed were the same as in Section 5.1. The results are presented in Table 4. As with the first experiment, the ACRE participants implemented marginally fewer protocols, though this difference was not statis-tically significant. Overall, fewer protocols were implemented compared to the first experiment. This may have been as a result of the shorter preparation time available to these students. For the lines of code per protocol metric, it can be seen that both groups of ACRE students wrote a very similar amount of code. However, it is interesting to note that the number of lines written per non-ACRE protocol in the second experiment is lower. Again, however, this difference is not statistically significant.

Table 4. Objective measures of programmer effort for the second experiment

	Protocols Implemented	Lines per Protocol
ACRE	4.4	18.93
Non-ACRE	4.67	14.87

Given the small sample size in the second experiment, it is difficult to draw concrete conclusions based on quantitative objective analysis. However, the metrics do add support to the argument that ACRE does not add to the amount of programmer effort required to create a communication-heavy agent program.

6.2 Subjective Analysis

For a subjective analysis of the second set of students' submitted code, it is interesting to determine the extent to which the issues that became apparent in the first experiment are also present in the second. Table 5 shows the prevalence of these issues in the non-ACRE code from the second experiment. The percentages in Table 5 are of the total of 9 non-ACRE students for the *Sender* and *Progress* issues. For the *Name* and *Address* issues, these are calculated from the 4 participants that were either totally or somewhat susceptible to the *Sender* issue. This is calculated in the same was as in Table 3.

Table 5. Issues present in non-ACRE code for the second experiment

	Sender	Progress	Name	Address
Totally Susceptible	56% (5)	78% (7)	100% (4)	0% (0)
Somewhat Susceptible	0% (0)	22% (2)	0% (0)	0% (0)
Not Susceptible	44% (4)	0% (0)	0% (0)	100% (4)

A notable difference between these results and those arising from the first experiment is that on this occasion, no student hard-coded addresses when checking message senders. It is of interest, however, that several students hard-coded addresses for some outgoing messages. This was not a feature of the code received for the first experiment.

As with the first experiment submissions, no solution was submitted that was completely immune from all of the common issues identified. Over half the participants failed to ever check the sender of incoming messages. Whenever this check was performed, it was always done by means of a hard-coded agent name. For the *Progress* issue, almost a quarter of subjects made some attempt to check for the correct message sequence. However, no student implemented this type of checking every time it was appropriate.

We believe that the findings of the two experiments described provide a strong argument in favour of the use of a conversation-handling technology such as ACRE that provides automated conversation checking and exception handling facilities without adding to the overall effort a programmer must go to when programming MASs in which communication plays a significant part.

7   Comparison with Jason

The issues identified above arose specifically within AOP code using one specific programming language (AF-AgentSpeak) on one agent platform (Agent Factory). To show that ACRE's conversation-handling capabilities could have a wider benefit than this single configuration, it was necessary to perform further analysis. To this end, we sought to examine how conversations are handled in a different agent framework that also lacks built-in conversation and protocol management. For this to be effective, we required that some best-practice conversation handling code must be available, so that any issues identified would not be as a result of poor coding practice or a lack of familiarity with the full capabilities of the language or platform.

Jason is a MAS development platform that makes use of an extended version of AgentSpeak(L) as its AOP language [4]. It supports inter-agent communication using KQML-like messages. However, it lacks built-in support for conversation handling and protocol definitions. Jason was chosen for this analysis for two principal reasons. Firstly, it is a popular, well-known platform. Secondly, a book is available that was written by Jason's developers that includes sample code for performing a variety of tasks, including inter-agent communication [4]. As this code is written by the platform's developers, we assume that it represents recommended best-practice.

Figure 4 is an extract from an implementation of a contract net protocol for Jason [4, p. 134]. This implementation is provided by the developers of Jason to illustrate how an interaction protocol may be implemented for that platform. The extract shows a plan that makes up part of the agent that initiates and coordinates the contract net. It is intended to be used when all bids have been received, so as to find the winner (line 7) and create an intention to announce the result to all the participants (line 9).

In the same way as the trading game presented in this paper, the sample MAS in which this agent was designed to run consists of a fixed set of agents with a particular purpose. Specifically, all other agents in the system were intended as participants in the contract net. As such, no allowance is made in the code for

```
1   @lc1[atomic]
2   +!contract(CNPId) : cnp_state(CNPId,propose) <-
3       -+cnp_state(CNPId,contract);
4       .findall(offer(O,A),propose(CNPId,O)[source(A)],L);
5       .print("Offers are ",L);
6       L \== []; // constraint the plan execution to at least one offer
7       .min(L,offer(WOf,WAg)); // sort offers, the first is the best
8       .print("Winner is ",WAg," with ",WOf);
9       !announce_result(CNPId,L,WAg);
10      -+cnp_state(Id,finished).
```

Fig. 4. Sample Jason rule forming part of an implementation for Contract Net protocol

proposals being received from agents that were not party to the initial call for proposals. This can be seen in line 4 of the extract, which creates a list of offers that have been received based on any proposal that has been received from any source. This is the same as the *Sender* issue identified above. Extending this code for a more open MAS would require modification of the code to check that agents sending proposals are expected to do so. Jason does provide a method named SocAcc (meaning "socially acceptable") that can prevent some types of message being processed if they are sent by inappropriate agents. Although this could be used to prevent non-participating agents from sending proposals, it is not sufficiently fine-grained to prevent an agent that is a party to one contract net from sending a proposal relating to another.

Figure 4 also illustrates that a Jason agent could also be susceptible to the "Progress" issue. The cnp_state belief in this extract is used to track the state of the conversation. As the code in question is written by experts, this belief is present in a number of plans so that the state of the contract net conversation is known at all times. However, as our evaluation has shown, less experienced programmers are more prone to omitting this type of checking.

Another issue arises in the choice of an identifier for the conversation (referred to as the CNPId variable in the extract shown). As presented, this ID is manually specified in the original intention that triggers the start of the contract net (not shown). ACRE assigns IDs to conversations automatically, meaning that the programmer need not be concerned with this aspect of conversation handling.

From this analysis, it can be seen that in the absence of integrated conversation handling, AOP developers using Jason are also susceptible to the issues outlined above. We believe that the type of conversation handling ACRE provides would help to avoid these pitfalls and so aid the development of reliable, scalable protocol implementations.

8   Conclusions and Future Work

We have described experiments whereby two groups of students were required to solve a communication-focused problem with and without the use of ACRE.

Objective metrics applied to the first experiment indicated that ACRE can reduce the amount of code required to implement the protocols provided when compared to implementing protocols without ACRE. However, similar metrics did not produce a statistically significant difference in the second case, although it should be noted that the sample size was much smaller. The metrics used did not indicate that ACRE adds to the effort required of programmers to implement conversations, which suggests that its learning curve is not overly steep.

On further subjective analysis, a number of issues arose with non-ACRE code. These would require substantial modification of the code if the scenario were extended by the addition of additional Player agents, duplicate core agents, similar protocols or malicious agents of any type. The issues observed cannot occur with the use of ACRE, as the automatic conversation management ensures that both message senders and sequence are checked without developer intervention. These issues were present in code submitted as part of both experiments and no submission was received that was immune from all problems identified.

We also analysed some best-practice conversation-handling code written for Jason and observed that the issues identified are applicable to that platform. We therefore suggest that a conversation management framework such as ACRE is generally desirable to aid the development of communication-heavy MASs.

8.1 Evolution of the Trading Game

The scenario as described has potential for further refinement in order to be usable as a more general-purpose evaluation platform.

- In its current guise, the trading scenario accommodates a single Player agent. A logical next step to take would be to allow a multi-player head-to-head to take place. This would mean that Player agents are in direct competition for auctions, as well as potentially creating a situation whereby one Player agent may take advantage of poorly-coded opponents by exploiting one or more of the issues identified in the above analysis.
- Although the facility to save and re-run particular games is possible, at present no predefined games have been created. A library of game configurations would allow for a variety of scenarios where, for example, auctions would take greater or lesser importance so a single strategy would not necessarily be best in all situations.
- The system agents provided as part of the trading game all behave as expected, meaning that none of them send out-of-sequence messages to test the error-handling of the Player agents. A more difficult trading game would require this to be handled.
- As an alternative to multi-player games, a malicious rogue system agent could be included. The behaviour of this agent would not be described in the specification other than to state that it may send any message at any time. This would attempt to impersonate the existing system agents to exploit agents that do not check messages senders. It would be interesting to measure the effect this additional requirement would have on the time taken to develop implementations of protocols.

References

1. Lillis, D., Collier, R.W.: Augmenting Agent Platforms to Facilitate Conversation Reasoning. In: Dastani, M., El Fallah Seghrouchni, A., Hübner, J., Leite, J. (eds.) LADS 2010. LNCS, vol. 6822, pp. 56–75. Springer, Heidelberg (2011)
2. Muldoon, C., O'Hare, G.M.P., Collier, R.W., O'Grady, M.J.: Towards Pervasive Intelligence: Reflections on the Evolution of the Agent Factory Framework. In: El Fallah Seghrouchni, A., Dix, J., Dastani, M., Bordini, R.H. (eds.) Multi-Agent Programming: Languages, Platforms and Applications and Applications, pp. 187–212. Springer US, Boston (2009)
3. Russell, S., Jordan, H., O'Hare, G.M.P., Collier, R.W.: Agent Factory: A Framework for Prototyping Logic-Based AOP Languages. In: Klügl, F., Ossowski, S. (eds.) MATES 2011. LNCS, vol. 6973, pp. 125–136. Springer, Heidelberg (2011)
4. Bordini, R.H., Hübner, J.F., Wooldridge, M.: Programming multi-agent systems in AgentSpeak using Jason. Wiley-Interscience (2007)
5. Bellifemine, F., Caire, G., Trucco, T., Rimassa, G.: JADE Programmer's Guide (JADE 4.0) (2010)
6. Barbuceanu, M., Fox, M.S.: COOL: A language for describing coordination in multi agent systems. In: Proceedings of the First International Conference on Multi-Agent Systems, ICMAS 1995, pp. 17–24 (1995)
7. Cost, R.S., Finin, T., Labrou, Y., Luan, X., Peng, Y., Soboroff, I., Mayfield, J., Boughannam, A.: Jackal: a Java-based Tool for Agent Development. Working Papers of the AAAI 1998 Workshop on Software Tools for Developing Agents. AAAI Press (1998)
8. Bradshaw, J.M., Dutfield, S., Benoit, P., Woolley, J.D.: KAoS: Toward an industrial-strength open agent architecture. Software Agents, 375–418 (1997)
9. Huget, M.P., Koning, J.L.: Interaction Protocol Engineering. Communications, 291–309 (2003)
10. Ancona, D., Drossopoulou, S., Mascardi, V.: Automatic Generation of Self-Monitoring MASs from Multiparty Global Session Types in Jason. In: Baldoni, M., Dennis, L., Mascardi, V., Vasconcelos, W. (eds.) DALT 2012. LNCS (LNAI), vol. 7784, pp. 76–95. Springer, Heidelberg (2013)
11. Hochstein, L., Basili, V.R., Vishkin, U., Gilbert, J.: A pilot study to compare programming effort for two parallel programming models. Journal of Systems and Software 81(11), 1920–1930 (2008)
12. Luff, M.: Empirically Investigating Parallel Programming Paradigms: A Null Result. In: Workshop on Evaluation and Usability of Programming Languages and Tools, PLATEAU, pp. 43–49 (2009)
13. Rossbach, C.J., Hofmann, O.S., Witchel, E.: Is Transactional Programming Actually Easier? ACM SIGPLAN Notices 45(5), 47–56 (2010)
14. VanderWiel, S.P., Nathanson, D., Lilja, D.J.: Complexity and performance in parallel programming languages. In: Second International Workshop on High-Level Programming Models and Supportive Environments, pp. 3–12 (1997)
15. Rao, A.S.: AgentSpeak (L): BDI agents speak out in a logical computable language. In: Van de Velde, W., Perram, J.W. (eds.) MAAMAW 1996. LNCS, vol. 1038, pp. 42–55. Springer, Heidelberg (1996)

Compact and Efficient Agent Messaging

Kai Jander and Winfried Lamersdorf

Distributed Systems and Information Systems
Computer Science Department, University of Hamburg
{jander,lamersd}@informatik.uni-hamburg.de

Abstract. Messages are considered to be a primary means of communication between agents in multi-agent systems. Since multi-agent systems
are used for a wide variety of applications, it also includes applications
like simulation and calculation of computer generated graphics which
need to employ a large number of messages or very large messages. In
addition, another set of applications target hardware which is resource
constrained in either bandwidth or processing capacity. As a result, these
applications have different requirements regarding their messages than
other agent message formats. This paper proposes useful properties of
agent messages and evaluates them with regard to different types of applications. Based on this evaluation a message format for Jadex called
Jadex Binary is proposed which emphasizes properties which are not
traditionally the focus of agent message formats and compare it to well-
known formats based on those properties.

1 Introduction

Multi-agent systems enable the development of scalable and highly dynamic
applications, which facilitates their deployment on infrastructure such as struc-
turally and spatially distributed systems and the integration of mobile devices
in such systems. An important means for coordinating agents within an application is the use of messages passed between agents. This mechanism is one of
the reasons that allow the autonomous behavior of agents which enables them
to be shielded from direct influence from the rest of the system and establish a
measure of robustness

Nevertheless, certain classes of applications deployed on such systems have
special requirements which appear to be in conflict with the focus of traditional
agent message formats. Examples of this type of applications include real-time
audio and video communication, distributed simulation and real-time distributed
computer generated image (CGI) animation.

Traditionally, these requirements have not been the focus of agent messaging,
which tends to target other useful properties that are important to other types
of applications. As a result, it would broaden the scope of agent systems to
specifically support such application by providing an alternative message format
that focuses on the requirements of those applications.

In the following section we will try to identify typical requirements for agent
messages and distill the ones that are especially important to the aforementioned

M. Dastani, J.F. Hübner, and B. Logan (Eds.): ProMAS 2012, LNAI 7837, pp. 108–122, 2013.
© Springer-Verlag Berlin Heidelberg 2013

classes of applications. We will then present some typical message formats and attempt to identify which criteria they attempt to fulfill. Finally, we will present a compact message format that caters to the special class of application with real-time and bandwidth-restricted sets of requirements and compare it to traditional agent message formats, demonstrating key advantages for this special set of applications.

2   Features of Agent Message Formats

Since multi-agent applications cover a large spectrum of potential applications, there are a number of features of agent messages which are particularly useful for different classes of applications. In addition to different application classes, different points in the development cycle may emphasize the importance of certain features over others. While there is a potentially large number of features that could be potentially useful, we will consider the following six features which appear to be features that are commonly requested for agent message:

- *Human Readability* allows humans to read messages with standard tools like text viewers without the help of decoders or other special tools.
- *Standard Conformance* requires messages to conform to a published message format standard or language standard, allowing interaction between systems conforming to those standards.
- A *Well-formed Structure* defines a valid form for messages, allowing the system to distinguish between valid and invalid messages.
- *Editability* goes beyond human readability by allowing users to edit and restructure messages using standard tools like text editors.
- *Performance* describes the computational requirements to encode and decode messages.
- *Compactness* defines the smallness of the encoded messages.

In order to evaluate these features we will use and example set of four common types of applications which are often used in practice. The first type are *real-time applications*, where latency becomes a primary concern. Examples of this type of application can be found in any real-time communication system such as voice or video conference systems. In those type of applications high latency has a considerable negative impact on the usefulness of the application and may make its use outright impossible.

The second type of applications are *cross-platform applications* such as applications using Agentcities (see [1]), which involves the use of multiple agent platforms and multiple types of agents. Being able to correctly interpret messages from other agents or platforms is key for such applications.

Another common type of applications are *enterprise backend applications*. These applications often run on application servers on high-performance intranets. It is key for such applications to provide quick access to the services required by the business in order to maintain high productivity.

The final type of applications are *mobile applications*, where a large number of nodes involved in the application are physically mobile and are typically connected using wireless connections. This means that the nodes are often restricted in terms of computational resources and network bandwidth. Energy supply is a key factor here, requiring modest use of resources even when more would be available.

	Real-time Applications	Cross-platform Applications	Enterprise Backend Applications	Mobile Applications
Human Readability	low	medium	low	low
Standard Conformance	low	high	medium	low
Well-formed Structure	low	high	low	low
Editable	low	medium	medium	low
Performance	high	low	high	high
Compactness	high	low	low	high

Fig. 1. Importance of message format features for different types of applications

Figure 1 shows the application types and the importance of the message format features. Some application types such as real-time applications and mobile applications have similar feature importance profiles for different reasons. While latency requires prudent use of resources for real-time applications, it is the energy and physical restrictions that make it a necessity for mobile applications. For cross-platform application the ability to interpret messages is key, so a standard-conformant and well-formed message format takes precedence over compactness and performance. Enterprise backend applications are more mixed, in that while the intranet typically provides abundant bandwidth, the large number of request still require good performance.

While an agent may have the option to open raw connection to other agents, bypassing the platform messaging service and supplying its own encoding and protocol, this is usually not advisable for the following reasons: On the one hand, developing an efficient transfer protocol involves a non-trivial amount of effort. It would therefore ease development effort if the agent message layer could be used. On the other hand, the agent system may be running within a restricted environment. For example, enterprise applications typically run on servers where the communication is tightly controlled for both support and security reason. As a result, an agent may not be allowed to make connections outside what is provided by the agent platform.

Furthermore, there is another aspect concerning application development. In practice, there is often a distinction between the development phase of an application and the production use in a business. For example, during development, applications often include additional logging and debug code to identify faults, includes the use of assertions to validate program invariants and the use of tests to validate functionality. During production use, these features are often omitted in favor of higher throughput or lower latency.

Figure 2 demonstrates this difference between the two stages with regard to agent message formats. During development being able to easily read and modify messages helps finding protocol errors and other implementation errors.

	Development	Production
Human Readability	high	low
Standard Conformance	medium	medium
Well-formed Structure	high	low
Editable	high	low
Performance	low	high
Compactness	low	high

Fig. 2. Importance of message format features during development and production use

In addition, a well-formed structure allows the use of validation tools to ensure message correctness. However, this changes during production use where good encoding and decoding performance and message compactness aids both system throughput and latency. While in use during production, this takes precedence over issues like message readability since, for the most part, it is no longer necessary for humans to read the agent messages.

The next section will take a look at common agent message formats that have been traditionally in use for multi-agent systems and show how well they support the proposed message format features. This will show that there is potential for improvements on both performance and compactness if the other features are less of a concern.

3   Related Work

Over time, multi-agent system have used a variety of message formats. Early system used simple ad-hoc languages in string-based formats, however, this resulted in languages that were specific to the application and made it difficult for multi-agent systems to communicate. As a result, languages were developed to allow interchange between agent applications and agent system. One early attempt at defining an agent language was the Knowledge Query and Manipulation Language (KQML - see [2]). However, it was quickly recognized that a standard language is useful for allowing communication between different agent system.

As a result, message formats and languages had to be standardized. The Foundation of Intelligent Physical Agents (FIPA) therefore proposed two standards, the FIPA Agent Communication Language (ACL - see [3] for the message structure and a specific language for the message content called FIPA SL (see [4]) with different levels of complexity reaching from FIPA SL0 to FIPA SL2, both of which are used in popular agent platforms such as JADE (see [5]).

This distinction between structure and content in later formats as well, for example, while the Jadex Agent Platform (cf. [6]) uses an XML-based format called Jadex XML, it distinguishes between message and content encoding. However, in case of Jadex, it uses Jadex XML for encoding both the message and content. Since the bulk of the message for the types of applications being targeted tends to be the content, the focus of this paper will be content encoding. However, like with Jadex XML, the same principles can be applied to the message encoding as well.

	FIPA SL	Java Serialization	Jadex XML	Jadex Binary
Human Readability	=	-	+	-
Standard Conformance	+	=	=	-
Well-formed Structure	+	=	=	-
Editable	=	-	+	-
Performance	-	+	-	+
Compactness	-	=	-	+

Fig. 3. Feature support by different methods of agent content encoding

When considering the agent format features proposed in Section 2, it becomes clear that while some features are well-supported, some other features were not the focus of those formats (cf. Fig. 3). For example, FIPA SL, being a text-based format, is fairly well readable and editable by humans, has a definition of a well-formed structure and is a standard for agent messaging with wide support for many agent platforms. Jadex XML on the other hand, while not being a widely-used standard, has a well-defined and openly accessible schema and allows a human user to easily read and edit agent messages.

However, neither compactness nor performance seem to be the focus of either language. This is likely to be the result of those features being in conflict with others. For example, a compact format tends to be hard for a human to read.

The need of certain application for the performance and compactness features is recognized by JADE. While discouraged due to standard non-conformance, JADE supports adding content objects to messages instead of a string-based content. It then uses the Java language serialization feature (see [7]). However, while this approach is fairly compact and certainly complying with the performance feature, it has multiple drawbacks. First, for a number of reasons listed in the specification it only supports classes that explicitly declare to implement a market interface. While it is trivial to add the interface, for legacy classes the source code may be unavailable.

In addition, some useful built-in classes like BufferedImage do not implement this marker interface and there is no way to easily retrofit the serialization system to support this class. Furthermore, there tend to be compatibility issues with serialization, requiring a versioning convention. The ObjectOutputStream class used to serialize object also uses some clever caching mechanisms which can be confusing to the user. For example, writing an object to the stream, modifying it, then writing it again results in the object reproduced twice in the unmodified state when unserialized unless an explicit reset is issued. Finally, as we will show, the compactness of the serialization format can be further improved upon, especially without an additional compression cycle.

In the next section we will introduce an agent message format for Jadex called Jadex Binary that focuses solely on the compactness and performance features. This message format will be an alternative to the default Jadex XML which can be used by application that have a strong need for those two features. We will then evaluate this new format based on those features and compare it to the other formats.

4   Format Description

Since the primary goal of the Jadex Binary format is to emphasize the compactness and performance properties of the format, it uses a binary instead of a string-based encoding for the messages. The primary concern is the serialization of the objects representing the message, such as, but not exclusively, ontology objects. In addition, some techniques are employed to prefer the compact encoding of common cases of data over the rare cases, providing some simple compression based on the meta-information available from the objects. The format is based on a set of techniques to encode primitive types which are then used to encode more complex data. The following subsections will start with the primitive types and then progress to more complex types such as bean objects.

4.1   Variable-Sized Integers

A key concept used in Jadex Binary are variable-sized integers. The goal is to encode unsigned integer values in a variable-sized format that encodes small values with less space than larger ones. The technique is based on the encoding technique of element IDs in the Extensible Binary Meta-Language (EBML - see [8]), which again is based on the variable Unicode-encoding UTF-8 (see [9]).

Bytes	Format	Value Range
1	1#######	0 to 127
2	01##### ########	128 to 16511
3	001#### ######## ########	16512 to 2113663
4	0001### ######## ######## ########	2113664 to 270549120

Fig. 4. Examples of variable-sized integers and their value ranges

A variable-sized integer is byte-aligned and consists of at least one byte (cf. Fig. 4). The number of zero bits starting from the highest-order bits before the first bit values one denotes the number of additional bytes called extensions that belong to this variable integer. The rest of the byte is then used to encode the highest-order bits of the integer value, the extensions then providing the lower order bits of the value, which is then shifted by a constant equal to the end of the previous value range plus one. This technique of storing integer value uses less space to encode small values at the expense of additional space of high values.

The next part will describe the encoding of boolean values in the format which can be used to extend variable integers to support negative values. Furthermore, variable integers are also heavily used for the string encoding.

4.2   Boolean Values

At first glance, encoding boolean values appears to be trivial since it only requires to store a single bit. However, a data stream which is not byte-aligned requires a considerable amount of processing to shift and pad bit during encoding and decoding, impacting the performance property of the format. As a result, a byte-aligned format is highly preferable. The Java language solves this issue by simply using a full byte to encode a single boolean value, however, this approach essentially wastes seven of the eight bits in the byte which is incompatible with the demand of a compact format.

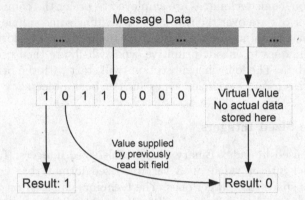

Fig. 5. Encoding of boolean values in the message: The first boolean value writes a byte-sized bit field that is reused by the next seven values

Therefore, multiple boolean values are packed into a single bit. This is accomplished by writing a full byte where the first boolean value is written and updating that byte whenever additional boolean values are added (cf. Fig. 5). When the byte is filled with eight boolean values, another byte is written to the stream when the ninth boolean value is written. While the update cycles require some additional overhead on part of the encoder by having to update an earlier part of the byte stream, it reduces overhead for the decoder. During decoding, the byte is read when its first boolean value is read and then buffered for later reads.

This enables efficient storage of boolean values. This can be combined with the variable integer encoding to provide support for signed variable integers. This is accomplished by writing a boolean sign flag before writing the absolute value as a variable integer.

4.3   Strings

String encoding is a key part in ensuring compactness since a large part of messages tend to be strings. When a string is written by the encoder, it is first checked whether the string is already known. If not, the string is assigned a unique numerical ID and added to the set of known strings called the *string pool*.

The encoder then uses variable integer encoding to write the ID to the stream (cf. Fig 6). The string is then encoded using UTF-8 and its encoded size is

First occurrence
in the message

Repeated occurrences
in the message

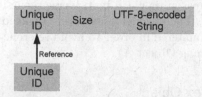

Fig. 6. When a string is occured for the first time in a message, it is encoded in full and assigned a unique ID allowing later occurences to be encoded by referencing the ID

written to the stream as a variable integer, followed by the encoded string itself. If the string is already known by the encoder, the encoder simply writes its ID as a variable integer, avoiding duplicate storage of the string.

Since the number of unique strings in a message is usually less than 128, a single byte is sufficient to encode any following occurence of a string using variable integer encoding. Furthermore, the size of strings tend to be short, generally less than 16511 bytes or even 127 bytes, especially if few characters are used outside the first 128 unicode characters is used, allowing the string size to be encoded in one or two bytes.

All strings share the same string pool, whether it is used to encode an actual string or if it is used for other internal purposes such as type encoding. This maximizes the chance of finding duplicate strings in the pool, reducing message size.

4.4   Other Primitives

Other primitive values consist of integer and floating point types byte, short, int, long, float and double. All of these values are simply translated into network byte order (see e.g. [10]) and added to the message. The only exception are 32-bit int value. In many cases, these values are used as a kind of default integer type. For example, the Java language treats all untyped integer literals as being of this type. This leads to a disproportionately large set of int-typed values to consists of small numbers.

As a result, we found it to be advantageous with regards to the compactness property to encode 32-bit int values as variable-sized integers in the message data. While this can lead to large values being encoded with more bytes than the 4 bytes such a value represents, for most values the size is actually lower than 4 bytes, providing an overall net advantage in terms of size.

4.5   Complex Objects

Complex objects are needed to encode messages containing ontology objects and their sub-objects. Aside from certain special cases which are discussed in the following subsections, complex objects have a type or class and contain a number of fields that can either be primitives or other complex objects.

For this reason they can be traverse recursively, encoding each sub-object when it occurs. The encoder only needs to keep track of objects that have already been encountered in order to avoid reference loops (Object A containing Object B containing Object A).

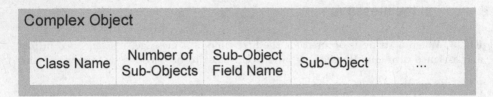

Fig. 7. A complex object is encoded using its class name, the number of sub-objects and pairs of field names and encoded sub-objects

As a result, the format for complex object can be straightforward (cf. Fig 7). It starts with the fully-qualified class name, defining the type of the object. This is written to the message data using the string writing technique described in Section 4.3. Since some sub-objects may not be defined (i.e. reference null), not all of the sub-objects need to be encoded. Therefore, the class name is followed by the number of encoded sub-objects. This number is written to the message data as a variable integer as describe in Section 4.1. Then the sub-objects are written by first writing the name of the field in the object containing the sub-object, then recursively encoding the sub-object itself. During decoding, the decoder first reads the class name and instantiates an object of that class. Then it reads the number of subobjects and finishes by decoding the sub-objects themselves, adding them to the object using the appropriate accessor methods.

Generally, it is expected that the objects offer accessor methods as described in the Java Bean specification [ref?] and the encoder will only encode fields for which such accessor methods are available. However, using annotations, a class may declare that the encoder should encode the field regardless of the existance of accessor methods. In this case the fields are access directly using the reflection API.

4.6 Arrays

Arrays are encoded in a manner similar to complex objects, starting with the array type and concatenating the number of array components and the components themselves. However, since the array type already provides information about the array components, this information can be used to reduce the amount of information that needs to be stored about the components. The array encoding therefore supports two modes, a raw mode which is used for primitive type values and a complex mode for objects. In raw mode, the components are just written without additional information about the type of each component. This can be done in case of primitive types for two reasons: First, primitive types cannot be subclassed, thus the array type is always sufficient to derive the component type and furthermore, primitive values are passed by value and thus do not have a null reference.

This is not the case for objects. The array type may only point at a superclass of the component object and the component object may simply be a null reference. This means that type information about each array component needs to be included. However, in most cases it is safe to assume that the array type describes the type of the component. Therefore, each component is preceded by a boolean value indicating whether further component type information is stored or if the type information can be derived from the array type. Only if this flag indicates that type information is stored, such in the case of subclasses or null values, the flag is followed by the type information. Otherwise, the component object is directly appended after the boolean flag.

In the next section we will evaluate Jadex Binary in terms of the performance and compactness features and compare it to three other message formats. This was done with a series of test in which the message formats were measured and evaluated.

5   Evaluation

In order to evaluate the performance and compactness feature of Jadex Binary, we conducted a series of tests. The experiments were conducted using an Intel i5 750 processor with four cores clocked at 2.67 GHz. The machine was supplied with 8 GiB of memory, however, the Java heap size was limited to 2 GiB. The Java environment used was the Oracle Java SE 6 Update 31 which was running on a current version of Gentoo Linux compiled for the x86-64 instruction set with an unpatched Linux 3.2.2 kernel.

The content formats used were FIPA SL, the built-in Java serialization, Jadex XML and Jadex Binary. The JADE agent platform 4.1.1 using the BeanOntology was used as a representative of Java SL encoding. An test class representing an agent action was used as data set to be encoded. The agent action sample contained a 514 byte string literal, a second string containing a randomized long value encoded as string, a single integer value, an array of 20 integer literals, an array of boolean values and finally an array of objects of the class itself to represent recursively contained sub-objects.

For the compactness tests, this array contained 100 further instances of the class, which themself had the field set to null. For the performance tests, the number of objects in that array was varied, starting at 10000 objects and increasing in steps of 10000 up to 100000 objects. The compactness was measured by counting the number of bytes of the encoded content. If the encoded content was a string, it was converted to a byte representation using UTF-8 encoding (other encodings like UTF-16 would have been possible but would have resulted in worse results). For the performance, the time between start and end of the encoding cycle was measured, other tasks like encoder and object setup was not considered.

In the following, we will present the results of both the performance and the compactness features. While the test data is certainly artificial, we have tried to supply what we think is a good cross-section of possible data cases.

5.1 Performance

In order to avoid interference with lazy initialization procedures and the just-in-time compilation of the Java VM, all performance tests were run twice, with the results of the first test run being discarded. This allowed the Java environment to compile the code and the encoding framing to initialize constants during the first pass so that the real performance figures could be obtained during the second pass.

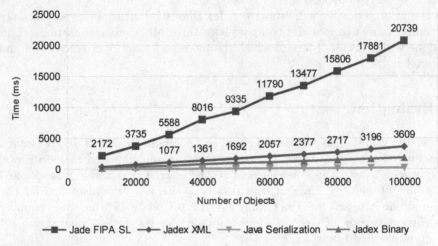

Fig. 8. Results for the performance test runs, the Jade FIPA SL encoding requiring an especially long time

The result of the tests can be seen in Figure 8. While the encoding times of all encoding seem to increase linearly, the FIPA SL encoding provided by JADE seems to require an unusually long time. As expected, both Jadex Binary and the Java serialization mechanism provide substantially better results, however, even Jadex XML which is not intended to be optimized for this format feature still offers substantially lower encoding times than the FIPA SL encoding.

Figure 9 gives a closer look to the three highest performing formats. While Jadex Binary clearly provides an advantage over Jadex XML by roughly a factor of two, the Java serialization is almost an order of magnitude faster. Initial analysis seems to suggest this is due to the use of the Java Reflection API used by both Jadex XML and Jadex Binary, which the Java serialization mechanism can avoid due to its built-in nature. However, Java serialization has further drawbacks as outlined in Section 3, meaning it is not a general solution to the problem and has a more narrow scope of environments in which it can be useful, for example, when dealing with highly homogeneous environments.

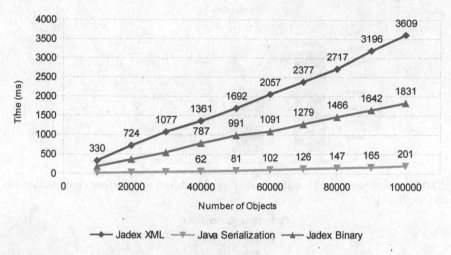

Fig. 9. Performance results using the same data set as Fig. 8 with JADE FIPA SL encoding excluded

5.2   Compactness

In order to test for content compactness, the test object was passed to the encoder and the number of bytes of the encoded object was measured. Since the test object contained a fair amount of test data, the resulting content sizes were expected to be large.

As can be seen in Figure 10, the differences between the four formats are quite substantial. Jadex XML is barely half the size of the FIPA SL encoding and both Java serialization and Jadex Binary are substantially smaller still. In fact, Jadex Binary clearly provided the most compact representation of the test object, being smaller than even the Java serialization format by a factor of roughly 2.5. A fair amount of this is likely to be due to redundant information, especially of string values, which Jadex Binary can exploit (though Jadex XML uses a similar mechanism). In addition, text-based formats like FIPA SL and Jadex XML use a large amount of redundant strings to represent their formatting, such as tags in the case of XML.

In order to test this assumption, another set of tests was performed, which were identical to the previous tests but added an additional compression pass, converting it to the gzip-format, which uses the DEFLATE algorithm (see [11]) to reduce data redundancy. The results shown in Figure 11 substantiate the assumption. The DEFLATE algorithm drastically reduced the redundancies in both FIPA SL and Jadex XML with FIPA SL now even coming out ahead of Jadex XML. Nevertheless, both Java serialization and Jadex binary still show an advantage in compactness with Jadex Binary maintaining a slim margin of Java serialization.

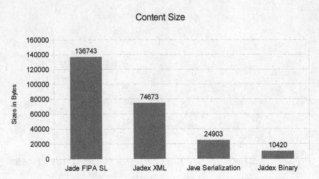

Fig. 10. Content sizes in bytes after encoding the object and further compressing the format with gzip

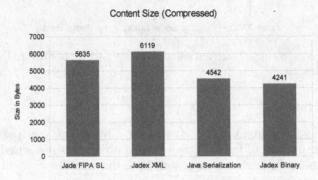

Fig. 11. Content sizes in bytes after encoding the object and further compressing the format with gzip

Since the compression pass substantially reduces the size of even verbose formats, it may suggest that starting out with a compact format only gives a marginal advantage. However, since data compression is not free in terms of computation time, this has to be weighed against the performance message feature. Despite the DEFLATE algorithm being a comparably fast compression algorithm, Figure 12 shows that it adds substantially to the total encoding time of the content. In fact, the additional time require seems to grow with the number of bytes in the uncompressed content, which appears reasonable considering the algorithm must evaluate every byte of the uncompressed data to produce a reversible output.

As a result, data compression does not appear to be generally beneficial when both performance and compactness are important, however, it is another useful tool to adjust the balance between the two language features. In the next section we will discuss further improvements and future work and provide a conclusion on the performance of Jadex Binary.

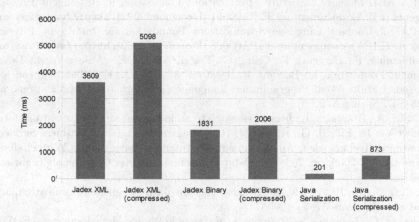

Fig. 12. An additional compression pass increases total encoding time

6 Future Work and Conclusion

The evaluation of Jadex Binary in Section 5 seems to give sufficient evidence that Jadex Binary already has significant advantages in both compactness and performance. However, the performance results of the Java serialization shows that further performance improvements may be possible. One way of further reducing the overhead of Jadex Binary is to reduce the use of the Java Reflection API to access complex objects. This could be accomplished by injecting bytecode-engineered delegate classes which use direct method calls to retrieve and set bean properties.

In addition, the encoder and decoder of Jadex Binary are largely independent of the Jadex platform. It would therefore be possible to port the message format to other agent platforms in order to offer an alternative compact format for agent communications for applications that require it.

Overall, Jadex Binary is able to represent agent messages in a compact form and performs in a reasonably fast manner. Since these two features were the primary goal of Jadex Binary, it does so by sacrificing others like human readability. Nevertheless, if those features are important, other language already provide sufficient support. This allows a developer of a multi-agent system to pick the kind of format that provides the best match for the requirements of the application.

References

1. Willmott, S., Dale, J., Burg, B., Charlton, P., O'Brien, P.: Agentcities: A Worldwide Open Agent Network. Agentlink News 8 (November 2001)
2. Finin, T., Weber, J., Wiederhold, G., Genesereth, M., McKay, D., Fritzson, R., Shapiro, S., Pelavin, R., McGuire, J.: Specification of the KQML agent-communication language – plus example agent policies and architectures. Tech. Rep. EIT TR 92-04 (1993)

3. FIPA ACL Message Structure Specification: Foundation for Intelligent Physical Agents (FIPA), document no. FIPA00061 (December 2002), http://www.fipa.org
4. FIPA SL Content Language Specification: Foundation for Intelligent Physical Agents (FIPA), document no. FIPA00008 (December 2002), http://www.fipa.org
5. Bellifemine, F., Bergenti, F., Caire, G., Poggi, A.: JADE - A Java Agent Development Framework. In: Bordini, R., Dastani, M., Dix, J., El Fallah Seghrouchni, A. (eds.) Multi-Agent Programming: Languages, Platforms and Applications, pp. 125–147. Springer (2005)
6. Pokahr, A., Braubach, L.: From a research to an industrial-strength agent platform: Jadex V2. In: Fill, H.-G., Hansen, H.R., Karagiannis, D. (eds.) Business Services: Konzepte, Technologien, Anwendungen - 9. Internationale Tagung Wirtschaftsinformatik, WI 2009, pp. 769–778. Österreichische Computer Gesellschaft (February 2009)
7. Gosling, J., Joy, B., Steele, G., Bracha, G.: The Java Language Specification, 3rd, 2nd edn. Addison-Wesley (2005)
8. Wiesner, C., Lhomme, S., Cannon, J.: Extensible Binary Meta-Language (EBML) (2012), http://ebml.sourceforge.net/
9. The Unicode Consortium. The Unicode Standard. Addison Wesley (2006)
10. Hoffman, P., Yergeau, F.: UTF-16, an encoding of ISO 10646. RFC 2781, Internet Engineering Task Force (February 2000), http://www.ietf.org/rfc/rfc2781.txt
11. Deutsch, L.P.: DEFLATE Compressed Data Format Specification version 1.3. RFC 1951, Internet Engineering Task Force (May 1996), http://www.ietf.org/rfc/rfc1951.txt

Query Caching in Agent Programming Languages

Natasha Alechina[1], Tristan Behrens[2], Koen V. Hindriks[3], and Brian Logan[1]

[1] School of Computer Science,
University of Nottingham,
Nottingham NG8 1BB UK
[2] Department of Informatics,
Clausthal University of Technology,
Germany
[3] Department of Intelligent Systems,
Delft University of Technology,
The Netherlands

Abstract. Agent programs are increasingly widely used for large scale, time critical applications. In developing such applications, the performance of the agent platform is a key concern. Many logic-based BDI-based agent programming languages rely on inferencing over some underlying knowledge representation. While this allows the development of flexible, declarative programs, repeated inferencing triggered by queries to the agent's knowledge representation can result in poor performance. In this paper we present an approach to query caching for agent programming languages. Our approach is motivated by the observation that agents repeatedly perform queries against a database of beliefs and goals to select possible courses of action. Caching the results of previous queries (memoization) is therefore likely to be beneficial. We develop an abstract model of the performance of a logic-based BDI agent programming language. Using our model together with traces from typical agent programs, we quantify the possible performance improvements that can be achieved by memoization. Our results suggest that memoization has the potential to significantly increase the performance of logic-based agent platforms.

1 Introduction

Belief-Desire-Intention (BDI) based agent programming languages facilitate the development of rational agents specified in terms of beliefs, goals and plans. In the BDI paradigm, agents select a course of action that will achieve their goals given their beliefs. To select plans based on their goals and beliefs, many logic-based BDI-based agent programming languages rely on inferencing over some underlying knowledge representation. While this allows the development of flexible, declarative programs, repeated inferencing triggered by queries to the agent's knowledge representation can result in poor performance. When developing multiagent applications for large scale, time critical applications such performance issues are often a key concern, potentially adversely impacting the adoption of BDI-based agent programming languages and platforms as an implementation technology.

In this paper we present an approach to query caching for agent programming languages. Our approach is motivated by the observation that agents repeatedly perform

M. Dastani, J.F. Hübner, and B. Logan (Eds.): ProMAS 2012, LNAI 7837, pp. 123–137, 2013.

queries against a database of beliefs and goals to select possible courses of action. Caching the results of previous queries (memoization) is therefore likely to be beneficial. Indeed caching as used in algorithms such as Rete [1] and TREAT [2] has been shown to be beneficial in a wide range of related AI applications, including cognitive agent architectures, e.g., [3], expert systems, e.g., [4], and reasoners, e.g., [5]. However that work has focused on the propagation of simple ground facts through a dependency network. In contrast, the key contribution of this paper is to investigate the potential of caching the results of arbitrary logical queries in improving the performance of agent programming languages. We develop an abstract model of the performance of a logic-based BDI agent programming language, defined in terms of the basic query and update operations that form the interface to the agent's knowledge representation. Using our model together with traces from typical agent programs, we quantify the possible performance improvements that can be achieved by memoization. Our results suggest that memoization has the potential to significantly increase the performance of logic-based agent platforms.

The remainder of the paper is organised as follows. In Section 2 we introduce an abstract model of the interface to a logic-based BDI agent's underlying knowledge representation and an associated performance model. Section 3 presents experimental results obtained from traces of typical agent programs and several key observations regarding query and update patterns in these programs. Section 4 introduces two models to exploit these observations and improve the efficiency of the use of Knowledge Representation Technologies (KRTs) by agent programs. Section 5 discusses related work, and Section 6 concludes the paper.

2 Abstract Performance Model

In this section, we present an abstract model of the performance of a logic-based agent programming language as a framework for our analysis. The model abstracts away details that are specific to particular agent programming languages (such as *Jason* [6], 2APL [7], and GOAL [8]), and focuses on key elements that are common to most, if not all, logic-based agent programming languages.

The interpreter of a logic-based BDI agent programming language repeatedly executes a '*sense-plan-act*' cycle (often called a *deliberation cycle* [9] or *agent reasoning cycle* [6]). The details of the deliberation cycle vary from language to language, but in all cases it includes processing of events (*sense*), deciding on what to do next (*plan*), and executing one or more selected actions (*act*). In a logic-based agent programming language, the *plan* phase of the deliberation cycle is implemented by executing the set of rules comprising the agent's program. The rule conditions consist of queries to be evaluated against the agent's beliefs and goals (e.g., plan triggers in *Jason*, the heads of practical reasoning rules in 2APL) and the rule actions consist of actions or plans (sequences of actions) that may be performed by the agent in a situation where the rule condition holds. In the *act* phase, we can distinguish between two different kinds of actions. *Query actions* involve queries against the agent's beliefs and goals and do not change the agent's state. *Update actions*, on the other hand, are either actions that directly change the agent's beliefs and goals (e.g., 'mental notes' in *Jason*, belief update actions in 2APL), or external actions that affect the agent's environment, and which may indirectly change the agent's beliefs and goals.

In a logic-based agent programming language, the agent's database of beliefs and goals is maintained using some form of declarative knowledge representation technology. Queries in the conditions of rules and query actions give rise to queries performed against the knowledge representation. Update actions give rise (directly or indirectly) to updates to the beliefs and goals maintained by the knowledge representation. For example, Figure 1 illustrates example rules from *Jason*, 2APL and GOAL agent programs, which select a move action to move a block in the Blocks World environment. While the rules appear quite different and have different components, the evaluation of

```
+!on(X,Y) <- !clear(X); !clear(Y); move(X,Y).
```

(a) *Jason*

```
allOnTable <- on(X,Y) and clear(X) and not(Y=table) |
    { @blocksworld(move(X,table),_); On(X,table) }
```

(b) 2APL

```
if a-goal(tower([X| T])) then move(X, table).
```

(c) GOAL

Fig. 1. Example Blocks World rules

the conditions of each rule gives rise to similar queries to the underlying knowledge representation. In this example, the terms on, clear and tower are predicates which are evaluated by querying the belief and goal bases of the agents. Similarly, the agent programs use logical rules (Horn clauses) to represent knowledge about the environment. For example, Figure 2 illustrates a rule used in the *Jason* Blocks World agent to determine whether a set of blocks constitutes a tower.

```
tower([X]) :- on(X,table).
tower([X,Y|T]) :- on(X,Y) & tower([Y|T]).
```

Fig. 2. Example *Jason* logical rule

The 2APL and GOAL agents use the same recursive rule in Prolog format with '&' replaced by ','. Similarly, in each case, execution of external actions such as move and internal belief and goal update actions give rise to updates to the agent's beliefs and goals, either indirectly through perception of the environment (in the case of external action) or directly (in the case of internal actions).

From the point of view of the agent's knowledge representation, the three steps in the *sense-plan-act* cycle can therefore be mapped onto two kinds of knowledge representation functionality. The knowledge representation must provide functionality for querying an agent's beliefs and goals when applying rules or executing query actions in the agent's plans, and for updating an agent's beliefs and goals upon receiving new information from other agents or the environment, or because of internal events that occur in the agent itself. Our performance model therefore distinguishes two key knowledge representation phases that are common to virtually all logic-based agent programming languages: a *query phase* and an *update phase*. The two phases together constitute an *update cycle*.

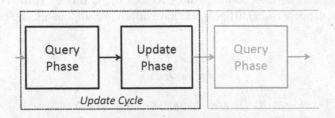

Fig. 3. Update Cycle

The model is illustrated in Figure 3. The query phase includes all queries processed by the agent's knowledge representation in evaluating rule conditions to select a plan or plans, and in executing the next step of the agent's plans (e.g., if the next step of a plan is a belief or goal test action). The update phase includes all updates to the agent's knowledge representation resulting from the execution of the next step of a plan, where this step changes the agent's state directly (e.g., the generation of subgoals or the addition or deletion of beliefs and goals), and updating the agent's state with new beliefs, goals, messages or events at the beginning of the next *sense-plan-act* cycle. Note that update cycles do not necessarily correspond one-to-one to deliberation cycles. For example, in *Jason* and 2APL the action(s) performed at the end of a deliberation cycle may be internal actions (such as test actions) that do not update the agent's beliefs and goals, and in these languages the query phase may include queries from several deliberation cycles. In what follows, we assume that the query phase occurs first and the update phase second, but our results do not depend on this particular order and a similar analysis can be performed if the order of the phases is reversed.

To develop our performance model in detail, we must first make the query/update interface to the agent's knowledge representation precise. Different agent programming frameworks utilise different types of databases to store different parts of the agent's state. For example, most logic-based agent programming languages use different databases for beliefs and for goals, and almost all languages (with the exception of GOAL) maintain bases that store plan-like structures or intentions. Here we focus on those aspects common to most logic-based agent programming languages, namely operations on the agent's beliefs and goals, and abstract away from the details of their realisation in a particular agent platform. In particular, we ignore operations performed on databases of intentions or plans. Although agent platforms do perform operations on intentions and plans that can be viewed as queries and updates, these operations vary widely from platform to platform and typically do not involve logical inference.

The first key KRT functionality is querying a database. A query assumes the presence of some inference engine to perform the query. In many agent platforms, a distinction is made between performing a query to obtain a single answer and to obtain all answers. In what follows, we abstract away from the details of particular inference engines provided by different agent platforms and represent queries by the (average) time required to perform the query. The second key functionality is that of modifying or *updating* the content of a database. With the exception of recent work on the semantic web and on theory progression in situation calculus, update has not been a major concern for classical (non-situated) reasoners. However it is essential for agents as they need to be able to represent a changing and dynamic environment. All the agent platforms we have investigated use a *simple* form of updating which involves simply adding or removing facts. In cases where the agent platform adopts the open world assumption, one needs to be slightly more general and support the addition and removal of literals (positive and negated facts).

Based on this model, we can derive an analysis of the *average case performance* for a single update cycle of an agent. Our analysis distinguishes between costs associated with the query phase and the update phase of an update cycle. We assume that the agent performs on average N queries in the query phase of an update cycle. If the average cost of a query is c_{qry}, then the average total cost of the query phase is given by

$$N \cdot c_{qry}$$

In general, the same query may be performed several times in a given update cycle. (We provide support for the fact that queries are performed multiple times in a cycle below.) If the average number of unique queries performed in an update cycle is K, then on average each query is performed $n = N/K$ times per cycle.

The total average cost of the update phase of an update cycle can be derived similarly. In logic-based agent programming languages, updates are simple operations which only add or remove facts (literals) from a database, so it is reasonable to consider only the total number of updates when estimating the cost of the update phase. If U is the average number of updates (i.e., adds and deletes) per cycle and c_{upd} is the average cost of an update, then the average total cost of the update phase is given by

$$U \cdot c_{upd}$$

Combining both the query and update phase costs yields:

$$N \cdot c_{qry} + U \cdot c_{upd} \tag{1}$$

3   Experimental Analysis

To quantify typical values for the parameters in our abstract performance model, we performed a number of experiments using different agent platforms and agent and environment implementations. We stress that our aim was not to determine the absolute or relative performance of each platform, but to estimate the relative average number of queries and updates performed by 'typical' agent programs, and their relative average costs on each platform, in order to determine to what extent caching may be useful as a general strategy for logic-based agent programming languages. To this end, we selected three well known agent platforms (Jason [6], 2APL [7] and GOAL [8]), and five existing agent programs/environments (Blocks World, Elevator Sim, Multi-Agent Programming Contest 2006 & 2011, and Wumpus World).

The agent platforms were chosen as representative of the current state of the art in logic-based agent programming languages, and span a range of implementation approaches. For example, both 2APL and GOAL use Prolog engines provided by third parties for knowledge representation and reasoning. 2APL uses the commercial Prolog engine JIProlog [10] implemented in Java, whereas GOAL uses the Java interface JPL to connect to the open source SWI-Prolog engine (v5.8) which is implemented in C [11]. In contrast, the logical language used in *Jason* is integrated into the platform and is implemented in Java.

The agent programs were chosen as representative of 'typical' agent applications, and span a wide range of task environments (from observable and static to partially observable and real-time), program complexity (measured in lines of code, LoC), and programming styles. The Blocks World is a classic environment in which blocks must be moved from an initial position to a goal state by means of a gripper. The Blocks World is a single agent, discrete, fully observable environment where the agent has full control. Elevator Sim is a dynamic, environment that simulates one or more elevators in a building with a variable number of floors (we used 25 floors) where the goal is to transport a pre-set number of people between floors [12]. Each elevator is controlled by an agent, and the simulator controls people that randomly appear, push call buttons, floor buttons, and enter and leave elevators upon arrival at floors. The environment is partially observable as elevators cannot see which buttons inside other elevators are pressed nor where these other elevators are located. In the 2006 Multi-Agent Programming Contest scenario (MAPC 2006) [13] teams of 5 agents explore grid-like terrain to find gold and transport it to a depot. In the 2011 Multi-Agent Programming Contest scenario (MAPC 2011) [14] teams of 10 agents explore 'Mars' and occupy valuable zones. Both MAPC environments are discrete, partially observable, real-time multi-agent environments, in which agent actions are not guaranteed to have their intended effect.

Finally, the Wumpus World is a discrete, partially observable environment in which a single agent must explore a grid to locate gold while avoiding being eaten by the Wumpus or trapped in a pit. For some of the environments we also varied the size of the problem instance the agent(s) have to deal with. In the Blocks World the number of blocks determines the problem size, and in the Elevator Sim an important parameter that determines the size of a problem instance is the number of people to be moved between floors. The size of problem instances that we have used can be found in the first column of Tables 2 through 6.

It is important to stress that, to avoid any bias due to agent design in our results, the programs were not written specially for the experiments. While our selection was therefore necessarily constrained by the availability of pre-existing code (in particular versions of each program were not available for all platforms), we believe our results are

Table 1. Agents and Environments

Environment	Agent Platform	Agent LoC	Deliberation Cycles
Blocks World	*Jason*	34	104-961
	2APL	64	186-1590
	GOAL	42	16-144
Elevator Sim	2APL	367	3187-4010
	GOAL	87	2292-5844
MAPC 2006	*Jason*	295	2664
MAPC 2011	GOAL	1588	30
Wumpus World	*Jason*	294	292-443

representative of the query and update performance of a broad range of agent programs 'in the wild'. Table 1 summarises the agents, environments and the agent platforms that were used in the experiments.

3.1 Experimental Setup

To perform the experiments, we extended the logging functionality of the three agent platforms, and analysed the resulting query and update patterns in the execution traces for each agent/environment combination. The extended logging functionality captured all queries and updates delegated to the knowledge representation used by the agent platform and the cost of performing each query or update.

In the case of 2APL and GOAL, which use a third party Prolog engine, we recorded the cost of each query or update delegated to the respective Prolog engine. In these languages, Prolog is used to represent and reason with percepts, messages, knowledge, beliefs, and goals. Action preconditions and test goals are also evaluated using Prolog. Prolog queries and updates to the Prolog database therefore account for all costs involved in the query and update phases of an update cycle. In the case of *Jason*, the instrumentation is less straightforward, and involved modifying the JASON belief base to record the time required to query and update percepts, messages, knowledge and beliefs.[1] The time required to process other types of *Jason* events, e.g., related to the intentions or plans of an agent, was not recorded.

We ran each of the agent/environment/platform combinations listed in Table 1 until the pattern of queries and updates stabilised (i.e., disregarding any 'start up' period when the agent(s), e.g., populate their initial representation of the environment). For different agent environments, this required different numbers of deliberation cycles (listed in the *Deliberation Cycles* column in Table 1). For example, fewer deliberation cycles are required in the Blocks World to complete a task than in other environments, whereas in the Elevator Sim environment thousands of deliberation cycles are required to reach steady state. For the real-time Multi-Agent Programming Contest cases, the simulations were run for 1.5 minutes; 1.5 minutes is sufficient to collect a representative number of

---

[1] In contrast to 2APL and GOAL, *Jason* does not have declarative goals.

cycles while keeping the amount of data that needs to be analysed to manageable proportions. For each agent/environment/platform run, the time required to perform each query or update resulting from the execution of the agent's program was logged, resulting in log files as illustrated in Figure 4. Here, add and del indicate updates, and

```
...
add on(b2,table) 30
add on(b9,b10) 43
del on(b4,b6) 21
query tower('.'(X,T)) 101
query tower('.'(b7,[])) 51
...
```

Fig. 4. Example log file

query indicates a belief or goal query, followed by the updated belief or goal, or query performed, and the time required in microseconds.

3.2 Experimental Results

In this section we briefly present the results of our analysis and highlight some observations relating to the query and update patterns that can be seen in this data. We stress that our aim is not a direct comparison of the performance of the agent programs or platforms analysed. The performance results presented below depend on the technology used for knowledge representation and reasoning as well as on the machine architecture used to obtain the results. As such the figures provide some insight in how these technologies perform in the context of agent programming but cannot be used directly to compare different technologies. Rather our main focus concerns the patterns that can be observed in the queries and updates that are performed by all programs and platforms, and the potential performance improvement that might be gained by caching queries on *each* agent platform.

We focus on the update cycles that are executed during a run of an agent. Recall that these cycles may differ from the deliberation cycle of an agent. An update cycle consists of a phase in which queries are performed which is followed by a subsequent phase in which updates are performed on the databases that an agent maintains. Note that update cycles do not correspond one-to-one to deliberation cycles. In particular, both *Jason* and 2APL agents execute significantly more deliberation cycles than update cycles as can be seen by comparing Table 1 with the tables below. The phases are extracted from log files by grouping query and add/del lines.

We analysed the log files to derive values for all the parameters in the abstract model introduced in Section 2, including the average number queries performed at each update cycle N, the average number of unique queries performed in an update cycle K, the average number of times that the same query is performed in an update cycle N/K, the average cost of a query c_{qry}, the average number of updates performed in an update cycle U, and the average cost of an update c_{upd}. We also report the number of update cycles for each scenario we have run. Finally, we report the average percentage of queries that are repeated in consecutive update cycles, p. That is, p represents the average percentage of queries that were performed in one cycle and repeated in the next update cycle.

The *Jason* and 2APL agents were run on a 2 GHz Intel Core Duo, 2 GB 667 MHz DDR2 SDRAM running OSX 10.6 and Java 1.6. The GOAL agents were run on a 2.66 GHz Intel Core i7, 4GB 1067 MHz DDR3, running OSX 10.6 and Java 1.6. Query and update costs are given in microseconds. The Size column in Tables 2a – 2c refers to the number of blocks in Blocks world. In Tables 3a and 3b for the Elevator Sim, Size refers to the number of people that randomly are generated by the simulator. The size column in Table 6 refers to the size of grid used: KT2 is a 6×5 grid with one pit, KT4 a 9×7 grid with 2 pits, and KT5 a 4×4 grid with 3 pits.

The results for the Blocks World environment are given in Tables 2a – 2c. Note that the average query and update costs for the GOAL agent decrease when the number of blocks increases. This effect can be explained by the fact that in this toy domain the overhead of translating queries by means of the JPL interface to SWI-Prolog queries is relatively larger in smaller sized instances than in larger sized ones. Also note that the costs found for GOAL agents cannot be used to draw conclusions about the performance of SWI-Prolog because of the significant overhead the Java interface JPL introduces.

Table 2. Blocks World

(a) *Jason*

Size	N	K	n	p	c_{qry}	U	c_{upd}	Update cycles
10	4.6	3.3	1.39	70%	485	1.1	376	16
50	4.8	3.3	1.46	82%	286	1.0	1057	79
100	5.1	3.3	1.54	82%	317	1.0	2788	152

(b) 2APL

Size	N	K	n	p	c_{qry}	U	c_{upd}	Update cycles
10	41.1	26.8	1.56	58%	8554	1.8	294	46
50	104.8	78.2	1.34	59%	22335	1.8	273	230
100	235.4	165.8	1.42	59%	49247	1.8	435	460

(c) GOAL

Size	N	K	n	p	c_{qry}	U	c_{upd}	Update cycles
10	26.0	17.6	1.48	59%	89	2.6	58	16
50	100.3	66.0	1.52	63%	64	2.7	35	70
100	153.3	105.7	1.45	70%	59	2.9	29	144

The results for the Elevator Sim environment are given in Tables 3a and 3b. Tables 4 and 5 give the results for the MAPC 2006 & 2011 environments, and the results for the Wumpus World environment are shown in Table 6.

Table 3. Elevator Sim

(a) 2APL

Size	N	K	n	p	c_{qry}	U	c_{upd}	Update cycles
10	11,214.3	290.3	38.63	52%	97979	2.0	2971	16
50	1,800.7	206.5	8.72	71%	88839	1.1	674	163
100	1,237.7	202.9	6.10	71%	82766	1.1	456	215

(b) GOAL

Size	N	K	n	p	c_{qry}	U	c_{upd}	Update cycles
10	29.5	12.1	1.16	92%	29	1.0	39	5844
50	28.44	23.7	1.20	92%	30	1.0	37	3636
100	34.3	28.6	1.20	90%	31	1.0	36	2292

Table 4. Multi-Agent Programming Contest 2006, Jason

Size	N	K	n	p	c_{qry}	U	c_{upd}	Update cycles
N/A	4.6	3.7	1.25	76%	256	1.1	96	379

Table 5. Multi-Agent Programming Contest 2011, GOAL

Size	N	K	n	p	c_{qry}	U	c_{upd}	Update cycles
N/A	80.5	66.0	1.22	82%	66	28.0	45	30

Table 6. Wumpus World, *Jason*

Size	N	K	n	p	c_{qry}	U	c_{upd}	Update cycles
KT2	8.9	7.4	1.2	59%	671	1.0	173	18
KT4	9.1	7.6	1.2	55%	1170	1.0	166	24
KT5	8.0	6.7	1.2	52%	664	1.0	428	18

As can be seen, even in simple environments like the Blocks World, agent programs may perform many queries in a single update cycle (see Table 2). In the Blocks World experiments, the total number of queries performed during a run ranges from 417 queries for the GOAL agent in the small 10 blocks problem instance in only 16 deliberation cycles to 108, 300 queries for the 2APL agent in the 100 blocks problem instance in 1590 deliberation cycles. Given that the Blocks World environment involves only a small number of beliefs and that the agents use only a few logical rules, this implies that the same query is repeated many times. A similar pattern can be seen in the other experiments. In all cases, the average number of times a query is performed in a single cycle is consistently larger than 1, with N/K ranging from 1.16 (Table 3b) up to 38.63 (3a). Our first observation is therefore that queries are consistently repeated in a single update cycle by all agents in all environments and across all the platforms investigated.

Observation 1. *In a single update cycle, the same query is performed more than once, i.e., we have $n > 1$.*

A second observation that follows consistently from the data is that large percentages of queries are repeated each update cycle. We have found that 22% up to even 92% of queries are repeated in consecutive update cycles.

Observation 2. *A significant number of queries are repeated at subsequent update cycles, i.e., $p > 20\%$.*

Secondly, in all agent/environment/platform combinations investigated, in a single deliberation cycle an agent performs only a few (perhaps only one) actions that directly or indirectly change the state of the agent. This is also supported by the fact that the number of deliberation cycles in most cases is larger than the number of update cycles. In other words, the execution of a deliberation cycle does not always result in an update. Comparing the average number of updates with the average number of unique queries, we consistently find that many more queries are performed than updates in each cycle.

Observation 3. *The number of updates U (add, deletes) performed in an update cycle is significantly smaller than the number of unique queries K performed in that cycle, i.e. $K \gg U$.*

Note that all three observations are independent of the size or complexity of the environment, the complexity of the agent program or the agent platform used. This strongly suggest that the query and update performance of agent programs in the platforms investigated can be significantly improved.

4   Query Caching

The observations in the previous section suggest that efficiency can be significantly increased by memoization, i.e. by caching query results. The cache stores answers to queries, so that if the same query is performed again in the same update cycle, the answers can be returned without recourse to the underlying knowledge representation.

In this section, we first show how to modify the interface to the underlying knowledge representation to incorporate caching. We then extend the abstract performance model introduced in Section 2 in order to analyse the potential increase in performance of caching, and derive a relationship between $n = N/K$ and the costs of maintaining the cache which characterises when caching is likely to be beneficial.

4.1   Extending the Knowledge Representation Interface

The most straightforward approach to exploit the fact that some queries are performed multiple times in a single update cycle, is to add the results of a query to the cache the first time it is performed in an update cycle, and then retrieve the results from the cache if the query is reevaluated at the same update cycle. Although very simple in requiring no information about the average number of times each unique query is repeated in a cycle, as we show below, if the cost of cache insertion is sufficiently low, significant performance improvements can be achieved. Moreover, such an approach requires only a very *loose coupling* between the cache and the underlying knowledge representation.

The cache simply acts as a filter: if a query is a cache hit the results are immediately returned by the cache; if a query is a cache miss, the query is delegated to the knowledge representation and the results stored in the cache, before being returned to the agent program.

The use of a cache requires an extension of the KRT interface with a cache operation `lookup` to lookup entries, an operation `put` to put entries into the cache, and an operation `clear` to clear the cache again. The basic approach can be implemented as shown in the algorithm below.

Listing 1.1. Query Cache

```
 1  % Query Phase
 2  clear(cache)
 3  FOR EACH query Q_i DO
 4     IF lookup(Q_i, answer, cache)
 5     THEN return(answer)
 6     ELSE DO
 7        answer = query(Q_i, beliefbase)
 8        put(Q_i:answer, cache)
 9        return(answer)
10     ENDDO
11  ENDDO
```

Of course, by only storing the query results, it is not possible to detect when cache entries are invalidated, so the cache needs to be cleared at the start of each query phase in an update cycle and rebuilt from scratch. In addition, when compiling an agent program, care is required to ensure that differences in variable names are resolved so that similar queries are retrieved from the cache instead of being recomputed. For example, the queries $q(X, Y)$ and $q(A, B)$ which represent the same query but use different variables should not result in a cache miss.

The cache can be implemented by a hash table. Given Observation 2, the size of the hash table can be tuned to optimal size after one or two cycles. By implementing the cache as a hash table, the insertion costs c_{ins} of an entry are constant and the evaluation costs of performing a query a second time are equal to the lookup costs, i.e. a constant c_{hit} that represents the cost for a cache hit. This results in the following performance model, adapted from the model in Section 2:

$$K \cdot (c_{qry} + c_{ins}) + N \cdot c_{hit} + U \cdot c_{upd} \qquad (2)$$

It follows that whenever

$$c_{qry} > \frac{K}{N - K} \cdot c_{ins} + \frac{N}{N - K} \cdot c_{hit} \qquad (3)$$

it is beneficial to implement a cache. That is, the cache increases performance whenever the average query cost is greater than the average lookup cost of a query plus the average insertion cost times the proportion of unique to non-unique queries (for $N > K$).

As expected, the larger the average number of times n a query is performed in a single cycle, the larger the expected efficiency gains. In the worst case in which all queries are only performed once in a cycle, i.e. $n = 1$, the cache will incur an increase in the cost which is linear in the number of queries, i.e. $N \cdot (c_{ins} + c_{hit})$.

4.2 Experimental Evaluation

To estimate values for c_{ins} and c_{hit} and the potential improvement in performance that may be obtained from caching, we implemented the caching mechanism described in algorithm 1.1 and evaluated its performance by simulating the execution of each agent platform with caching using the query and update logs for the Blocks World and Elevator Sim experiments. The cache is implemented as a single hash table that is filled the first time a query is performed in a query phase and cleared when the first update is performed in the subsequent update phase.

As might be expected, the cost of both cache insertions and hits were low. For our implementation, the cost c_{hit} was about 1 microsecond ($0.45 - 1.16\mu s$) with a similar value for c_{ins} ($0.29 - 0.83\mu s$).

Even in the experiment with the lowest value of n (the Elevator Sim agent programmed in GOAL with 10 people to be transported) the condition of equation 3 is satisfied and performance is improved by caching. In this case, $n = 1.16$ and $c_Q = 29$ (see Table 3b), and we have $29 > 1/0.16 + 1 = 7.25$. The average estimated gain per cycle in this case is $42\mu s$, which can be computed using equation 2 and subtracting the first from the last. The performance gained even in this case is about 10%. In all other cases the gains of using single cycle caching are substantially larger.

5   Related Work

There is almost no work that directly relates to our study of the performance of knowledge representation and reasoning capabilities incorporated into agent programming. As far as we know, our study is the first to investigate patterns in the queries and updates that are performed by agent programs. In [15] it was observed that agent programs appear to spend most of their time in evaluating conditions for adopting plans, although the author's proposed solution was to adopt a plan indexing scheme, rather than to optimize query evaluation in general. In [16] the performance of the FLUX and GOLOG agent programming languages is studied. Another GOLOG-style language, Indi-GOLOG, implements caching [17]. GOLOG-like languages, however, do not implement a deliberation cycle based on the BDI paradigm.

Performance issues of BDI agents have been studied in various other contexts. To mention just a few examples, [18] proposes an extended deliberation cycle for BDI agents that takes advantage of environmental events and [19] proposes the incorporation of learning techniques into BDI agents to improve their performance in dynamic environments. The focus of these papers is on integrating additional techniques into an agent's architecture to improve the performance of an agent instead of on the KRT capabilities of those agents.

6   Conclusion

We presented an abstract performance model of the basic query and update operations that define the interface to a logic-based BDI agent's underlying knowledge representation. Using this model, we analysed the performance of a variety of different agent programs implemented using three different agent platforms. To the best of our knowledge, our study is the first to analyse query and update patterns in existing agent programming languages. Although preliminary, our results suggest that in logic-based agent platforms, knowledge representation and reasoning capabilities account for a large part of the execution time of an agent. In particular, three key observations suggest that integrating memoization into agent programming languages have the potential to significantly increase the performance of logic-based agent platforms: the same queries are performed more than once in a single update cycle, large number of queries are repeated in subsequent cycles, and the number of queries is typically much larger than the number of updates performed.

We showed how the interface to the underlying knowledge representation of an agent platform can be modified to incorporate caching, and extended the abstract performance model to quantify the potential performance improvements that can be achieved by memoization of queries. Our results indicate that even simple query caching techniques have the potential to substantially improve the performance across a wide range of application domains.

The work presented here is limited to a single agent update cycle. Our results, and in particular the observation that a significant number of queries are repeated in subsequent agent cycles, suggests that further performance improvements may be obtained by extending caching to multiple cycles. Extending our abstract performance model and implementation to account for such queries is an area of further work.

References

1. Forgy, C.: Rete: a fast algorithm for the many pattern/many object pattern match problem. Artificial Intelligence 19(1), 17–37 (1982)
2. Miranker, D.P.: TREAT: A better match algorithm for AI production systems. In: Proceedings of the Sixth National Conference on Artificial Intelligence, AAAI 1987, pp. 42–47. AAAI Press (1987)
3. Laird, J.E., Newell, A., Rosenbloom, P.S.: SOAR: An architecture for general intelligence. Artificial Intelligence 33, 1–64 (1987)
4. Software Technology Branch, Lyndon B. Johnson Space Center Houston: CLIPS Reference Manual: Version 6.21 (June 2003)
5. Jena (2011), http://jena.sourceforge.net/
6. Bordini, R.H., Hubner, J.F., Wooldridge, M.: Programming Multi-Agent Systems in AgentSpeak using Jason. Wiley (2007)
7. Dastani, M.: 2APL: a practical agent programming language. International Journal of Autonomous Agents and Multi-Agent Systems 16(3), 214–248 (2008)
8. Hindriks, K.V.: Programming Rational Agents in GOAL. In: Multi-Agent Programming, pp. 119–157. Springer (2009)
9. Dastani, M., de Boer, F.S., Dignum, F., Meyer, J.J.C.: Programming agent deliberation. In: Proceedings of the Second International Joint Conference on Autonomous Agents and Multiagent Systems, pp. 97–104. ACM (2003)

10. JIProlog (2011), http://www.ugosweb.com/jiprolog/
11. SWI-Prolog (2011), http://www.swi-prolog.org/
12. Elevator Simulator (2011),
    http://sourceforge.net/projects/elevatorsim/
13. Dastani, M., Dix, J., Novak, P.: The first contest on multi-agent systems based on computational logic. In: Toni, F., Torroni, P. (eds.) CLIMA 2005. LNCS (LNAI), vol. 3900, pp. 373–384. Springer, Heidelberg (2006)
14. Behrens, T., Dix, J., Köster, M., Hübner, J. (eds.): Special Issue about Multi-Agent-Contest II. Annals of Mathematics and Artificial Intelligence, vol. 61. Springer, Netherlands (2011)
15. Dennis, L.A.: Plan indexing for state-based plans. In: Sakama, C., Sardina, S., Vasconcelos, W., Winikoff, M. (eds.) DALT 2011. LNCS, vol. 7169, pp. 3–15. Springer, Heidelberg (2012)
16. Thielscher, M.: Pushing the envelope: Programming reasoning agents. In: AAAI Workshop Technical Report WS-02-05: Cognitive Robotics. AAAI Press (2002)
17. Giacomo, G.D., Lespérance, Y., Levesque, H.J., Sardina, S.: IndiGolog: A high-level programming language for embedded reasoning agents. In: Bordini, R.H., Dastani, M., Dix, J., Fallah-Seghrouchni, A.E. (eds.) Multi-Agent Programming: Languages, Platforms and Applications, pp. 31–72. Springer (2009)
18. Koch, F., Dignum, F.: Enhanced deliberation in BDI-modelled agents. In: Demazeau, Y., Dignum, F., Corchado, J.M., Pérez, J.B. (eds.) Advances in PAAMS. AISC, vol. 70, pp. 59–68. Springer, Heidelberg (2010)
19. Singh, D., Sardina, S., Padgham, L., James, G.: Integrating learning into a BDI agent for environments with changing dynamics. In: Proceedings of the International Joint Conference on Artificial Intelligence, IJCAI, pp. 2525–2530 (2011)

Typing Multi-agent Programs in simpAL

Alessandro Ricci and Andrea Santi

DISI, University of Bologna
via Venezia 52, 47023 Cesena, Italy
{a.ricci,a.santi}@unibo.it

Abstract. Typing is a fundamental mechanism adopted in mainstream programming languages, important in particular when developing programs of a certain complexity to catch errors at compile time, before executing a program, and to improve the overall design of a system. In this paper we introduce typing also in agent-oriented programming, by using a novel agent programming language called simpAL, which has been conceived from scratch to have this feature.

1   Introduction

Typing is an important mechanism introduced in traditional programming languages, particularly useful if not indispensable when developing programs of a certain complexity [19,16,6,4]. Generally speaking, the definition of a (strong and static) type system in a programming language brings two main benefits. First, it enables compile time error checking, greatly reducing the cost of errors detection—from both a temporal and economic point of view. Second, it provides developers with a conceptual tool for modeling generalization/specialization relationships among concepts and abstractions, eventually specializing existing ones through the definition of proper sub-types and making it possible to fully exploit the principle of substitutability [29] for supporting a safe extension and reuse in programming.

We argue that these features could be very useful and important also for agent-oriented programming (AOP), in particular as soon as AOP is investigated as a paradigm for developing software systems in general [25]. To authors' knowledge, there are no agent-oriented programming languages (APLs) in the state-of-the-art that fully support typing and related features. Consequently, the support which is provided by existing languages to catch errors *before* executing the system is quite weak. To this purpose, in this paper we describe an approach that introduces typing in agent-oriented programming, in particular by means of a novel agent programming language called simpAL, which has been conceived from scratch to have this feature. simpAL, whose general design and concepts have been recently introduced elsewhere [26], has been conceived on the one side drawing inspiration from existing APLs based on the BDI model [23] – AgentSpeak(L) [22] / Jason [2] in particular – and existing meta-models such as the A&A [18] (Agents and Artifacts), along with related frameworks such as

M. Dastani, J.F. Hübner, and B. Logan (Eds.): ProMAS 2012, LNAI 7837, pp. 138–157, 2013.
© Springer-Verlag Berlin Heidelberg 2013

CArtAgO [24]. On the other side, it has been designed having in mind agent-oriented programming as an evolution of Object-Oriented Programming, to be explored as a paradigm for general-purpose computing and software development [25]. Generally speaking, simpAL is not meant to be as flexible and effective as existing APLs for tackling the development of agent-based systems in the context of Distributed Artificial Intelligence, but it is meant to provide more robust and effective features for the development of general software systems yet characterized by elements of complexity related to concurrency, distribution, decentralization of control, reactivity, etc. In that perspective, typing – as well as other mechanisms not considered in the paper such as *inheritance* – is considered an essential feature.

The remainder of the paper is organized as follows: In Section 2, first we briefly remind the role of typing for programming in general, then we discuss what kind of errors we aim at detecting by introducing typing in agent-oriented programming, as an improvement of the current error checking support provided by existing APLs in the state-of-the-art. Section 3 contains the core contribution of the paper, which is about introducing typing in agent-oriented programming, taking simpAL as target programming language. Finally, in Section 4 we discuss related work and in Section 5 we provide concluding remarks.

2 Bringing Types in Agent-Oriented Programming: Desiderata

2.1 On the Role of Typing for Programming

In the context of programming and software development, typing plays an important role in helping programmers organise computational structures and use them correctly [19,17]. In general, a *type* is a collection of computational entities that share some common property. A *type system* can be defined as *a tractable syntactic method for proving the absence of certain program behaviours by classifying phrases according to the kinds of values they compute* [19]. In the most general case, type systems and type theory refer to a broad field of study in logics, mathematics and philosophy. Here we consider their specific applications in programming languages, where three main uses of types can be identified [17]:

- *Detecting errors* – type errors occur when a computational entity, such as a function or a data value, is used in a manner that is inconsistent with the concept it represents. For instance, in the case of OO programming languages, invoking a method which is not part of the object (class) interface or passing wrong parameters, or rather assigning wrong values to an object's instance fields. Static type checking allows early detection of these kind of errors, that can be fixed then before running the program.
- *Program organisation and documentation* – in modern programming languages types can be used to represent concepts related to the problem to be solved and their relationships, providing an important support for the high-level organisation of programs, improving their readability, understanding

and maintenance. For instance, in a object-oriented CAD program using an interface/type *Shape* with some *draw* method to represent geometrical shapes, and different classes (*Rectangle*, *Circle*, etc.) – one for each specific concrete shape and a concrete draw behavior. Type systems enforce disciplined programming and this is important in particular in the context of large-scale software composition, where they typically form the backbone of the modules used to package and tie together the components of a large system. Module's interfaces are typically seen as the types of the module.

– *Efficiency* – typing makes it possible to avoid (some) error checking at runtime (since it has been done already at compile time), so improving performance. Generally speaking, types provide information to the compiler about the computational entities in the program that could be useful to produce optimized code to be executed.

These uses are not bound to any *specific* programming language or paradigm, so an interesting question for us is if and how they could be exploited also in the context of agent-oriented programming. In this paper we focus in particular on error detecting, even if the notion of type introduced in simpAL (that will be presented in Section 3) has been devised to be of help also for improving organisation and optimisations of programs.

2.2   Detecting Errors in Current APLs

The support for (static) error detecting in current state-of-the-art APLs is quite limited, much weaker indeed compared to what we have e.g. in (statically) typed object-oriented programming languages.

Besides mere syntactical controls, there are APLs – e.g. Jason [2] – that do not provide any particular kind of checks, while others – such as 2APL [7], GOAL [11] and AFAPL [28] – provide some basic mechanisms for static errors detection. For example in 2APL warnings are generated when undefined *belief update actions* are referenced in the agent code. Similar controls are present in GOAL where a check is done about non-existing *user-defined actions* referenced in agent programs. For what concerns AFAPL instead, an old version of the language provides a quite rich set of static controls [3] (e.g. for incorrectly specified *activity identifiers*, for mistyped *imports*, etc.), nevertheless such controls have been removed – or just not re-implemented yet – in the current version of the language.

Overall, MAS developers are forced to deal *at runtime* with a set of programming errors that should be detected instead statically, before running the MAS program. In the following we provide some main examples of such programming errors, using a set of simple Jason source code snippets. We intentionally choose to consider samples written in only one APL just for making the description simple and terse. However, beside mere syntactical differences related to specific language constructs, through these samples we are able to outline a set of general considerations related to programming errors that do not hold only for Jason, but also apply to others state-of-the-art APLs.

```
1   // agent ag0
2   iterations("zero").
3
4   !do_job.
5
6   +!do_job
7     <-  ...
8         -+iterations(N+1);
9         ...
10        ?num_iterations(N).
11
12  +msgbel
13    <-  .print("Message received").
14
15  // agent ag1
16  !send_msg.
17
18  +!send_msg
19    <- .send(ag0, tell, msg_bel).
```

```
1   // agent ag2
2   !do_job.
3
4   +!do_job
5     <-  .send(ag3,achieve,floor_cleaned);
6         ...
7         !dojob.
8
9   //agent ag3
10  +!car_cleaned
11    <-  ...
```

```
1   // agent a4
2   iterations("zero").
3
4   +envPerceptA(ValueA)
5     <-  ...
6         actionA(10,20);
7         ?iterations(I)
8         actionA(10,I);
9         actionB(I);
10        actionB(10);
11        ?envPerceptC(ValueC);
12        nonExistingAction("hello").
13
14  +envPerceptC(Value)
15    <- ...
```

Fig. 1. Source code snippets showing a set of typical programming errors in Jason concerning: belief-related errors (on the left), goal-related errors (on top right) and agent-environment interaction errors (on bottom right)

First we consider issues related to beliefs, using the the snippet shown in Fig. 1 on the left. One of the most common belief-related errors concerns referencing non-existing beliefs in agent code, causing: *(i)* plan failures – e.g. line 10 where, due to a typo, we try to retrieve the belief iterations(N) using the predicate num_iterations(N) – and, *(ii)* the disabling of meaningful plans due to triggering events referring to non-existing perceivable events—e.g. the triggering event of the plan reported at lines 12-13 does not match the event generated by the reception of the message (+msg_bel) sent by agent ag1 (line 19). Another beliefs-related issue concerns the possibility to write agent programs in which the same beliefs are bound to different value types in the course of agent execution. We argue that this can be problematic both from a conceptual viewpoint – i.e. a belief meant to be used for storing numeric information should not be used later also for storing strings literals – and also because such a permission can cause different runtime errors. For example the belief update action reported at line 8, being the belief iterations initialized with a string value (line 2), is not semantically correct and it hence produces, when executed, a runtime error.

We consider now issues related to goals, and in particular to goals assignment. It is possible to write correct MAS programs from a syntactical point of view, in which however wrong goals are assigned to agents at runtime, where wrong means e.g. goals that are unknown by the agents. Let's consider the case of agent ag2 requesting to agent ag3 the achievement of the goal `floor_cleaned` (line 5 in Fig. 1, top right). Agent `ag3` is not able to achieve such a goal and the programmer can detect this issue only at runtime, by properly investigating why the MAS is not behaving as it is supposed to. As another example, the wrong goal self-assignment made by `ag2` (line 7 in Fig. 1, top right) – i.e. goal `!do_job` is referred as `!dojob` – is detected only at runtime when the agent realizes that it has no plan for dealing with the goal `!dojob`.

Finally we consider issues related to agent-environment interactions in agent programs. To this end we refer to the source code snippet reported in Fig. 1 on bottom right in which an agent `ag4` works in a classical Jason environment providing to the agent the external actions `actionA(<int>,<int>)` and `actionB(<String>)`; and generating percepts `envPerceptA(<int>)` and `envPerceptB(<String>)`. Even for what concerns agent-environment interactions it is quite simple to write source code that is correct from a mere syntactical perspective that however contains several errors from the semantic one. The source code reported in Fig. 1 on bottom right shows a set of the most common errors that can be made, and that can not be detected statically, when interacting with the environment in an agent program. In detail such errors are: *(i)* the invocation of environment actions providing arguments of the wrong type (e.g. line 8 and line 10), *(ii)* the invocation of non-existing environment actions (line 12), and *(iii)* the referencing of non existing percepts in both plan bodies (line 11) and in plan triggering events (line 14).

Some of the errors presented here – e.g. referencing a belief/goal that does not exists – may be detected statically quite easily, by enforcing the declaration of all the symbols in the MAS program in order to be effectively used. These errors are mainly related to the presence of typos, and they could be easily detected at compile time by constructing proper symbol tables to be used for the managing of symbols resolutions. For other kinds of errors instead – such as invoking an environment action with wrong arguments types, sending to an agent a message that exists but that the agent can not understand, etc. – the previous assumption is no longer sufficient. The introduction of typing would allow to detect even this kind of errors in a static manner, before running the MAS program.

3   Typing in simpAL

Before concentrating on the typing issue, first we give a brief overview of the main elements of the simpAL language. A prototype version of the simpAL platform – implemented in Java, including a compiler, an interpreter/virtual machine and an Eclipse-based IDE providing an editor with typical features such as context-assist, code completion, etc.[1] – is available for download as an open-source project[2], and can be used to test the examples discussed in this section. Because of lack of space, only those aspects of the language that are important

---

[1] Some snapshots of the IDE at work are available on the simpAL web site at
   `http://tinyurl.com/832o8hk`
[2] `http://simpal.sourceforge.net`

for this paper will be considered—the interested reader can refer to [26] and to the technical documentation on the web site for a more extensive account.

3.1   simpAL Overview

The main inspiration for simpAL abstractions comes – on the one side – from the A&A model [18] and from the BDI (Belief-Desire-Intention) model, in particular from its implementation in existing APLs, Jason in particular. On the other side, differently from existing BDI-based APLs, simpAL has been conceived conceptually as an extension of OOP languages with a further separated abstraction layer based on agent-oriented abstractions. The OOP layer – based on Java, but it could be any OOP language – is meant to be used solely to represent and manipulate abstract data types and data structures in general. All the other issues that, for instance, are related to concurrent programming (e.g. threads, synchronized methods, etc.) or I/O programming (e.g. network, GUI, OS related functionalities, etc.) are meant to be tackled using the agent-oriented abstraction layer.

By adopting a typical anthropomorphic and social view of computation, a simpAL program is given by an organization composed by a dynamic set of agents concurrently working in a shared, possibly distributed, environment. Agents are those components of the program (system) designed to perform autonomously *tasks*, that can be assigned both statically and dynamically to them. Autonomously means in this case that given a task to do, they pro-actively decide what actions to do and when to do them, promptly reacting to relevant events from their environment, fully encapsulating the control of their behavior. To perform their tasks, agents can create and use resources and tools, called generically *artifacts*. Artifacts are useful to represent those non-autonomous components of our program, the basic bricks composing the environment of the organization, providing some kind of functionality or service—such as easing agent communication and coordination (e.g. a blackboard), or interfacing agents with external environment or the user (e.g. a GUI, a socket), or wrapping external systems (e.g. a data-base, a web-service) or even simply helping agent work (e.g. a shared counter). An artifact can be used by a single agent or can be designed to be concurrently and safely used by multiple agents (e.g. a shared knowledge base, a shared calendar for alarms, etc.).

Agent interactions can occur in two basic ways that can be combined together: either indirectly through the environment (by using the same artifacts), or directly by means of asynchronous messages. In particular, agents have a basic set of communicative actions, that allow for sending messages either to inform or ask about some data or to assign/work with tasks. Agent-artifact interaction is based instead on the concept of *use* and *observation*, reminding the way in which artifacts are used by people in human environments. In order to be used, an artifact provides a set of *operations*, corresponding to the set of actions available to agents to use it. This implies that the repertoire of an agent's actions at runtime depends on the artifacts that the agent knows and can use. Besides operations, the usage interface of an artifact includes also *observable properties*, as observable information concerning the dynamic state of the artifact which may be perceived and exploited by agents accordingly.

The overall (dynamic) set of agents and artifacts can be organized in one or multiple logical containers called *workspaces*, possibly in execution on different nodes of the network. An agent can also use – concurrently and transparently – artifacts located in different workspaces, not necessarily only those that belong to the workspace where the agent is running.

The computational model/architecture adopted for simpAL agents is a simplified version of the BDI one, implementing a sense-plan-act like execution cycle [26,27], but using OOP instead of logic programming to represent and manipulate data structures. An agent has a belief base, as a long term private memory storing information about: *(i)* the private state of an agent, *(ii)* the observable state of the environment, and *(iii)* information communicated by other agents. In simpAL the belief base is composed by a set of beliefs represented by simple variable-like information items, characterized by a name, a type, and a value—which could be any data object[3]. To perform tasks, an agent exploits the *plans* available in its plan library. Plans are modules of procedural knowledge specifying how to act and react to the events of the environment in order to accomplish some specific task. The set of plans in the plan library depends on the *scripts* loaded by the agent. As detailed later on, scripts are modules containing the description of set of plans, written by the agent programmers. An agent can handle multiple tasks in execution at a time.

3.2 Typing Agents with Tasks and Roles

In a software engineering perspective, a type defines a contract about what one can expect by some computational entity. In the case of objects, this concerns their interface, i.e. what methods can be invoked (and with which parameters) or – in a more abstract view – what messages can be handled by the objects. Conceptually, messages are the core concept of objects: receiving a message is the reason why an object moves and computes something. This is actually true also for active objects and actors.

Agents introduce a further level of abstraction. An agent does something because – first of all – it has a task to do (or rather a goal to achieve or maintain). It is quite intuitive then to define the type of an agent as its *contract* w.r.t. the organizational environment where it is immersed. In other words, conceiving the type of an agent as what one can expect by the agent in terms of the set of possible tasks that can be assigned to that agent. Following this idea we introduce the notion of *role* to explicitly define the type of an agent as the set of

---

[3] It is worth remarking that in existing agent-oriented languages beliefs are typically represented by first-order logic literals, denoting information that can be used by reasoning engines. However the logic representation is not necessarily part of the belief concept, as remarked by Rao and Georgeff in [23]: *"[beliefs] can be viewed as the informative component of the system state"* and *"[beliefs] may be implemented as a variable, a database, a set of logical expressions, or some other data structure"*([23], p. 313).

```
1   role Thermostat {
2
3       task AchieveTemperature {
4         input-params {
5             targetTemp: double;
6             threshold: double;
7       }}
8
9       task KeepTemperature {
10        input-params {
11          inputView: UserView;
12        }
13        understands {
14          newThreshold: double;
15      }}
16
17      task DoSelfTest {
18        talks-about {
19          malfunctionDescr:
20                  MalfunctionInfo;
21      }}}
```

```
1   usage-interface Conditioner {
2     obs-prop isHeating: boolean;
3     obs-prop isCooling: boolean;
4
5     operation startHeating(speed: double);
6     operation startCooling(speed: double);
7     operation stop();
8   }
```

```
1   usage-interface Thermometer {
2     obs-prop currentTemp: double;
3   }
```

```
1   usage-interface UserView {
2     obs-prop desiredTemp: double;
3     obs-prop threshold: double;
4     obs-prop thermStatus:
5             acme.ThermostatStatus;
6   }
```

Fig. 2. Definition of an agent role (on the left) and artifact interfaces (on the right)

the possible types of tasks that any agent playing that role is able to do. Fig. 2 on the left shows the definition of a role in simpAL. A role is identified by a name (e.g. Thermostat) and it includes the definition of the set of *task types*. A task type is identified by a unique identifier (name) inside the role. It defines a *contract* between the task *assigner* and *assignee*, in terms of a set of typed input/output parameters – input-params block and output-params block (not shown on this simple example) – and set of messages that can be understood by the task assignee – understands block – and the task assigner—talks-about block. A task type instance is like a record with the parameters assigned to some value. Typed attributes may contain any value/object of any Java class, plus also the identifiers of entities that are first-class simpAL abstractions, such as artifacts, agents, tasks, etc., which are typed too.

In simpAL information exchanges are always contextualized to tasks: so an agent A can send an information to another agent B only referring to a task instance t, without explicitly referring to B. A predefined action for exchanging messages among agents (tell) is provided:

```
1   /* the assigner tells a newThreshold msg to the assignee */
2   tell achieveTempTaskInstance.newThreshold = 100
3   /* the assignee tells a malfunctionDescr msg to the assigner */
4   tell doSelfTestTaskInstance.malfunctionDescr = new MalfunctionInfo(..)
```

The concept of role defining the agent type allows us to do error checking on: *(a)* the behavior of the agent implementing the role, checking that the agent implementation (the *how*) conforms to role definition (the *what*); *(b)* the behavior of the agents that aim at interacting with agents implementing a particular role, checking that: *(i)* they would request the accomplishment only of those tasks that are specified by the role, and *(ii)* they would send only those messages that the tasks' assignee can understand.

. Case *(a)* concerns performing two different controls when compiling *agent scripts*, which are the basic construct used to define agent concrete behavior (a brief description of agent scripts is reported in a separate box following Fig. 3). The first control is responsible of validating the script's plans w.r.t. the task types defined in the roles implemented by the script. The error checking rule states informally:

– for an agent script S, for each type of task T defined in any role R implemented by S, it must exist (at least) one plan P for T.

Given this rule, the `ACMEThermostat` script implementing the `Thermostat` role reported in Fig. 3 is correct, while a script like the following one:

```
1    agent-script IncompleteThermostatImpl implements Thermostat {
2        plan-for AchieveTemperature { ... }
3        plan-for DoSelfTest { ... }
4    }
```

would report an error message about missing a plan for a declared task, i.e. `KeepTemperature`.

The second control concerns checking messages that an agent playing certain roles tells to its tasks assigners (how assign a task to an agent is described below). This can be done by using the set of messages listed in the `talks-about` block of tasks definition. The checking rule in this case states:

– in a plan P related to a task type T, the messages sent by the *assignee* to the task *assigner* can only be the ones listed in T's `talks-about` block. In addition, the type of the messages sent must be compatible w.r.t. the message types defined in T.

Referring to the `ACMEThermostat` script, the only message that can be sent to tasks' assigners is the message `malfunctionDescr` in the context of the task type `DoSelfTest` (Fig. 3 line 66, where the prefix `this-task.` is used to identify the assignee's task instance—i.e, the task instance for which the plan will be instantiated at runtime), a task that can be used to check the correct functioning of the thermostat.

Case *(b)* concerns instead checking: *(i)* the assignment of tasks to agents playing a certain role R, and *(ii)* messages sent by a task assigner to the task assignee. Task assignment can be done in two ways.

```
1    assign-task taskInstanceTodo to: AgentId
2    do-task taskInstanceTodo task-recipient: AgentId
```

The first is through a predefined action `assign-task`. The action succeeds as soon as the task is successfully assigned to the assignee. It can also be used without specifying the target agent, so as for an agent to allocate the task to itself. The second is through a predefined action named `do-task`, which instead waits for the completion of the specified task instance—i.e. the action succeeds only when the task instance is successfully completed by the assignee.

```
1   agent-script ACMEThermostat implements Thermostat in SmartHome {
2
3     savedThreshold: double
4
5     plan-for AchieveTemperature  {
6       #using: console@mainRoom, thermometer@bedRoom, conditioner@bedRoom
7
8       println(msg: "Achieving temperature "
9         + this-task.targetTemp + " from " + currentTemp);
10      savedThreshold = this-task.threshold;
11      {
12        #completed-when:
13          java.lang.Math.abs(this-task.targetTemp - currentTemp) < savedThreshold
14
15        every-time currentTemp > (this-task.targetTemp + savedThreshold)
16          && !(isCooling in conditioner) =>  startCooling(speed: 1) on conditioner
17        every-time currentTemp < (this-task.targetTemp - savedThreshold)
18          && !(isHeating in conditioner) =>  startHeating(speed: 1) on conditioner
19      };
20      stop()
21    }
22
23    plan-for KeepTemperature {
24      #using: console@mainRoom, thermometer, conditioner, userView@mainRoom
25
26      quitPlan : boolean = false;
27      {
28        #completed-when: quitPlan
29
30        achiveTempTask: AchieveTemperature =
31          new-task AchieveTemperature(targetTemp: desiredTemp in userView,
32                              threshold: threshold in userView);
33        assign-task achiveTempTask
34
35        every-time changed desiredTemp => {
36          drop-task achiveTempTask;
37          achiveTempTask = new-task AchieveTemperature(targetTemp: desiredTemp,
38                                            threshold: threshold);
39          assign-task achiveTempTask
40        }
41
42        every-time changed currentTemp : !is-doing-any AchieveTemperature => {
43          assign-task new-task AchieveTemperature(targetTemp: desiredTemp,
44                                            threshold: savedThreshold)
45        }
46
47        every-time changed thermStatus
48          : thermStatus.equals(acme.ThermostatStatus.OFF) => {
49          if (isCooling || isHeating){
50            stop()
51          };
52          drop-task achiveTempTask;
53          quitPlan = true
54        }
55
56        every-time told this-task.newThreshold => {
57          #atomic
58          savedThreshold = this-task.newThreshold
59        }
60      }
61    }
62
63    plan-for DoSelfTest {
64      ...
65      if (someCondition) {
66        tell this-task.malfunctionDescr = new MalfunctionInfo( ... )
67      }
68      ...
69    }
70  }
```

Fig. 3. Definition of a script in simpAL

Defining Agent Scripts in simpAL (Fig. 3)

The behavior of an agent can be programmed in simpAL through the definition of scripts, that are loaded and executed by agents at runtime. Here we give a very brief account directly by using the ACMEThermostat example Fig. 3. The definition of an agent script includes the script name, an explicit declaration of the roles played by the script and then the script body, which contains the declaration of a set of *beliefs* and the definition of a set of *plans*. Beliefs in simpAL are like simple variables, characterized by a name, a type and an initial value. The ACMEThermostat script has just one belief, to keep track of the current threshold temperature to consider while doing its job. Beliefs declared at the script level are a sort of long-term memory of the agent, useful to keep track of information that could be accessed and updated by any plan in execution, and whose lifetime is equal to the one of the agent (script). Plans contain the recipe to execute tasks. The ACMEThermostat script has three plans, to achieve a certain temperature value (lines 5-21), to maintain a temperature value (lines 23-61), and to do some self test (lines 63-69). To do the AchieveTemperature task, the plan starts cooling or heating – using the conditioner – as soon as the current temperature is too high (lines 15-16) or too low (lines 17-18) compared to the target one (and the threshold)—the current temperature is observed by the thermometer. The information about the target temperature (this-task.targetTemp) derives from the related parameter of the task, while the belief about the current temperature (currentTemp) is related to the observable property of the thermometer artifact used in the plan. As soon as the current temperature is in the good range, the plan completes—stopping the conditioner if it was working. To do the KeepTemperature task, the plan achieves the desired temperature by immediately self-assigning the sub-task AchieveTemperature (line 33), which is executed also as soon as the desired temperature changes (lines 35-40) or the current temperature changes and the agent is not already achieving the temperature (line 42-45). The belief about the desired temperature (desiredTemp) comes from the observable property of the userView artifact used in the plan. Also, as soon as a message about a new threshold is told by the task assigner, the internal value of the threshold is updated (lines 56-59). The plan quits if the agent perceives from the userView artifact that the user has switched off the thermostat (lines 47-54). In that case, before quitting the plan, the conditioner is stopped if it was working. Finally, to do the SelfTest task, the agent performs some diagnostic operations (not reported in the sources) and if some malfunction condition is verified, a report containing the malfunction description is sent to the task assigner (line 66).

Explanations about some key elements of the syntax and semantics of plans follow—a more comprehensive description can be found here [26,27] and on simpAL technical documentation. The definition of a plan includes the specification of the type of task for which the plan can be used and a plan body, which is an action rule block. The action rule block contains the declaration of a set of local beliefs – that are visible only inside the block, as a kind of short-term memory – and a set of *action rules* specifying *when* executing *which* action. In the simplest case, an action rule is just an action and a block could be a flat list of actions. In that case, actions are executed in sequence, i.e. every action in the list is executed only after perceiving the event that the previous one has completed. In the most general case, an action rule is of the kind: every-time | when *Event* : *Condition* => *Action* meaning that the specified action can be executed every time or once that (when) the specified event occurs and the specified condition – which is a boolean expression over the agent beliefs base – holds. If not specified, the default value of the condition is true. Events concern percepts related to either one of *(i)* the environment, *(ii)* messages sent by agents or *(iii)* actions execution. All events are actually uniformly modeled as changes to some belief belonging to agent belief base, given the fact that observable properties, messages sent, and action state variables are all represented as beliefs. Furthermore, the syntax for specifying events related to a change of an observable property is changed *ObsProp* (e.g. line 35), the one for specifying the update of a belief about an information told by another agent is told *What* (e.g. line 56). If no event is specified, the predefined meaning is that the rule can be triggered immediately, but only once. Given that, the execution of a flat list of actions can be obtained by a sequence of action rules with only the action specified, separated by a semicolon (;). Actions can be: *(i)* external actions to affect the environment, i.e. operations provided by some artifact, *(ii)* communicative actions to directly interact with some other agent (to tell some belief, to assign a task, etc.), or *(iii)* predefined internal actions (to update internal beliefs, to manage tasks in execution, etc). An action can be also an action rule block { ... }, which allows then to nest action blocks. Finally, the definition of an action rule block includes the possibility to specify some predefined attributes, for instance: the #using: attribute to specify the list of artifacts identifiers used inside the block (an artifact can be used/observed only if explicitly declared), the #completed-when: attribute to specify the condition for which the action rule block execution can be considered completed, the #atomic attribute to specify that the action rule block must be executed as a single action, without being interrupted or interleaved with blocks of other plans in execution (when the agent is executing multiple tasks at a time).

In both cases, we can enforce, statically, that:

- given a belief *Id* of type *R*, storing the identifier of some agent playing the role *R*, then for any action **assign-task** *t* **to:** *Id* or **do-task**
  t **task-recipient:** *Id*, there must exist a task type *T* in *R* such that *t* is
  a value (instance) of *T*. In case of task self-assignment the belief *Id* storing
  the agent identifier is implicit (it refers to the current agent).

Then, given a script fragment with a belief **myThermostat: Thermostat**, we
have the following list of the main errors that can be caught at compile time:

```
1    /* compilation ok */
2    assign-task AchieveTemperature(targetTemp:21, threshold:2) to: myThermostat
3
4    /* error: no tasks matching CleanTheRoom in role Thermostat */
5    do-task CleanTheRoom() task-recipient: myThermostat
6
7    /* error: no targetT param in AchieveTemperature */
8    /* error: missing threshold param */
9    assign-task AchieveTemperature(targetT: 21) to: myThermostat
10
11   /* error: wrong type for the param value targetTemp */
12   /* error: missing threshold param */
13   do-task AchieveTemperature(targetTemp: "21") task-recipient: myThermostat
```

The definition of a task type includes also the type of messages that the assigner can send to the task assignee. Given that, we can then check in agent
scripts that the beliefs specified in the assigner's **tell** actions – those in which
the task instance identifier is not **this-task**. – are among those listed in the
understands block of the assignee role *R*, and that the types of the beliefs are
compatible. In the example, when doing the task **KeepTemperature**, an agent
playing the **Thermostat** role can be told about the new threshold to adopt –
which is represented by the message **newThreshold** – by the assigner. Examples
of checks follow:

```
1    keepTempTask: KeepTemperature
2    /* compilation ok */
3    tell keepTempTask.newThreshold = 2
4
5    /* error: aMsg is not listed in KeepTemperature understands block */
6    tell keepTempTask.aMsg = "hello"
7
8    /* error: wrong type for the belief newThreshold
9     * told to an agent playing the role Thermostat */
10   tell keepTempTask.newThreshold = "2"
```

Finally, some other kinds of errors can be checked in scripts at compile time
thanks to the explicit declaration of beliefs (and their types): finding errors in
plans about beliefs that are not declared neither as beliefs at the script level,
nor as local beliefs of plans, nor as parameters of the task; or about beliefs that
are assigned with expressions of wrong type.

3.3 Typing the Environment

On the environment side, we introduce the notion of *usage interface* defining
the type of the artifacts, separated from its implementation provided by *artifact*

```
1   artifact ACMEConditioner implements Conditioner {
2     nTimesUsed: int;
3
4     init(){
5       isCooling = false; isHeating = true; nTimesUsed = 0;
6     }
7
8     operation startCooling(speed: double){
9       nTimesUsed++;
10      isCooling = true;  isHeating = false;
11      ...
12    }
13
14    operation startHeating(speed: double){...}
15
16    operation stop(){
17      isCooling = false; isHeating = false;
18      ...
19    }}
```

Fig. 4. Definition of an artifact template in simpAL. Artifact templates are used like classes in OOP, i.e. as templates to create instances of artifacts, defining then their internal structure and behavior. This figure shows the implementation of the toy ACMEConditioner artifact, implementing the Conditioner interface. The definition of a template includes the name of the template, the explicit declaration of the interfaces implemented by the template and then a body containing the declaration of the instance typed state variables of the artifact (e.g. nTimesUsed, line 2) – which are hidden, not observable – and the definition of operations' behavior. An operation is defined by a name (e.g. startCooling) (line 8), a set of keyword-based parameters (e.g. speed) and a body. The body is very similar to the one found in imperative OO languages – Java in this case is taken as main reference – so it is a block with a sequence of statements, including local variable declarations, control-flow statements, object related statements (object creation, method invocation, etc) and some pre-defined statements related to artifact functioning, that allow, for instance, for suspending the execution of the operation until some specified condition is met, or to terminate with a failure the operation execution.

templates. A usage interface is identified by a name and includes the specification of *(i)* the observable properties, and of *(ii)* the operations provided by all the artifacts implementing that interface—which correspond to the actions that agent can do on those kind of artifacts.

Fig. 2 on the right shows the definition of the artifacts used in the ACMEThermostat script, namely Conditioner – representing the interface of conditioner devices modeled as artifacts, used by agents to heat or cool – Thermometer – used by agents to be aware of the current temperature – and UserView – representing the interface of those GUI artifacts used to interact with the human users, in particular to know what is the desired temperature. Fig. 4 shows the skeleton of the definition of an artifact template implementing the Conditioner interface.

The introduction of an explicit notion of type for artifacts allows us to define a way to address two main issues: *(a)* on the agent side, checking errors about the actions (i.e. artifacts operations) and percepts (related to artifacts observable state); *(b)* on the environment side, checking errors in artifact templates (i.e. the implementation), controlling that they conform to the implemented usage interfaces (i.e the type specification).

The case *(a)* concerns checking the action (rules) in plan bodies, so that: for each action *OpName*(Params) on *Target*, specified in an action rule, meaning the execution of an operation *OpName* over an artifact identifier *Target* whose type is *I*:

- there must exist an operation defined in the interface *I* matching the operation request;
- the action rule must appear in an action rule block (or in any of its parent block) where *Target* has been explicitly listed among the artifact used by the agent through the #using: attribute.

Examples of checks, given a fragment of a script with e.g. a belief cond: Conditioner:

```
1   /* compilation ok */
2   startCooling (speed: 1) on cond
3
4   /* error: unknown operation switchOn */
5   switchOn () on cond
6
7   /* error: unknown parameter time in startCooling operation */
8   startCooling (speed: 2 time: 10) on cond
9
10  /* error: wrong type for the param value speed */
11  startCooling (speed: "fast") on cond
```

The target of an operation (e.g., on cond) can be omitted (as it happens in some points in plans of ACMEThermostat shown in Fig. 3) when there is no ambiguity with respect to the target of the artifacts that are currently used by the agent (specified in the #using: attribute).

On the event/percept side, we can check beliefs representing artifact observable properties in the event template of rules and in any expression appearing either in the context or in action rule body, containing such beliefs. For what concerns event templates, given an action rule: updated *Prop* in *Target* : Context => Action, where the event concerns the update of the belief about an observable property *Prop* in the artifact of type *I* denoted by *Target*, then the following checks apply:

- there must exist an observable property defined in *I* which matches *Prop*;
- the action rule must appear in an action rule block (or in any of its parent block) where *Target* has been explicitly listed among the artifacts used by the agent through the #using: attribute.

As in the case of operations, in *Target* can be omitted if there is no ambiguity about the artifact which is referred.

Examples of checks follow, supposing to have a fragment of a script with beliefs cond: Conditioner and therm: Thermometer about a conditioner and thermometer artifact:

```
1   /* compilation ok */
2   updated currentTemp => println(msg: "the temperature has changed")
3   updated currentTemp : isHeating
4          => println(msg: "the temperature has changed while heating...")
5   sum: double = currentTemp in therm + 1
6
7   /* error: unknown obs property isHeating  in Thermometer type */
8   updated isHeating in therm => ...
9
10  /* error: wrong type */
11  bak: boolean = currentTemp in therm
```

On the environment side (case *(b)*) the definition of the interface as a type allows for checking the conformance of artifact templates that declare to implement that interface, so that:

- for each operation signature Op declared in any of the interfaces I implemented by the template, the template must contain the implementation of the operation;
- for any observable property $Prop$ that appears in expressions or assignments in operation implementation, then the declaration of the observable property must appear in one of the interfaces implemented by the template and the corresponding type expression must be compatible.

Finally, the explicit declaration of observable properties (in interfaces) and (hidden) state variables in artifact templates – the latter can be declared also as local variable in operations – allow for checking errors in the implementation of operations about the use of unknown observable properties/variables or about the assignment of values with a wrong type.

3.4   Typing the Overall Program Structure

In simpAL we use the notion of organization (recalling the human organization metaphor) to define the *main* of the overall multi-agent program. We introduce then the type of an organization, called *organization model*. An organization model is identified by a name and it used to explicitly define the workspace-based logic structure of the application. Besides the definition of its name, a workspace declaration in an organization model can include the explicit declaration of the identifiers (*literals*) of instances of artifacts and agents – along with their types – that are known to be available in that workspace[4]. Such identifiers are like global references that can be then referred in any agent script – so as to identify *"well-known"* agents to communicate with or artifacts to use – which explicitly declares to play a role R inside that organization model.

As a simple example, Fig. 5 (on the left) shows the definition of the SmartHome organization model, with: *(i)* a mainRoom workspace hosting the userView artifact and an agent majordomo of type HomeAdmin, and *(ii)* a

---

[4] In general, a workspace can contain at runtime also agents/artifacts not declared in the organization model: both can be dynamically created by agents by means of specific actions.

```
1  org-model SmartHome{
2
3    workspace mainRoom {
4      userView: UserView
5      majordomo: HomeAdmin
6    }
7
8    workspace bedRoom {
9      thermostat: Thermostat
10     conditioner: Conditioner
11     thermometer: Thermometer
12   }}
```

```
1  org ACMESmartHome implements SmartHome{
2
3    workspace mainRoom {
4      majordomo = Majordomo()
5                     init-task: AdminHouse()
6      userView = ACMEControlPanel()
7    }
8
9    workspace bedRoom {
10     thermostat = ACMEThermostat()
11     conditioner = ACMEConditioner()
12     thermometer = ACMEThermometer()
13   }}
```

Fig. 5. Example of the definition of an organization model in simpAL (on the left) and the a main organization file implementing the model (on the right)

bedRoom workspace hosting the remaining agents and artifacts. Given this organization model definition, then it is possible e.g. in the plan for the task KeepTemperature of the ACMEThermostat script (Fig. 3) to refer directly to the artifact userView@mainRoom.

Then a notion of *concrete organization* is introduced to define a concrete application instance, referring to an existing *organization model*. An example of organization definition is shown in Fig. 5 (on the right), sketching the definition of an ACMESmartHome concrete organization. A simpAL program in execution is a running instance of an organization.

The notion of organization model, defining the type for a simpAL organization, allows us to: *(a)* perform additional error checking controls in scripts *explicitly declared* in the context of an organization of a certain type, and *(b)* control that a concrete organization (i.e. the implementation) is conform w.r.t. its type specification (i.e. organization model). The case *(a)* allows to check, in those scripts sources declared inside an organizational context, that all the used literals refer to existing symbols defined in the related organization model.

On the organization side (case *(b)*), the definition of an organization model *OrgModel* as a type allows for checking the conformance of a concrete organization instance *Org* that declares to implement that model, so that:

- each workspace Wsp declared in $OrgModel$ must be defined also in Org;
- each artifact literal $ArtLit$ of type I defined inside a workspace Wsp in $OrgModel$ must be must be correctly instantiated in the concrete organization Org. In particular such literal must be instantiated in Wsp, specifying an artifact template $ArtTempl$ implementing the usage interface I and, if needed, providing the initial parameters required by $ArtTempl$;
- each agent literal $AgLit$ of type R defined inside a workspace Wsp in $OrgModel$ must be must be correctly instantiated in the concrete organization Org. In particular such literal must be instantiated in Wsp, specifying an agent script $AgScript$ implementing the role R.

It is worth remarking that in the definition of a concrete organization Org implementing an organization model $OrgModel$, additional workspaces, agent and artifact instances can be added to the ones initially declared in *OrgModel*. Examples of static checks that can be done follow, supposing to have a fragment of an organization that declares to implement the SmartHome organization model defined in Fig. 5.

```
1   org DummyHome implements SmartHome {
2     /* compilation ok: new workspace */
3     workspace newWsp {
4       otherConsole = Console()
5     }
6     workspace bedRoom {
7       /* error: missing instantiation of thermostat agent */
8       conditioner = ACMEConditioner() /* compilation ok */
9       /* error: wrong type. ACMEConditioner does
10             not implement the required Thermometer role */
11      thermometer = ACMEConditioner()
12    }}
13    /* error: missing mainRoom workspace */
```

As a final remark, the notion of organization used here is not meant to be as rich as the one that appears in MAS organization modelling. The main objective of introducing this concept here is to have a way to define rigorously the structure of the overall multi-agent program and to introduce some typing also at this level, in order to check errors at compile time related to the implementation of the overall program structure.

4   Related Work

As far as authors' knowledge, types and type systems have not received particular attention so far in the context of agent programming languages and agent-oriented programming.

In [10,9] a discussion about integrating algebraic data types, roles, and session types in the context of agent-oriented programming is sketched, starting from high-level similarities between certain aspects of an agent programming language (2APL) and a functional programming language (Haskell). Algebraic data types are used to constrain the content of messages; roles to constrain how particular agents interact, and sessions, to describe slices of the global interactions in the agent system. Together, these language features are introduced to support organisational concepts, as devised in agent-oriented methodologies and frameworks. Howver, the paper does not introduce an explicit notion of type for agents so as to improve static error checking.

Those agent-oriented platforms that are based or integrated with object-oriented languages / environments (e.g. JACK [14], Jade [1], Jadex [21]) can benefit of typing and static type checking provided by the lower-level OO layer (e.g. Java); however, such benefits are typically limited to the OO computational entities used in agent programs. So, it is not possible to detect at compile time errors related to e.g. the assignment of wrong tasks to agents or sending wrong messages—as far as authors' knowledge based on papers and official documentation.

Active Components are a recent development of the Jadex project, aiming at providing programming and execution facilities for distributed and concurrent systems [20]. The general idea is to consider systems to be composed of active (autonomous) components acting as service providers and consumers, following the Service Component Architecture (SCA) defined in the context of service oriented architectures. Communication among active components is preferably done then using service invocations, as defined by the service/component interfaces. Even if the approach does not clearly define a notion of type for agents (it is not its objective), this makes it possible to improve the kind of errors that could be detected at compile time by exploiting the service/component interfaces.

Besides sequential programming languages, type systems have been widely used for analyzing the behavior also of concurrent programs and systems of concurrent processes, to reason about deadlock-freedom, safe usage of locks, etc. [30,15]. In particular, the notion of *session type* has been introduced to specify complex interaction protocols, verified by static type checking [12]. Session types, and in particular multiparty session types [13], could be used to impose (and verify statically) restrictions on the pattern of interaction. These aspects are important indeed also in the context of programming languages based on agent-oriented abstractions and will be considered in our future work.

5   Concluding Remarks

The definition of a notion of type for agents, artifacts and organizations makes it possible to clearly separate the specification from the implementation, getting a first kind of substitutability. In particular, in every context of the program in which an agent playing some role R is needed, we can (re-)use any concrete agent equipped with a script – whose source code can be unknown, having only the compiled version – implementing the role R. Also, in every context of the program where an artifact providing the functionalities described by the I interface is needed, we can (re-)use any concrete artifact instance of an artifact template implementing the interface I. This enables a first level of reuse and evolvability, without the need of having the source codes. Improved version of agents and artifacts implementing some roles/interfaces can be introduced without doing any change in the other components that interact with them —if the roles and interfaces are not changed.

Indeed this is just a first step towards fully supporting the principle of substitutability, as defined in the context of OOP [29]. This requires the definition of a proper *subtyping* relationship, to define roles/interfaces as extensions of existing ones. This is part of our future work, exploring subtyping as a mechanism providing a sound and safe way to conceive the incremental modification and extension of agents/artifacts and their conceptual specialization.

Other important works in our agenda include: the definition of a proper formal model of the type system described in this paper – following a previous work introducing a core calculus for agents and artifacts [5] – so as to rigorously analyze its properties; and the improvement of typing for messages and communication protocols, eventually exploiting results available both in agent-oriented programming literature and outside, such as the work on session types [8].

Finally, many of the concepts and abstractions on which simpAL is based can be found also in agent-oriented software engineering methodologies (an easy example is the very notion of role): these will be used then as a main reference for eventually refining and enriching how such concepts are currently modeled in simpAL.

References

1. Bellifemine, F., Caire, G., Poggi, A., Rimassa, G.: Jade: A software framework for developing multi-agent applications. Lessons learned. Information & Software Technology 50(1-2), 10–21 (2008)
2. Bordini, R., Hübner, J., Wooldridge, M.: Programming Multi-Agent Systems in AgentSpeak Using Jason. John Wiley & Sons, Ltd. (2007)
3. Collier, R.: Debugging agents in agent factory. In: Bordini, R.H., Dastani, M., Dix, J., El Fallah Seghrouchni, A. (eds.) PROMAS 2006. LNCS (LNAI), vol. 4411, pp. 229–248. Springer, Heidelberg (2007)
4. Cook, W.R., Hill, W., Canning, P.S.: Inheritance is not subtyping. In: Proceedings of the 17th ACM SIGPLAN-SIGACT Symposium on Principles of Programming Languages, POPL 1990, pp. 125–135. ACM, New York (1990)
5. Damiani, F., Giannini, P., Ricci, A., Viroli, M.: A calculus of agents and artifacts. In: Cordeiro, J., Ranchordas, A., Shishkov, B. (eds.) ICSOFT 2009. CCIS, vol. 50, pp. 124–136. Springer, Heidelberg (2011)
6. Danforth, S., Tomlinson, C.: Type theories and object-oriented programmimg. ACM Comput. Surv. 20(1), 29–72 (1988)
7. Dastani, M.: 2apl: a practical agent programming language. Autonomous Agents and Multi-Agent Systems 16(3), 214–248 (2008)
8. Dezani-Ciancaglini, M., Mostrous, D., Yoshida, N., Drossopoulou, S.: Session types for object-oriented languages. In: Thomas, D. (ed.) ECOOP 2006. LNCS, vol. 4067, pp. 328–352. Springer, Heidelberg (2006)
9. Grigore, C., Collier, R.: Supporting agent systems in the programming language. In: Hübner, J.F., Petit, J.-M., Suzuki, E. (eds.) Web Intelligence/IAT Workshops, pp. 9–12. IEEE Computer Society (2011)
10. Grigore, C.V., Collier, R.W.: Af-raf: an agent-oriented programming language with algebraic data types. In: Proceedings of the Compilation of the Co-located Workshops on DSM 2011, TMC 2011, AGERE! 2011, AOOPES 2011, NEAT 2011, & VMIL 2011, SPLASH 2011 Workshops, pp. 195–200. ACM, New York (2011)
11. Hindriks, K.V.: Programming rational agents in goal. In: Multi-Agent Programming, pp. 119–157. Springer US (2009)
12. Honda, K., Vasconcelos, V.T., Kubo, M.: Language primitives and type discipline for structured communication-based programming. In: Hankin, C. (ed.) ESOP 1998. LNCS, vol. 1381, pp. 122–138. Springer, Heidelberg (1998)
13. Honda, K., Yoshida, N., Carbone, M.: Multiparty asynchronous session types. In: POPL, pp. 273–284 (2008)
14. Howden, N., Rönnquist, R., Hodgson, A., Lucas, A.: JACK intelligent agents^{TM} — summary of an agent infrastructure. In: Proc. of 2nd Int. Workshop on Infrastructure for Agents, MAS, and Scalable MAS (2001)

15. Kobayashi, N.: Type systems for concurrent programs. In: Aichernig, B.K., Maibaum, T. (eds.) Formal Methods at the Crossroads. From Panacea to Foundational Support. LNCS, vol. 2757, pp. 439–453. Springer, Heidelberg (2003)
16. Meyer, B.: Static typing. In: ACM SIGPLAN OOPS Messenger, vol. 6, pp. 20–29. ACM (1995)
17. Mitchell, J.: Concepts in Programming Languages. Cambridge University Press (2002)
18. Omicini, A., Ricci, A., Viroli, M.: Artifacts in the A&A meta-model for multi-agent systems. Autonomous Agents and Multi-Agent Systems 17(3) (December 2008)
19. Pierce, B.C.: Types and programming languages. MIT Press, Cambridge (2002)
20. Pokahr, A., Braubach, L., Jander, K.: Unifying agent and component concepts: Jadex active components. In: Dix, J., Witteveen, C. (eds.) MATES 2010. LNCS, vol. 6251, pp. 100–112. Springer, Heidelberg (2010)
21. Pokahr, A., Braubach, L., Lamersdorf, W.: Jadex: A BDI reasoning engine. In: Bordini, R., Dastani, M., Dix, J., Seghrouchni, A.E.F. (eds.) Multi-Agent Programming. Kluwer (2005)
22. Rao, A.: AgentSpeak (L): BDI agents speak out in a logical computable language. In: Van de Velde, W., Perram, J.W. (eds.) MAAMAW 1996. LNCS, vol. 1038, pp. 42–55. Springer, Heidelberg (1996)
23. Rao, A.S., Georgeff, M.P.: BDI Agents: From Theory to Practice. In: First International Conference on Multi Agent Systems, ICMAS 1995 (1995)
24. Ricci, A., Piunti, M., Viroli, M.: Environment programming in multi-agent systems: an artifact-based perspective. Autonomous Agents and Multi-Agent Systems 23, 158–192 (2011)
25. Ricci, A., Santi, A.: Agent-oriented computing: Agents as a paradigm for computer programming and software development. In: Proc. of the 3rd Int. Conf. on Future Computational Technologies and Applications, Future Computing 2011, Rome, Italy. IARIA (2011)
26. Ricci, A., Santi, A.: Designing a general-purpose programming language based on agent-oriented abstractions: the simpAL project. In: Proc. of AGERE! 2011, SPLASH 2011 Workshops, pp. 159–170. ACM, New York (2011)
27. Ricci, A., Santi, A.: From actors to agent-oriented programming abstractions in simpal. In: Proceedings of the 3rd Annual Conference on Systems, Programming, and Applications: Software for Humanity, SPLASH 2012, pp. 73–74. ACM, New York (2012)
28. Ross, R., Collier, R., O'Hare, G.M.P.: AF-APL – bridging principles and practice in agent oriented languages. In: Bordini, R.H., Dastani, M., Dix, J., El Fallah Seghrouchni, A. (eds.) PROMAS 2004. LNCS (LNAI), vol. 3346, pp. 66–88. Springer, Heidelberg (2005)
29. Wegner, P., Zdonik, S.B.: Inheritance as an incremental modification mechanism or what like is and isn't like. In: Gjessing, S., Chepoi, V. (eds.) ECOOP 1988. LNCS, vol. 322, pp. 55–77. Springer, Heidelberg (1988)
30. Yoshida, N., Hennessy, M.: Assigning types to processes. Inf. Comput. 174(2), 143–179 (2002)

Learning to Improve Agent Behaviours in GOAL

Dhirendra Singh and Koen V. Hindriks

Interactive Intelligence Group, Delft University of Technology, The Netherlands

Abstract. This paper investigates the issue of adaptability of behaviour
in the context of agent-oriented programming. We focus on improving
action selection in rule-based agent programming languages using a reinforcement learning mechanism under the hood. The novelty is that
learning utilises the existing mental state representation of the agent,
which means that (i) the programming model is unchanged and using
learning within the program becomes straightforward, and (ii) adaptive
behaviours can be combined with regular behaviours in a modular way.
Overall, the key to effective programming in this setting is to balance
between constraining behaviour using operational knowledge, and leaving flexibility to allow for ongoing adaptation. We illustrate this using
different types of programs for solving the Blocks World problem.

Keywords: Agent programming, rule selection, reinforcement learning.

1 Introduction

Belief-Desire-Intention (BDI) [1] is a practical and popular cognitive framework
for implementing practical reasoning in computer programs, that has inspired
many agent programming languages such as AgentSpeak(L) [2], JACK [3], Jason [4],
Jadex [5], CANPLAN [6], 3APL [7], 2APL [8], and GOAL [9], to name a few. Despite
its success, an important drawback of the BDI model is the lack of a learning ability, in that once deployed, BDI agents have no capacity to adapt and
improve their behaviour over time. In this paper, we address this issue in the
context of BDI-like rule-based agent programming languages. Particularly, we
extend the GOAL agent programming language [9] for practical systems [10, 11]
with a new language primitive that supports adaptive modules, i.e., modules
within which action choices resulting from programmed rules are learnt over
time. While we have chosen GOAL for this study, our approach applies generally
to other rule-based programming languages. We use an off-the-shelf reinforcement learning [12] mechanism under the hood to implement this functionality.

Our aim is to allow agent developers to easily program adaptive behaviours
using a programming model that they are already familiar with, and without
having to explicitly delve into machine learning technologies. Our idea is to leverage the domain knowledge encoded into the agent program, by directly using the
mental state representation of the agent for learning purposes. This has the key
benefits that (i) the programmer need not worry about knowledge representation
for learning as a separate issue from programming; (ii) the programming model

M. Dastani, J.F. Hübner, and B. Logan (Eds.): ProMAS 2012, LNAI 7837, pp. 158–173, 2013.
© Springer-Verlag Berlin Heidelberg 2013

for adaptive behaviours remains the same as before; and (iii) learning and programming become truly integrated in the sense that their effectiveness depends directly on the mental state representation used by the programmer.

The key idea is that learning may exploit the *underspecification* that is inherent in agent programming [13]. That is, agent programs often generate multiple options for actions without specifying how to make a final choice between these options. This is a feature of agent programming because it does not require a programmer to specify action selection to unnatural levels of detail. The motivation of our work is to exploit this underspecification and potentially optimize action selection by means of automated learning where it may be too complicated for a programmer to optimize code. The first challenge is to add a learning mechanism to agent programming in a generic and flexible way and to naturally integrate such a mechanism in a way that burdens the programmer minimally. The second challenge is to do this in such a way that the state space to be explored by the learning mechanism can still be managed by the program. Our approach addresses both challenges by re-using the mental state representation available in the agent program. Although our approach also facilitates managing the state space, there remain issues for future work that need to be dealt with in this area in particular. To this end, we draw some lessons learned from our work and discuss some options for dealing with this issue.

One of the aims of our work is to explore the impact of various representations or program choices on the learning mechanism. Even though our objective is to impose minimal requirements on the programmer's knowledge of machine learning, the program structure will have impact on the learning performance. Ideally, therefore, we can give the programmer some guidelines on how to write agent programs that are able to effectively learn. It is well-known that the representation language is a crucial parameter in machine learning. Given an adequate language, learning will be effective, and given an inadequate one learning will be difficult if not impossible [14]. Applied to agent-oriented programming this means that it is important to specify the right predicates for coding the agent's mental state and to provide the right (modular) program structure to enhance the effectiveness of learning. If the programmer is not able to use knowledge to guide program design, one may have to search a larger space, may require more examples and time, and in the worst case, learning might be unsuccessful.

The remainder of the paper is as follows. Section 2 introduces the GOAL language and reinforcement learning, followed by an overview of related works in Section 3. Section 4 describes the integration of GOAL and reinforcement learning and Section 5 presents experiments in the Blocks World. We conclude with a discussion of limitations and future directions of this work in Section 6.

2   Preliminaries

We now briefly discuss how agent programs and cognitive architectures select the action to perform next. In other words, we discuss how the mechanism we want to extend with a learning capability works. Following this, we introduce the reinforcement learning framework that we have used in this work.

2.1   Agent Programming Languages

Agent programming languages (APLs) based on the BDI paradigm are rule-based languages [15, 16]. Rules may serve various purposes but are used among others to select the actions or plans that an agent will perform. An agent program may perform built-in actions that are provided as programming constructs that are part of the language itself or it may perform actions that are available in an environment that the agent is connected to. Environment actions give the agent some control over the changes that occur in that environment. The types of rules that are used in APLs varies. Generally speaking, however, rules have a condition that is evaluated on the agent's mental state (rule head) and have a corresponding action or plan that is instantiated if the rule fired (rule body).

Rules are evaluated and applied in a reasoning cycle that is part of the agent program's interpreter. Agent interpreters for APLs implement a sense-plan-act cycle or a variant thereof. In a typical interpreter, for example, the percepts received from an environment are processed by some predefined mechanism. Most often this is an automatic mechanism (that may be customisable as in Jason) [4], but not necessarily; in GOAL, for example, so-called percept rules are available for processing incoming percepts and similar rules are available for processing messages received from other agents (2APL has similar rules [8]). During this stage, either before or after processing the percepts, typically the messages received from other agents are processed. These steps are usually performed first to ensure the mental state of the agent is up to date. Thereafter, the interpreter will evaluate rules against the updated mental state and select applicable rules. After determining which rules are applicable one or more of these rules is fired, resulting in one or more options to perform an action or add a plan to a plan base. Some selection mechanism (that again may be customised as e.g. in Jason) then is used to arbitrate between these multiple options, or, as is the case in for example GOAL, a choice is randomly made. Finally, an action is executed either internally or an action is sent to the environment for execution.

One aspect of these interpreters is that they may generate multiple applicable rules and options for performing actions. If multiple options are available, then the agent program is *underspecified* in the sense that it does not determine a unique choice of action. It is this feature of agent architectures that we will exploit and can be used by a learning mechanism for optimising the agent's choice of action [17, 18].

2.2   Reinforcement Learning

Reinforcement learning [12] is a formal framework for optimally solving multistage decision problems in environments where outcomes are only partly attributed to decision making by the agent and are partly stochastic. The general idea is to describe the *value* of a decision problem at a given time step in terms of the payoffs received from choices made so far, and the value of the remaining problem that results from those initial choices. Formally, at each time step t in a multistep problem, the agent perceives state $s \in S$ of the environment and chooses an action $a \in A_s$ that causes the environment to transition to state s' in the next time step $t+1$ and return a reward with the expected value $r \in R(s,a)$. Here S is the set of all possible states, A_s is the set of all possible actions in a given state s, and $R(s,a)$ is the function that determines the reward for taking an action a in state s. The probability that the process advances to state s' is given by the state transition function $P(s'|s,a)$. The agent's behaviour is described by a policy π that determines how the agent chooses an action in any given state. The optimal value in this setup can be obtained using dynamic programming and is given by Bellman's equation (Equation 1) [19], that relates the value function $V^*(s)$ in one time step to the value function $V^*(s')$ in the next time step. Here, $\gamma \in [0,1)$ is the discount factor that determines the importance of future rewards.

$$V^*(s) = R(s,a) + \max_{a \in A_s} \gamma \sum_{s'} P(s'|s,a)V^*(s'). \tag{1}$$

In the reinforcement learning setting both $P(s'|s,a)$ and $R(s,a)$ are unknown. So the agent has little choice but to physically act in the environment to observe the immediate reward, and use the samples over time to build estimates of the expected return in each state, in the hope of obtaining a good approximation of the optimal policy. Typically, the agent tries to maximise some cumulative function of the immediate rewards, such as the *expected discounted return* $R^\pi(s)$ (Equation 2) at each time step t. $R^\pi(s)$ captures the infinite-horizon discounted (by γ) sum of the rewards that the agent may expect (denoted by E) to receive starting in state s and following the policy π.

$$R^\pi(s) = E\{r_{t+1} + \gamma r_{t+2} + \gamma^2 r_{t+3} + \ldots\}. \tag{2}$$

One way to maximise this function is to evaluate all policies by simply following each one, sampling the rewards obtained, and then choosing the policy that gave the best return. The obvious problem with such a brute force method is that the number of possible policies is often too large to be practical. Furthermore, if rewards were stochastic, then even more samples will be required in order to estimate the expected return. A practical solution, based on Bellman's work on value iteration, is Watkins' Q-Learning algorithm [20] given by the action-value function (Equation 3). The Q-function gives the expected discounted return for taking action a in state s and following the policy π thereafter. Here α is the learning rate that determines to what extent the existing Q-value (i.e., $Q^\pi(s,a)$) will be corrected by the new update (i.e., $R(s,a) + \gamma \max_{a'}(Q(s',a'))$), and $\max_{a'}(Q(s',a'))$ is the maximum possible reward in the following state, i.e., it is the reward for taking the optimal action thereafter.

$$Q^\pi(s,a) \leftarrow Q^\pi(s,a) + \alpha \left[R(s,a) + \gamma \max_{a'}(Q(s',a')) - Q^\pi(s,a) \right]. \tag{3}$$

In order to learn the Q-values, the agent must try out available actions in each state and learn from these experiences over time. Given that acting and learning are interleaved and ongoing performance is important, a key challenge when choosing actions is to find a good balance between exploiting current knowledge to get the best reward known so far, and exploring new actions in the hope of finding better rewards.

3   Related Work

In most languages for partial reinforcement learning programs, the programmer specifies a program containing choice points [21]. Because of the underspecification present in agent programming languages, there is no need to add such choice points as multiple options are generated automatically by the agent program itself. There is little existing work in integrating learning capabilities within agent programming languages. In PRS-like cognitive architectures [2, 4, 22, 3] that are based in the BDI tradition, standard operating knowledge is programmed as abstract recipes or *plans*, often in a hierarchical manner. Plans whose preconditions hold in any runtime situation are considered applicable in that situation and may be chosen for execution. While such frameworks do not typically support learning, there has been recent work in this area. For instance, in [23] the learning process that decides when and how learning should proceed, is itself described within plans that can be invoked in the usual manner. Our own previous investigations in this area include [24–26] where decision tree learning was used to improve hierarchical plan selection in the JACK [3] agent programming language. That work bears some resemblance here in that the aim was to improve choice of instantiated plans as we do for bound action options in this study. In [17] we integrated GOAL and reinforcement learning as we do in this paper, with the key difference that now (i) a learning primitive has been added to the GOAL language to explicitly support adaptive behaviours, and (ii) a much richer state representation is used, i.e., the mental state of the agent.

Among other rule-based systems, ACT-R [27, 28] is a cognitive architecture primarily concerned with modelling human behaviour, where programming consists of writing production rules [29] that are condition-action pairs to describe possible responses to various situations. Learning in ACT-R consists of forming entirely new rules from sample solutions encountered, as well as updating the utilities of existing rules from ongoing experience. While not a programming language per se, ACT-R learning is nevertheless quite related in that Q-Learning is also used to learn rule preferences. SOAR [30] also uses production rules to capture procedural knowledge about the domain. It uses a process called chunking to create new production rules based on the results of subgoals, in a kind of explanation-based learning. SOAR-RL [31] integrates reinforcement learning to improve operator selection based on experience, similar to learnt utilities in ACT-R. ICARUS [32] is a cognitive architecture that incorporates ideas from work on production systems, hierarchical task networks, and logic programming. It uses a form of explanation-based learning to find the task hierarchy in hierarchical task networks. Overall, ACT-R, SOAR and our work share similarities in the way reinforcement learning is used to learn rule preferences, however the motivations are quite different. While ACT-R is heavily used in cognitive psychology research to model human behaviour, and SOAR is a general cognitive architecture for building intelligent systems, GOAL is an agent programming language in the BDI tradition. For us, the key motivation for integrating learning is to make adaptive technologies more accessible to agent programmers.

4   The GOAL Agent Programming Language

GOAL is a logic-based agent programming language similar to 2APL [8] and Jason [4]. GOAL agents maintain a dynamic mental state consisting of beliefs and goals that are represented in Prolog. GOAL agents also have a static knowledge base that is part of their mental state and consists of domain knowledge. They may perform built-in actions that update their mental state or send a message as well as actions that are available in the environment that the agent is connected to. Environment actions are specified using a STRIPS-like pre- and post-condition specification. A GOAL agent derives its choice of action from its beliefs and goals (in combination with its knowledge) by means of rules. Rules consist of a condition that is evaluated on the mental state of the agent and one or more actions that may be executed if the condition holds. In addition, GOAL supports multiple types of rules, rule evaluation strategies, and modules that facilitate structured programming.

Figure 1 provides a listing of a simple example GOAL agent program for the Blocks World [33]. We have used this program also in our experiments to evaluate the learning mechanism we have added to the language. The Blocks World is a well studied toy domain that has been used extensively in artificial intelligence research. The setup consists of a fixed number of blocks that are sitting on a table big enough to hold them all. Each block exists on top of exactly one other object that can either be another block or the table itself. Each block is considered to be *clear* when no other block exists on top of it. There is only one type of action that is possible in this domain: move a single clear block, either from another block onto the table, or from an object onto another clear block. A problem specification in this domain consists of an initial configuration of blocks, as well as the desired configuration. The task for the agent is to move blocks around one at a time until the final configuration is realised.

The program processes percepts and randomly selects an action that is enabled in the Blocks World environment. The init module consists of code to initialize the mental state of the agent and a single action specification for the move(X,Y) action that the agent can perform in the Blocks World. The Prolog rules in the knowledge section of this module define the concepts of a block and a block being clear. An initial goal is specified in the goals section. Initially the agent has no beliefs; the agent must first perceive the environment to obtain information about the blocks' configuration. The event module is executed at the start of each decision or reasoning cycle of an agent. Its purpose is to process received percepts (and messages). The two forall rules part of this module process the percepts received at the start of the cycle of the form percept(on(X,Y)). The first rule checks whether the agent sees that a block X is on top of a block Y and inserts this fact if the agent does not currently believe it; the second rule removes facts that are believed but not perceived (assuming full observability this is a sound rule).

```
1  init module {
2    knowledge{
3      block(X) :- on(X,_).
4      clear(X) :- block(X), not( on(_,X)).
5      clear(table).
6    }
7    actionspec{
8      move(X,Y) {
9        pre{ clear(X), clear(Y), on(X,Z), not(on(X,Y)) }
10       post{ not(on(X,Z)), on(X,Y) }
11     }
12   }
13   goals{ on(b1,table), on(b2,b1), on(b3,b2), on(b4,b3). }
14   beliefs{}
15 }
16 event module { program {
17   forall bel(percept(on(X,Y)), not(on(X,Y))) do insert(on(X,Y)).
18   forall bel(on(X,Y), not(percept(on(X,Y)))) do delete(on(X,Y)).
19 }}
20 main module { program[order=random] {
21   if bel(true) then move(X,Y).
22 }}
```

Fig. 1. A simple GOAL agent for solving the Blocks World problem

The **main** module consists of the decision logic for acting in the environment and selects actions after the mental state has been updated with the most recent perceptual information. The option **order=random** associated with the program section of the module indicates that rule evaluation occurs in random order (other options are to evaluate in linear order and to evaluate all rules in either linear or random order). In the example agent of Figure 1 there is only one rule that is always applicable because the condition **bel(true)** always holds and there is always an action enabled in a Blocks World environment. Note that a rule is evaluated by evaluating its condition *and* the precondition of the (first, if there are more) action of the rule. A rule that is applicable generates a non-empty set of *options* which are actions that may be performed by the agent. Only one of these actions is performed in a rule of the form **if ... then ...** and the action is randomly selected in that case. One might say that the program underspecifies what the agent should do. This may be useful if a programmer does not know how to select or care for a unique action and may be exploited by a learning mechanism to optimise the behavior of the agent, which is exactly the focus of this paper. Where more than one action is applicable, the agent must decide which one to choose and execute. In this work we are concerned with improving this action selection based on the ongoing experiences of the agent.

Implementing Adaptive Behaviours in GOAL

There are two key aspects of the adaptive framework in GOAL that we describe now, (i) the programming model that describes how adaptive behaviour modules can be specified by the agent programmer using the language of GOAL, and (ii) the underlying reinforcement learning implementation that makes it all possible.

Let us start with how adaptive behaviours can be specified in the programming model of GOAL. An important consideration for us when deciding what the programming interface should consist of was to keep as much of the machine learning technologies insulated from the programmer as possible. The motivation for this was to keep the programming model as simple and as close to the existing model as possible in order to allow easy uptake by existing GOAL programmers. Our stance here has been that agent programmers are not experts in machine learning and so they will be reluctant to try a new feature of the language if it required new expertise and significant changes to their programming style.

The first design choice for us was how the knowledge representation aspect of machine learning should be combined in the agent programming model without sacrificing programming flexibility and avoiding significant overhead. *We achieve this by making the knowledge representation for learning to be the same as the knowledge representation for the agent program.* That is to say that the "state" in the reinforcement learning sense is the mental state of the agent that comprises of its beliefs and goals. All that is required is to provide a translation function that automatically maps the mental state of the agent to a suitable state id (a number) used for reinforcement learning. The second decision was to make learning a modular feature in line with the GOAL philosophy of modular programming, to allow regular and adaptive behaviours to be easily combined.

The result is a very easy to use programming model where learning can simply be enabled as desired using a new `order=adaptive` option in the program section of a module. For example, to change the regular program module in the agent of Figure 1 to an adaptive one, we only have to change `order=random` as follows:

```
main module { program[order=adaptive] {
  if bel(true) then move(X,Y).
}}
```

With this specification, all possible action bindings will be evaluated by the underlying learning mechanism and action selection will be governed by the Q-values derived over repeated runs, rather than being random as it was before.

The benefit is that the agent programmer does not have to explicitly think about learning as being separate from programming, bar adhering to some basic guidelines. The only recommendation we have for the programmer is to not use the belief base of the agent as a long term memory store if learning is to be used. This means to not keep adding belief facts that only serve to keep a history of events. For example, a programmer may choose to store the history of every choice it made in a maze solving problem. If the programmer then enables learning such as to optimise the maze exploration strategy, then it will likely not deliver any useful results quickly due to the very large state space created by the belief base. A similar argument also applies for adding new goals to the mental state, but it is generally not as much of a problem since programs do not add new goals during execution to the same extent as they do beliefs. We must add here that in some problems this representation is unavoidable. In future work, we hope to address such cases by allowing learning to select a more appropriate context by decoupling the mental state into relevant and not relevant parts using a dependency graph that is already part of the GOAL implementation. For instance, in the maze example, if the exploration module code does not depend on the history of beliefs being added, then it should be possible to automatically isolate them from the state representation for learning purposes.

The final decision was on how rewards should be specified for reinforcement learning within the GOAL programming framework. We do this using the existing Environment Interface Standard (EIS) that GOAL uses to connect to external environments. The addition is a new "reward" query from GOAL that, if implemented by the environment, returns the reward for the last executed action. If, however, the plugged environment does not support this query, then the reward is simply an evaluation of the goals of the agent: if all the goals have been achieved, then the reward is 1.0, otherwise it is 0.0. The idea is that learning can be enabled regardless of whether a reward signal is available from the environment, in which case the agent tries to optimise the number of steps it takes to achieve its goals. A future extension might be to give partial rewards between 0.0 and 1.0 based on how many independent goals have been satisfied. However, it is unclear if rewards based solely on the agent's goals are always useful in learning, such as in programs that add or remove goals from the mental state.

In this study we use a Q-Learning implementation where the precise action-value function is maintained in memory. It should be noted here that this implementation does not scale well to large state spaces. Of course, we could use an approximation of the action-value function, such as a neural network, to store this in a compact manner. However, our focus here is not so much to use an efficient reinforcement learning technology as it is to see how such learning can be integrated into agent programming in a seamless manner. For this reason, in this version of the work, we have kept the basic Q-Learning implementation.

A simple action-selection strategy is to select the best known action most of the time, but every once in a while choose a random action with a small probability, say ϵ. This strategy is well known as ϵ-greedy and is the one we use in this work. In future work we plan to experiment with more advanced strategies. For instance, in the so-called Boltzmann selection strategy, instead of picking actions randomly, weights are assigned to the available actions based on their existing action-value estimates, so that actions that perform well have a higher chance of being selected in the exploration phase.

Under the hood we have implemented a Java-based interface that allows us to plug in a generic reinforcement learning algorithm into GOAL. The idea is to be able to offload the task of providing and maintaining the machine learning technology to the relevant expert. It will also allow us to easily update the default Q-Learning implementation with a more efficient one in the future.

5 Experiments

Here we describe the Blocks World domain that we used as a testbed for our experiments, and then the three different programs to solve it. We analyse the results quantitatively in terms of the average number of steps taken by the agent to achieve its goal, as well as qualitatively in terms of how the design of the program impacts learning performance.

We have chosen the Blocks World domain for our experiments for several reasons. First, the domain is simple to understand and programming strategies are easy to describe and compare at a conceptual level. Second, despite its simplicity, finding optimal solutions in this domain is known to be an NP-hard problem [34]. Finally, decisions in this domain often involve choosing between several options that could potentially be optimised using learning.

There are various ways of programming a strategy for solving the Blocks World. For example, one way would be to dismantle all blocks onto the table one by one, and then stack them into the desired configuration from there. This is in fact a reasonable "baseline" strategy because it is easy to see that the upper bound for the number of steps needed to solve a problem with n blocks is $2(n-1)$ which is the case when one must dismantle a single tower (which takes $n-1$ moves for a tower of height n) to construct a different single tower (that takes another $n-1$ moves). The average number of steps for this algorithm is less intuitive but has been shown to be $2(n - \sqrt{n})$ [33]. For this work, we will compare three other solutions to the problem, and see how they compare amongst themselves and against this baseline strategy.

Program A. A very simple strategy for solving the Blocks World is to randomly select some block that is clear and move it to some randomly chosen place on top of another object. Effectively, this strategy tries to achieve the final configuration by randomly changing the current configuration for as long as needed until it eventually stumbles upon the solution. This strategy is given by the program listing in Figure 1, and is contained in the following code segment:

```
main module { program[order=random] {
  if bel(true) then move(X,Y).
}}
```

This is certainly not the most effective way to solve the problem, and while it works reasonably well for small problems of two to four blocks, it quickly becomes unusable beyond six blocks. Nevertheless it is useful for this study since we are interested in improving action selection using learning, and one would imagine there is a lot of room for improvment in this strategy.

Program B. An improvement on the random strategy is this actual Blocks World program written in GOAL by an agent programmer:

```
main module { program[order=random] {
  if bel(on(X,Y), clear(X), clear(Z)), a-goal(on(X,Z)) then move(X,Z).
  if bel(on(X,Y), not(clear(X))), a-goal(on(X,Z)) then adopt(clear(X)).
  if a-goal(on(X,Z)), bel(on(X,Y), not(clear(Z))) then adopt(clear(Z)).
```

```
   if bel(on(X,Y), clear(X)), a-goal(clear(Y)) then move(X,table).
   if bel(on(X,Y), not(clear(X))), a-goal(clear(Y)) then adopt(clear(X)).
}}
```

This strategy uses the following line of thought: If the agent has a goal to have some block X on top of Z, then move X onto Z if possible. If not possible because X cannot be moved, then clear whatever block is obstructing X. On the other hand, if it is Z that is blocked then clear it first. Finally, repeatedly clear blocks that are obstructing other blocks that are to be cleared.

Program C. A more sophisticated solution that comes bundled with the GOAL distribution uses a higher level notion of *misplaced blocks* to decide if a block should be moved. To do this it provides a recursive definition of a *Tower*. Then a block is considered misplaced if the agent still has a goal to have a tower with block X on top. Given these definitions, the strategy is relatively simple and uses only two rules. The idea is to either move a misplaced block onto the table, or move a block onto another block if the move is constructive, i.e., results in a desired tower configuration.

```
knowledge[
  ...
  tower([X]) :- on(X, table).
  tower([X, Y| T]) :- on(X, Y), tower([Y| T]).
}
program[order=linear] {
 #define misplaced(X) a-goal(tower([X| T])).
 #define constructiveMove(X,Y) a-goal(tower([X, Y| T])), bel(tower([Y| T])).
 if constructiveMove(X, Y) then move(X, Y).
 if misplaced(X) then move(X, table).
}
```

We conducted several experiments with the three example programs A, B, and C, for problems with upto 10 blocks. Each run of the experiment consisted of a series of randomly generated problems that were solved using the program first in its original form and then using adaptive ordering (i.e., by substituting [order=adaptive] in the program module options). Since problems are randomly generated and the number of moves required to solve them can vary significantly, we used a moving average of 20 results over the series of generated problems to get the average number of steps for *any* problem of a given size. Finally, we ran 20 repeats of each experiment and report the average number of moves taken to achieve the fixed goal of building a given tower configuration.

For all of our experiments, we used the following parameters' settings. The ϵ value for the action selection strategy was set to always explore 10% of the time. For Q-Learning we set the learning rate α to 1.0 and the discount factor γ to 0.9. It should be noted that these settings will obviously impact learning, and these default values may not work as well in other domains. An option in the future might be to setup learning "profiles" that the programmer can select between based on some basic usage guidelines.

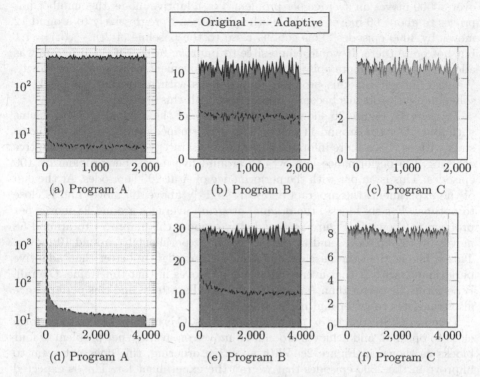

Fig. 2. Comparison of the number of moves (y-axis) over successive episodes (x-axis) to solve randomly generated worlds of four (top row) and six (bottom row) blocks, with original (light shade) and adaptive (dark shade) rule ordering

Results

Figure 2 shows the results of running the programs A, B, and C, with and without adaptive behaviours enabled (in dark and light shading respectively). Figure 2a, Figure 2b, and Figure 2c are results for problems with four blocks, while Figure 2d, Figure 2e, and Figure 2f are for problems with six blocks.

Program A: In Figure 2a, the light shading shows that the average number of steps taken by the original A to solve problems with four blocks is around 350 moves. This is not very surprising since A is really only trying to solve the problem using random moves. The dark shading shows the results for the same set of problems and the same A, but using adaptive rule ordering. While initially the program performs similarly as it tries to find the first few solutions, it improves to around seven moves per problem by 100 episodes. Beyond that it improves progressively and by the end of the experiment at 2000 episodes the program takes around five moves per problem. Compared to our baseline program that averages $2(n - \sqrt{n}) = 4$, i.e., four moves for a problem with four blocks, we can already see that the learnt ordering gives competitive performance. Figure 2d shows the same A for problems with six blocks using adaptive ordering. We have not included results for the original program since it takes over 30000 moves on average per problem. For adaptive mode, this number improves to about 60 moves by the 100th episode, and progressively to around 12 moves by 4000 episodes. This gets us close to the baseline of $2(n - \sqrt{n}) = 7.1$ but not quite there. It would be possible to improve further if the program was allowed to run for more episodes, but the improvement will occur very slowly. We also did not run this program for problems with more than six blocks as solving larger problems becomes impractical with this strategy.

Program B: Figure 2b shows the performance of the original B for problems with four blocks at around 11 moves. The performance is already reasonable to start with as it is a more informed programmed strategy than A. With adaptive ordering, the performance improves to around five moves per problem by 100 episodes. This is on par with the performance of A at 2000 episodes. At the end of the experiment, the program performs slightly above 4.5 moves and is close to optimal. For six blocks, the original program averages around 28 moves per problem as shown in Figure 2e. In adaptive mode, this improves to around 58 moves by 100 episodes, and at the end of the experiment to around 10 moves. This is higher than the baseline of 7.1 moves but slightly better than adaptive performance with A that averages around 12 moves in that timeframe. Overall, B performs far better than A due to its informed strategy, and this performance also translates to faster and better learning.

Program C: In contrast to the other programs, C is already known to perform close to optimal, and achieves around 4.5 moves on average per problem of four blocks as shown in Figure 2c. With adaptive ordering, this does not seem to improve in the 2000 episodes that we ran the experiment for. This is expected since the program is already performing close to optimal. However, interestingly we know from previous studies that C does not perform optimally for certain "deadlock" cases. We would have hoped to overcome this using learning but from the averaged results this is not evident as there is no significant difference in the performance with and without learning. Importantly, for six blocks, for the first time in the experiments we see that the adaptive ordering actually performs worse than the original program in Figure 2f, albeit by only 0.25 moves per problem on average at its worst. On closer analysis this seems to be because we simply have not run the experiment long enough. Certainly the difference between the two modes of execution is diminishing as the experiment progresses and is evident in Figure 2f. We should note that regardless, the performance of C with or without learning is significantly better than the other programs at around 8 moves and only slightly higher than the baseline case of $2(n-\sqrt{n}) = 7.1$. Overall, we can conclude that C is already very informed about the domain, so learning is not very useful in this case.

Interestingly, in all experiments, adaptive mode does not do any worse than the default behaviour. This is a useful insight for agent programmers who may otherwise feel reluctant to try a "black box" technology that directly impacts the performance of the agent but that they do not really understand. Another important point is that the performance improvement with adaptive mode is very much tied to the problem at hand and does not necessarily generalise to other related problems. For instance, the learning from four-block problems does not generalise to six-block problems and the agent programmer should be aware that one cannot simply plug-and-play learnt values between problems. While this feature may be desirable in many domains, it is nevertheless a shortcoming that comes with the ease of use of the programming model that completely insulates the programmer from the knowledge representation used for learning.

6   Discussion and Conclusion

In this paper we have shown how the mental state representation of an agent program may be exploited to significantly increase the effectiveness of the program through ongoing learning. The novelty is that this performance improvement comes almost for free since the programming model remains relatively unchanged. In particular, we presented an enhancement to the GOAL agent programming language that allows adaptive behaviours to be easily programmed. The new language primitive is implemented using a Q-Learning mechanism under the hood, and allows action choices resulting from programmed rules to be improved over time based on the ongoing experience of the agent. A key feature of this enhancement is that it can be readily used by agent programmers who are non-experts in machine learning, since the learning feature has little impact on the programming model. We demonstrated the usability of the framework in the Blocks World domain and analysed the programmer's role in balancing between fixed and flexible behaviour using three sample solutions for the problem.

The results in Section 5, however, also indicate that scalability (i.e. managing the size of the state space) remains an important challenge. The main tool a programmer currently has in our approach to integrating learning into GOAL to reduce the state space is to add and exploit knowledge about the environment in the agent program. Even though the use of domain knowledge may reduce the size of the state space, which corresponds one-to-one with the number of beliefs and goals of the agent, the state space still quickly becomes very large in the Blocks World environment with an increasing number of blocks [33].

We have used and integrated a standard Q-Learning approach to reinforcement learning. It is well-known that such an approach is unable to handle all but the smallest state spaces [14]. Our approach, however, does not depend on this particular choice of learning technique that has been used here mainly to demonstrate the viability of the approach. In order to handle bigger state spaces it is clear that we need some abstraction technique.

The ease of use of the new adaptive functionality in GOAL is appealing from a programming point of view as shown in this study. The downside is that a programmer may waste valuable time in trying to improve performance where it is simply not possible within the constraints of the learning framework and the mental state representation used. For example, in a maze world, the only way to distinguish between two T-junctions that "look" identical is to trace back the history of actions that led to the junctions. Here the underlying reinforcement learning framework is inadequate for learning if the mental state only consists of the current percepts of the agent. Keeping the history in the mental state would help but will make the learning impractical even for simple problems.

This drawback also highlights the need for future work to better understand how aware a programmer needs to be of the learning model. It would be useful in this context to develop design patterns that serve as guidelines for implementing adaptive behaviours in typical scenarios. Another avenue for future work is in deciding which mental state atoms are more relevant than others, in order to improve learning times in large state spaces. One option is to automatically learn such useful "features" of the agent's mental state using regularization techniques [35].

Acknowledgments. This research is supported by the 2011 Endeavour Research Fellowship program of the Australian government.

References

1. Rao, A., Georgeff, M.: Modeling rational agents within a BDI-architecture. In: International Conference on Principles of Knowledge Representation and Reasoning, KR, pp. 473–484. Morgan Kaufmann (1991)
2. Rao, A.: Agentspeak(l): BDI agents speak out in a logical computable language. In: Van de Velde, W., Perram, J.W. (eds.) MAAMAW 1996. LNCS, vol. 1038, pp. 42–55. Springer, Heidelberg (1996)
3. Busetta, P., Rönnquist, R., Hodgson, A., Lucas, A.: JACK intelligent agents: Components for intelligent agents in Java. AgentLink Newsletter 2, 2–5 (1999)
4. Bordini, R., Hübner, J., Wooldridge, M.: Programming multi-agent systems in AgentSpeak using Jason. Wiley-Interscience (2007)
5. Pokahr, A., Braubach, L., Lamersdorf, W.: JADEX: Implementing a BDI-infrastructure for JADE agents. EXP - in Search of Innovation (Special Issue on JADE) 3(3), 76–85 (2003)
6. Sardina, S., Padgham, L.: A BDI agent programming language with failure recovery, declarative goals, and planning. Autonomous Agents and Multi-Agent Systems 23(1), 18–70 (2010)
7. Hindriks, K., Boer, F.D., Hoek, W.V.D., Meyer, J.: Agent programming in 3APL. Autonomous Agents and Multi-Agent Systems 2(4), 357–401 (1999)
8. Dastani, M.: 2APL: A practical agent programming language. Autonomous Agents and Multi-Agent Systems 16(3), 214–248 (2008)
9. Hindriks, K.: Programming Rational Agents in GOAL. Multi-Agent Tools: Languages, Platforms and Applications, 119–157 (2009)
10. Hindriks, K.V., van Riemsdijk, B., Behrens, T., Korstanje, R., Kraayenbrink, N., Pasman, W., de Rijk, L.: UNREAL GOAL bots - conceptual design of a reusable interface. In: Dignum, F. (ed.) Agents for Games and Simulations II. LNCS, vol. 6525, pp. 1–18. Springer, Heidelberg (2011)
11. Hindriks, K., Neerincx, M.A., Vink, M.: The iCat as a natural interaction partner. In: Dechesne, F., Hattori, H., ter Mors, A., Such, J.M., Weyns, D., Dignum, F. (eds.) AAMAS 2011 Workshops. LNCS, vol. 7068, pp. 212–231. Springer, Heidelberg (2012)
12. Sutton, R.S., Barto, A.G.: Reinforcement Learning: An Introduction. The MIT Press (1998)
13. Rao, A., Georgeff, M.: BDI agents: From theory to practice. In: Proceedings of the First International Conference on Multi-Agent Systems (ICMAS), San Francisco, pp. 312–319 (1995)
14. Džeroski, S., Raedt, L.D., Driessens, K.: Relational reinforcement learning. Machine Learning 43, 7–52 (2001), doi:10.1023/A:1007694015589

15. Bordini, R.H., Dix, J., Dastani, M., Seghrouchni, A.E.F.: Multi-Agent Programming: Languages, Platforms and Applications. Multiagent Systems, Artificial Societies, and Simulated Organizations, vol. 15. Springer (2005)
16. Bordini, R.H., Dix, J., Dastani, M., Seghrouchni, A.E.F.: Multi-Agent Programming: Languages, Tools and Applications. Springer (2009)
17. Broekens, J., Hindriks, K., Wiggers, P.: Reinforcement Learning as Heuristic for Action-Rule Preferences. In: Collier, R., Dix, J., Novák, P. (eds.) ProMAS 2010. LNCS, vol. 6599, pp. 25–40. Springer, Heidelberg (2012)
18. Hindriks, K.V., van Riemsdijk, M.B.: Using temporal logic to integrate goals and qualitative preferences into agent programming. In: Baldoni, M., Son, T.C., van Riemsdijk, M.B., Winikoff, M. (eds.) DALT 2008. LNCS (LNAI), vol. 5397, pp. 215–232. Springer, Heidelberg (2009)
19. Bellman, R.E.: Dynamic Programming. Princeton University Press (1957)
20. Watkins, C.J.: Learning from delayed rewards. PhD thesis, King's College London (1989)
21. Andre, D., Russell, S.J.: State abstraction for programmable reinforcement learning agents. In: Eighteenth National Conference on Artificial Intelligence, Menlo Park, CA, USA, pp. 119–125. American Association for Artificial Intelligence (2002)
22. Pokahr, A., Braubach, L., Lamersdorf, W.: Jadex: A BDI reasoning engine. In: Multi-Agent Programming. Multiagent Systems, Artificial Societies, and Simulated Organizations, vol. 15, pp. 149–174. Springer (2005)
23. Subagdja, B., Sonenberg, L., Rahwan, I.: Intentional learning agent architecture. Autonomous Agents and Multi-Agent Systems 18, 417–470 (2009)
24. Singh, D., Sardina, S., Padgham, L.: Extending BDI plan selection to incorporate learning from experience. Robotics and Autonomous Systems 58, 1067–1075 (2010)
25. Singh, D., Sardina, S., Padgham, L., Airiau, S.: Learning context conditions for BDI plan selection. In: Proceedings of Autonomous Agents and Multi-Agent Systems (AAMAS), pp. 325–332 (May 2010)
26. Singh, D., Sardina, S., Padgham, L., James, G.: Integrating learning into a BDI agent for environments with changing dynamics. In: Toby Walsh, C.K., Sierra, C. (eds.) Proceedings of the International Joint Conference on Artificial Intelligence (IJCAI), Barcelona, Spain, pp. 2525–2530. AAAI Press (July 2011)
27. Anderson, J., Bothell, D., Byrne, M., Douglass, S., Lebiere, C., Qin, Y.: An integrated theory of the mind. Psychological Review 111(4), 1036 (2004)
28. Fu, W., Anderson, J.: From recurrent choice to skill learning: A reinforcement-learning model. Journal of Experimental Psychology: General 135(2), 184 (2006)
29. Klahr, D., Langley, P., Neches, R.: Production system models of learning and development. The MIT Press (1987)
30. Laird, J., Rosenbloom, P., Newell, A.: Chunking in soar: The anatomy of a general learning mechanism. Machine Learning 1(1), 11–46 (1986)
31. Nason, S., Laird, J.: Soar-rl: Integrating reinforcement learning with soar. Cognitive Systems Research 6(1), 51–59 (2005)
32. Nejati, N., Langley, P., Konik, T.: Learning hierarchical task networks by observation. In: International Conference on Machine Learning, pp. 665–672. ACM Press (2006)
33. Slaney, J., Thiébaux, S.: Blocks world revisited. Artificial Intelligence 125(1-2), 119–153 (2001)
34. Gupta, N., Nau, D.: On the complexity of blocks-world planning. Artificial Intelligence 56(2-3), 223–254 (1992)
35. Guyon, I., Elisseeff, A.: An introduction to variable and feature selection. The Journal of Machine Learning Research 3, 1157–1182 (2003)

The Multi-Agent Programming Contest 2012

Michael Köster, Federico Schlesinger, and Jürgen Dix

Department of Informatics, Clausthal University of Technology,
Julius-Albert-Str. 4, 38678 Clausthal-Zellerfeld, Germany
{dix,michael.koester,federico.schlesinger}@tu-clausthal.de

Abstract. The Multi-Agent Programming Contest, MAPC, is an annual, community-serving competition that attracts groups from all over the world. Its aim is to facilitate advances in programming multiagent systems (MAS) by (1) developing benchmark problems, (2) enabling head-to-head comparison of MAS's and (3) supporting educational efforts in the design and implementation of MAS's. We report about its eighth edition and give a detailed overview of the participants strategies and the overall contest.

1 Introduction

This paper serves as an introduction to the subsequent papers in this proceedings volume, each of which describes a team that participated in this years edition. We give a comprehensive overview of the Multi-Agent Programming Contest[1] 2012, an annual international event that has started in 2005 as an attempt to stimulate research in the field of programming multi-agent system by 1) identifying key problems, 2) collecting suitable benchmarks, and 3) gathering test cases which require and enforce coordinated action that can serve as milestones for testing multi-agent programming languages, platforms and tools. In 2012 the competition was organised and held for the eighth time.

Research communities in general benefit from competitions that attempt to evaluate different aspects of the systems under consideration and furthermore allow for comparing state of the art systems, act as a driver and catalyst for developments and pose challenging research problems.

In this paper we (1) briefly introduce the Contest and its infrastructure, (2) elaborate on the 2012 scenario and its differences with the 2011 edition, (3) introduce the seven teams that took part in the tournament, and (4) present results and findings acquired before, during and after the tournament.

More detailed information about the strategies of the teams are to be found in the remaining six papers in this volume.

1.1 Related Work

The Multi-Agent Programming Contest has generated quite a few publications over the years [9,10,11,3,4,1,8]. For a detailed account on the history of the

---

[1] http://multiagentcontest.org

M. Dastani, J.F. Hübner, and B. Logan (Eds.): ProMAS 2012, LNAI 7837, pp. 174–195, 2013.
© Springer-Verlag Berlin Heidelberg 2013

contest as well as the underlying simulation platform, we refer to [1,8,5,6]. A quick non-technical overview appears in [2].

Similar contests, competitions and challenges have taken place in the past few years. Among them we mention *Google's AI challenge*[2], the *AI-MAS Winter Olympics*[3], the *Starcraft AI Competition*[4], the *Mario AI Championship*[5], the *ORTS competition*[6], and the *Planning Competition*[7]. Every such competition rests in its own research niche. Originally, our Contest has been designed for problem solving approaches that are based on formal approaches and computational logics. But this is not a requirement to enter the competition.

1.2   The Contest from 2005–2012

From 2005 to 2007 we used a classical gold miners scenario [10] and introduced the *MASSim* platform: A platform for executing the Contest tournaments.

From 2008 to 2010 we developed the cows and cowboys scenario which has been designed to enforce cooperative behavior among agents [4]. The topology of the environment was represented by a grid that contained, besides various obstacles, a population of simulated cows. The goal was to arrange agents in a manner that scared cows into special areas, called corrals, in order to get points. While still maintaining the core tasks of environment exploration and path planning, we also made the use of cooperative strategies an obligation.

The agents on Mars scenario, used during the 2012 edition and discussed in this paper, was firstly introduced in 2011 [5]. In short, we have generalized the environment topology to a weighted graph. Agents were expected to cooperatively establish a graph covering while standing their ground in an adversarial setting and reaching achievements.

2   MAPC 2012: Agents on Mars

In this section we give a detailed overview of the 2012 agents on Mars scenario and point out differences to the scenario from 2011.

2.1   The Scenario

It is now a tradition to accompany the technical description of each scenario with a motivating little story:

> *In the year 2033 mankind finally populates Mars. While in the beginning the settlers received food and water from transport ships sent from earth*

---

[2] http://aichallenge.org/
[3] http://www.aiolympics.ro/
[4] http://eis.ucsc.edu/StarCraftAICompetition
[5] http://www.marioai.org/
[6] http://skatgame.net/mburo/orts/
[7] http://ipc.icaps-conference.org/

shortly afterwards – because of the outer space pirates – sending these ships became too dangerous and expensive. Also, there were rumors going around that somebody actually found water on Mars below the surface. Soon the settlers started to develop autonomous intelligent agents, so-called All Terrain Planetary Vehicles (ATPV), to search for water wells. The World Emperor – enervated by the pirates – decided to strengthen the search for water wells by paying money for certain achievements. Sadly, this resulted in sabotage among the different groups of settlers.

Now, the task of your agents is to find the best water wells and occupy the best zones of Mars. Sometimes they have to sabotage their rivals to achieve their goal (while the opponents will most probably do the same) or to defend themselves. Of course the agents' vehicle pool contains specific vehicles. Some of them have special sensors, some are faster and some have sabotage devices on board.

Last but not least, your team also contains special experts, e.g. the repairer agents, that are capable of fixing agents that are disabled. In general, each agent has special expert knowledge and is thus the only one being able to perform a certain action. So your agents have to find ways to cooperate and coordinate among them.

The environment's topology is constituted by a weighted graph. Each vertex has a unique identifier and a number that indicates its value. Each edge has a number that represents the costs of moving from one of its vertices to the other. These vertex-values are crucial for calculating the values of zones. A zone is a subgraph that is covered by a team of agents according to a coloring algorithm that is based on a domination principle.

Several agents can stand on a single vertex. If a set of agents dominates such a vertex, the vertex gets the color of the dominating team. A previously uncolored vertex that has a majority of neighbors (at least 2) with a specific color, inherits this color as well. Finally, if the overall graph contains a colored subgraph that constitutes a frontier or border, all the nodes that are inside this border are colored as well. This means that agents can color or cover a subgraph that has more vertices than the overall number of agents. Figure 1 shows a screenshot of a relatively small map, depicting, amongst other things, the graph coloring.

Before elaborating on the agent roles we have to specify the effectoric capabilities of the agents. Each agent, or vehicle, has a state that is defined by its position on the map, its current energy available for executing actions and its current health. On top of that, each team has a budget for equipping the vehicles during the simulation. These actions[8] are defined by the scenario:

- skip is the noop-action, which does not change the state of the environment,
- recharge increases the current energy of a vehicle by a fixed factor and can be performed at any time without costs,

---

[8] Of course, all the actions that cost energy will fail if the vehicle under consideration does not have enough energy.

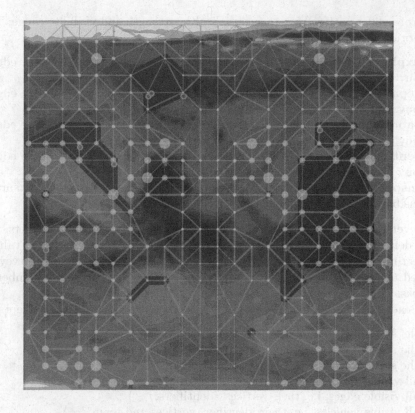

Fig. 1. A screenshot of the agents on Mars scenario

- **attack** decreases the health of an opponent, standing on the same vertex, if successfully executed and decreases the current energy of the attacker,
- **parry** parries an attack and decreases the energy of the defending agent,
- **goto** moves the vehicle to a neighboring vertex while decreasing its energy by the weight of the traversed edge,
- **probe** yields the exact value of the vertex the vehicle is standing on and decreases the probing vehicle's energy,
- **survey** yields the exact weights of visible edges while decreasing the energy,
- **inspect** costs energy and yields the internals of all visible opponents,
- **buy** equips the vehicle with new components, which increase its performance, and cost money, and
- **repair** repairs a teammate, which again costs energy.

We have defined five different roles. Each team consists of four vehicles for each role, that is a total of twenty vehicles per team. This number increased from the 2011 edition, where teams were composed by 2 vehicles for each role, totaling 10 vehicles. Each role defines the vehicle's internals and its capabilities.

The roles differ with respect to energy, health, strength and visibility range. The effectoric capabilities are as follows:

- **explorer** can skip, move to a vertex, probe a vertex, survey visible edges, buy equipment and recharge its energy,
- **repairer** can skip, move to a vertex, parry an attack, survey visible edges, buy equipment, repair a teammate and recharge its energy,
- **saboteur** can skip, move to a vertex, parry an attack, survey visible edges, buy equipment, attack an opponent and recharge its energy,
- **sentinel** can skip, move to a vertex, parry an attack, survey visible edges, buy equipment and recharge its energy,
- **inspector** can skip, move to a vertex, inspect visible opponents, survey visible edges, buy equipment and recharge its energy.

Achievements are tasks that, if fulfilled, contribute to the teams' budgets. We have defined a set of achievements that includes having zones with fixed values, inspecting a specific number of vehicles, probing a number of vertices, surveying a fixed number of edges and successfully performing and parrying a number of attacks.

In each step, each vehicle is provided with its currently available percepts:

- the state of the simulation, i.e. the current step,
- the state of the team, i.e. the current scores and money,
- the state of itself, i.e. its internals,
- all visible vertices, i.e. identifier and team,
- all visible edges, i.e. their vertices' identifiers,
- all visible vehicles, i.e. their identifier, vertices and team,
- probed vertices, i.e. their identifier and values,
- surveyed edges, i.e. their vertices' identifiers and weights, and
- inspected vehicles, i.e. their identifiers, vertices, teams and internals.

After sending percepts, the server grants some time for deliberation. After that the new state is computed. The simulation state transition is as follows:

1. collect all actions from the agents,
2. let each action fail with a specific probability,
3. execute all remaining **attack** and **parry** actions,
4. determine disabled agents,
5. execute all remaining actions,
6. prepare percepts,
7. deliver the percepts.

The introduction of the agents on Mars scenario was also accompanied by the release of an environment interface that has been developed to be compatible with the *environment interface standard* [7]. This standard allows Java based problem solving approaches to make use of a jar-file provided by the organizers that facilitated connecting to and communicating with the *MASSim* server. This is done my mapping the whole communication to Java-method invocations and callbacks.

2.2 Changes and Modifications to the Scenario from 2011

As already mentioned, we increased the number of agents to 20 and provided them with more energy. This results in less recharging and gives them more freedom: in 2011, recharge was by far the most used action.

The visualisation was improved a lot (zones as well as high-valued vertices are highlighted, costs of the edges are depicted by their thickness. The last action from an agent at each vertex is illustrated: (1) green circle: successful sense action (probe, survey, inspect), (2) red circle: last action failed, (3) yellow star: successful attack, (4) indigo star: successful parry, (5) pink star: successful repair, and (6) crossed out: disabled.

Agents are now getting feedback as to why their actions failed (if they did). The (automatic) generation of maps has been improved (a map contains now several centers).

3 The Tournament

During past editions of the Contest, stability (i.e., the capacity to send actions to the MASSim server in time) was a big problem for some teams. It also affected the overall quality of the Contest and the possibility to draw conclusions about the strategies by looking at the results. To address this, we decided for the 2012 edition to implement a *qualification round*, in which teams were required to show that they were able to maintain good stability (i.e. timeout-rates below 5%) during a round of test matches. Only then they were allowed to take part in the tournament.

3.1 Participants and Results

Nine teams from all around the world registered for the Contest. Seven of them were able to pass the qualification round and took part in the tournament (see Table 1). Full introductions of the teams can be found in [12] and in the papers included in this volume.

Table 1. Participants of the 2012 edition

Team	Affiliation	Platform/Language
AiWYX	Sun Yat-Sen University, China	C++
PGIM	Islamic Azad University of Malayer, Iran	Prometheus, JACK
LTI-USP	University of Sao Paulo, Brazil	Jason, CArtAgO, Moise
SMADAS-UFSC	Federal University of Santa Catarina, Brazil	Jason
Python-DTU	Technical University of Denmark	Python
Streett	- , USA	Java
TUB	TU Berlin, Germany	JIAC

Team AiWYX was a single-developer team from Sun Yat-Sen Univerity, China. The agents were developed in C++, using no agent-specific technologies. The approach used is centralized, where one agent gets all the percepts from the other agents and makes the decisions for the whole team.

Team PGIM comes from the Islamic Azad University of Malayer, Iran. The 3 developers used agent-specific technologies for developing their team: Prometheus, JACK. Nevertheless the team organization is not distributed, and agents broadcast their percepts.

Team LTI-USP from University of Sao Paulo, Brazil had three developers. Agents were implemented using Jason, CArtAgO and Moise. There is one agent that determines the best strategy, but each agent has its own thread, with its own beliefs, desires and intentions. Agents broadcast new percepts, but communication load decreases over time.

Team SMADAS-UFSC is from Federal University of Santa Catarina, Brazil. It had six team members. The language of choice for agent development was Jason. Besides normal agent-communication provided by Jason, agents shared a common data-structure (blackboard) for storing the graph topology.

Team Python-DTU from the Technical University of Denmark is a regular contender of the Multi-Agent Programming Contest. For this edition it registered 6 members. As team's name suggest, Python was the language of choice. The agents follow a decentralized approach, where coordination is achieved through distributed algorithms, e.g. for auction-based agreement.

Team Streett was composed by a single independent developer from the USA. Agents were developed in Java, based on the sample agents provided with the MASSim platform. Agents shared only vital information and coordination was achieved by sharing location data.

Team TUB, TU Berlin, Germany, is another regular contender of the Multi-Agent Programming Contest, that presented for this edition as a single-developer team. The agents are developed in the JIAC platform (which won the contest several times in previous years).

The tournament took place from 10th to 12th September 2012. Each day each team played against two other teams so that in the end all teams played against all others. We started the tournament each morning at 10 am and finished at around 3 pm. A match between two teams consisted of 3 simulations only differing in the size of the graph. For a win the team got 3 points and for a draw 1 point. The results of this year's Contest are shown in Table 2.

Table 2. Results

Pos.	Team	Score	Difference	Points
1	SMADAS-UFSC	2778057 : 1043023	1735034	51
2	Python-DTU	2738397 : 1095251	1643146	48
3	TUB	2090849 : 1600914	489935	30
4	LTI-USP	1627177 : 1845601	-218424	27
5	AiWYX	2301358 : 1526768	774590	24
6	PGIM	1130432 : 2047735	-917303	9
7	Streett	192694 : 3699672	-3506978	0

Two teams, *SMADAS-UFSC* and *Python-DTU*, stood out from the rest and the tournament winner was decided by the match that confronted them, during the second day of the competition. *SMADAS-UFSC* won two of three simulations of that match and was crowned champion, leaving *Python-DTU* as runner-up for the second consecutive year. Both teams won all the matches they played against the rest of the teams without losing any simulations. The mid-table teams *TUB*, *LTI-USP* and *AiWYX* where relatively close while playing against each other. They could not catch up with the first two teams but clearly differentiated from the last two.

Thanks to the qualification round (as well as the optional test matches offered before it), there were no stability issues during the Contest. This was a great improvement compared to previous editions. Although some of the teams experimented a few crashes from time to time, the promptness of the developers to restart their agents ensured that the results of the simulation were not affected by these isolated events.

3.2   Overview of the Teams' Strategies

In this section we collect a few facts about the participating teams. For more detailed information we refer to the articles in these proceedings.

SMADAS: The winner of this years contest, from Brazil, used Jason, a dedicated MAS programming language. For some algorithms, Java was used to implement them, rather than Jason. The development needed 500 person hours distributed among 6 people. They used 7900 lines of code, 2400 of which were written in Java. Communication with the server was done through the EISMASSIM interface.

The system is decentralized. Agents were executed on the same machine to use shared memory (blackboard programming). But updating the blackboard was computationally difficult and thus could only be done every 3 steps.

The strategy was first to explore the map, find the best potential zones (high values) and then to conquer and defend them. An interesting idea was to make the opponents spend their money using a special agent: Hulk. If the team detects that there is no particular buying strategy, then the Hulk agent changes its behaviour.

They claim that the good performance is based on the various strategies that make the team very flexible against different opponents. Defending of the zones can still be improved.

Python-DTU: The danish team ended as runner-up for the second time in a row. The team did not use a dedicated platform or MAS programming language. They choose Python for efficiency and to have complete control over all features in the implementation. However, the team used the organizational model of *Moise.*

The solution they implemented is decentralized and heavily based on communications between the agents and on an auction-based agreement algorithm. They invested 300 person hours distributed among 6 people. 1500 lines of codes were written.

The strategy is based on dividing the game in three phases: randomly trying for achievements in the first phase, taking control of high valued areas and sending out explorers in the second phase, and trying to expand in the third phase.

The team claims that their buying algorithm has been detected in the qualification phase and a clever counter strategy was developed by another team that eventually led to the defeat.

TUB: The german team TUB, winner of several contests in the past, entered the contest for the 4th time (but with different team members). They use a centralized approach where agents share all their perceptions and intentions. It required 640 person hours (and 8000 lines of code)

First the agents probe and survey the whole graph. Explorers, attackers, repairers and inspectors only contribute to the zoning algorithm, if they have done their dedicated tasks. The team tries to find a balance between zoning and achievements points.

The team claims that they did not foresee very aggressive playing methods and that this led to several lost games.

LTI-USP: The motivation of the second brazilian team, (one professor and 2 students without previous experience in this scenario, was to test the Ja-CaMo framework (CArtAgO, Jason and Moise). They used a centralized approach for coordinating the agents and communication via speech-acts. 300 person-hours were invested and 3000 lines of code (a third in AgentSpeak, the rest in Java) were written.

The strategy was not to divide the game into phases but the agents into three subgroups: two for occupying zones and one for sabotaging the enemy. Communication with the server was through the EISMASSIM interface. The repairer agents stay where they are and wait until damaged agents come and see them. The sentinels always parry when an opponent saboteur is there and the own saboteurs always attack opponents in the same vertex.

No defense strategy has been implemented and the team claims that this was responsible for not doing better in the contest (zones were instable).

AiWYX: The chinese team consisted of just one person, a bachelor of science. He has a background in knowledge representation, game theories and distributed algorithms and used just plain C++. He invested ca. 250 person-hours and wrote 10000 lines of code. No agent programming technology was used at all, the system was centralized, all agents share their knowledge to build the map.

The strategy is to first go for areas where nobody else is and trying to expand them. If enemies attack, the agents draw back and look for better zones rather than attacking the enemies. Agents can dynamically change their behaviour at run-time. A big problem was that the agents did not attack the enemy team and that attacks from the enemy were not parried in a suitable way which resulted in instability of the zones.

PGIM: The iranian team consisted of one scientist and three students. They invested 8000 person-hours in total, using 7000 lines of code, to develop a decentralized system. After careful evaluation they chose Prometheus and Jack.

Due to licensing problems, they could not use Jack and had to redo all in Java. Due to some misunderstanding of the scenario, they chose to first attack and destroy the opponents repairer agent, then to attack other agents and only in the third place to consider building zones.

Instability of the zones and not being able to conquer zones of some value were the main drawbacks.

Streett: This team consisted of an american student who, unfortunately, did not provide us with any information about his team.

4   Interesting Simulations

In this section we analyse three of the most interesting games using our newly developed statistics module. This involves analysing the following charts: (1) summed-up scores, (2) zone scores and achievement scores, (3) zone stabilities.

The summed-up score consists of the achievement-score plus the zone-score. Note that the achievement score decreases, when the buy action is executed.

Summed-Up Scores: This chart depicts the summed-up score of each team in each step of the current simulation.

Zone Scores and Achievement Scores: This chart combines the charts for the step-score (zone-scores + achievement-scores) and the achievement-scores. The zone-score derives from the number and value of the currently dominated nodes, while the achievement score sums up (across all categories) all the achievements so far.

Zone Stabilities: This chart depicts the zone stabilities of each team in each step of the current simulation. The zone stability increases for one team, if the team can hold all conquered nodes over a longer period of time. If nodes are lost, the value decreases. The exact computation is as follows: For each node that is dominated by a team in a certain step the counter is increased by one. If the team does not dominate the node anymore the counter is reset. The overall zone stability is then the sum of all node counter values.

4.1   SMADAS-UFSC vs. Python-DTU – Simulation 1

The first simulation of the match between SMADAS-UFSC and Python-DTU was a close victory for the winners of the contest, by 127.546 to 121.312. The complete visualization of the simulation can be downloaded from our webpage[9]. Both teams started even, with a very small edge to Python-DTU in the first few steps. Then, SMADAS-UFSC took over from step 35 until step 259. Python-DTU managed to recover the lead at that point for around 50 steps but with no considerable difference. Finally, SMADAS-UFSC took over again from step 309 until the end of the simulation, with a tendency to further increase the score difference. Figure 2, which shows the summed scores at each step, presents this visually.

---

[9] http://www.multiagentcontest.org/downloads?func=fileinfo&id=1133

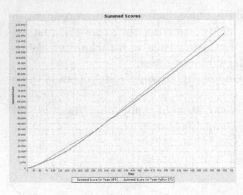

Fig. 2. SMADAS-UFSC vs. Python-DTU (Sim 1): Summed scores

Fig. 3. SMADAS-UFSC vs. Python-DTU (Sim 1): Step-scores and Achievement points

Figure 3 shows the *step-score* at each step (i.e., the value of the zone plus the unused achievement points at each step). To better display how the score is composed, also the unused achievement points at each step are displayed in the figure. Changes in step-score suggest that both teams attempted to conquer differentiated overlapping zones, as both teams maintained their zone value always above a relatively high minimum, but at several points in the graph the increase in the score for one team is correlated with a decrease in the opponent's score.

Achievements and Buying Strategy. Also from Figure 3 it becomes clear that the difference in achievement points is much more significant than the difference in the total score. Even though Python-DTU had more valuable zones during most steps of the simulation, SMADAS-UFSC earned more points per step because of achievement points. The buying strategy proved to be crucial: the clever strategy implemented by SMADAS-UFSC, which consisted in buying improvements for only one of their saboteurs in an attempt to drive the other teams to spend more achievement points in more agents, worked perfectly in this case. Both teams earned the same number of achievements points: 68. But Python-DTU spent 48 of those points improving the saboteurs, whereas SMADAS-UFSC only used 16 for improving one of theirs. This meant a difference that at the end of the match was of 32 extra points per step for SMADAS-UFSC with little variations after step 350, which was not easily compensated by the zone-score. A point to remark here is that doubling the number of agents per team with regards to the previous edition of the Multi-Agent Programming Contest increased the efficacy of this strategy.

It is worth noticing that, while SMADAS-UFSC attempted to start their buying strategy as early as possible (and also to earn as many achievements as early as possible), Python-DTU's approach was to compensate for the aggressive buying strategy by delaying the first round of buys until step 150. Half of the 16 achievement points spent by SMADAS-UFSC were spent before step 10. Their strategy also attempted to detect whether the other time was buying improvements to limit their own buys, and that explains the later buys at step 175.

Nevertheless, even when in general the buying strategy played in favor of UFSC-SMADAS, there seems to be a correlation between the first bulk of buys for Python-DTU at step 150 and an increase in their step scores. On the other hand, at that point of the simulation both teams were still scattered on the map and had not yet committed to defend a certain area.

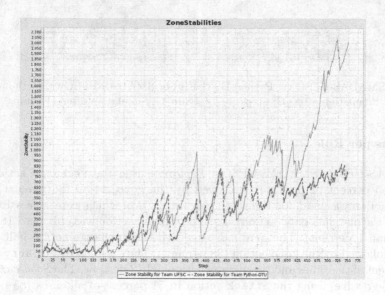

Fig. 4. SMADAS-UFSC vs. Python-DTU (Sim 1): Zones' Stability

Zone Stability. The *zone-stability*[10] graph in Figure 4 reaffirms the idea of overlapping but differentiated zones. Both teams' zone-stability have a clear tendency towards increasing, which means that a number of nodes remain unchallenged. At the same time, none of the zone-stability lines is smooth, which means that several nodes were being lost and recovered during simulation.

Two examples of area domination, one for each team, are presented in Figures 5 and 6. In Figure 5, at step 338 the value of the zone for Python-DTU was 223 and 140 for SMADAS-UFSC. In Figure 6, at step 417 those were respectively 160 and 219.

---

[10] The *zone-stability* is a measure that increases when a team keeps dominance of a node, without taking into account the values of the nodes. It was designed for post-match analysis only, as it is not used for computing the scores.

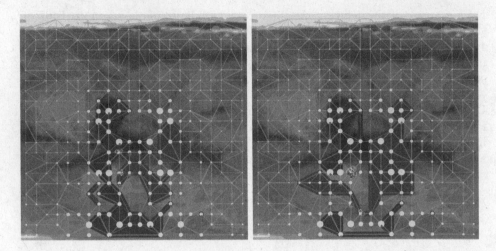

Fig. 5. SMADAS-UFSC vs. Python-DTU (Sim 1): Simulation after 338 steps

Fig. 6. SMADAS-UFSC vs. Python-DTU (Sim 1): Simulation after 417 steps

Actions per Role

SMADAS-UFSC. SMADAS-UFSC's *Explorers* used the `recharge` action the most, 55 percent of the times, followed by the `goto` action (35 percent). The `probe` action was used 303 times (10 percent), 302 of which were successful even though the map had only 300 vertices. The `survey` action was only used 16 times (less than 1 percent). The *Sentinels* executed the `recharge` action half of the times, followed by the `goto` action (38 percent). They also used the `parry` action 10 percent of the times and the `survey` action only 2 percent. The *Saboteurs* were quite aggressive, using the `attack` action in 51 percent of all cases (85 percent of the attacks were successful). The `recharge` action was used 32 percent of the times, And the `goto` action in only 16 percent of the cases, meaning they were somehow static. The `survey` action was also only used in less than 1 percent of the times (18) and the `buy` action, as mentioned before, was used 8 times. The *Repairers* executed `goto`, `recharge` and `repair` close to a third of the times each (39 percent, 30 percent, and 28 percent respectively). They also chose the `survey` action and the `parry` action around 1 percent of the times each. Finally, the *Inspectors* used mainly the `recharge` action (58 percent) followed by the `goto` action (38 percent). The `survey` action was used only 63 times (2 percent) and the `inspect` action even less, 33 times (1 percent).

Python-DTU. The *Explorers* from Python-DTU used the `recharge` action extensively, 75 percent of the times. The `goto` action, in contrast, was used 15 percent of the times. The `probe` action was used on 305 occasions (10 percent), of which 300 were successful (the number of vertices on the map). The `survey` action was used only in two occasions. The *Sentinels* also used the `recharge` action 75 percent the times. It was followed by the `parry` action, 13 percent of the times, although less than half of the parries were successful. They used the goto action even less than the Explorers, only 8 percent of the times. They also used the survey action 5 percent of the times. The *Saboteurs* used the attack action 38 percent of the times (76 percent of the attacks were successful). The recharge and goto actions were used 30 percent of the times each. The buy action was used 24 times. They used the survey action only once. The *Repairers* executed the goto action 35 percent of the times and the repair action 34 percent. The third choice was the recharge action, 26 percent of the times. They opted for the parry action 83 times (3 percent, less than half of the parries were successful) and for the survey action 36 times (1 percent). Finally, the *Inspectors* used the recharge action the most (67 percent). They used the inspect action much more than they rivals (24 percent) and the goto action much less (9 percent). They only surveyed in 4 occasions.

4.2 SMADAS-UFSC vs. Python-DTU – Simulation 2

The second simulation of the match between the winners and runner-ups of the contest was won by the latter, by an even closer score of 120.450 to 115.076. Thus Python-DTU maintained the lead during the whole simulation, although SMADAS-UFSC reduced that difference to just 2.474 points at step 578. This is shown in Figure 7. The complete visualization of the simulation can be downloaded at our webpage [11].

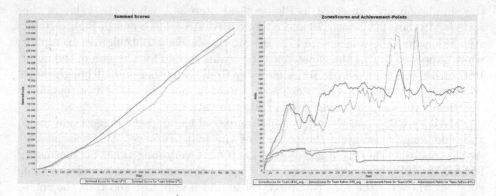

Fig. 7. SMADAS-UFSC vs. Python-DTU (Sim 2): Summed scores

Fig. 8. SMADAS-UFSC vs. Python-DTU (Sim 2): Step-scores and Achievement points

Zone Scores and Stability. Figure 8 presents the Step-scores and achievement points at each step of simulation 2. In spite of the two high peaks in the score for SMADAS-UFSC, the advantage for Python-DTU was clear during most of the simulation.

---

[11] http://www.multiagentcontest.org/downloads?func=fileinfo&id=1120

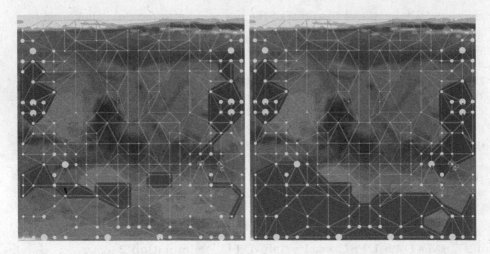

Fig. 9. SMADAS-UFSC vs. Python-DTU (Sim 2): Simulation after 362 steps

Fig. 10. SMADAS-UFSC vs. Python-DTU (Sim 2): Simulation after 481 steps

The map in this simulation has different characteristics compared to the first simulation: The most valuable nodes were scattered towards the outer edges of the graph. A clear pattern of which zones each team would attempt to dominate and keep, did not emerge until around step 250. Two different moments during the simulation are presented in Figure 9, at step 362, where the value of the zone for Python-DTU was 176 and 64 for SMADAS-UFSC; and in Figure 10, at step 481, where the values were 172 and 243 respectively. Both figures exemplify what happened during the game, once the teams settled for a region of the map: Python-DTU conquered two zones far away from each other, and although those zones were not very big, they were very stable: In fact, one of the two remained practically unchanged during most of the simulation.

SMADAS-UFSC, on the other hand, managed to build the biggest and most valuable zone by isolating the bottom of the map. However, this was an unstable zone that they were not able to keep for a very long time. Furthermore, SMADAS-UFSC's agents were not standing on the most valuable nodes of that zone, so whenever the zone collapsed, those nodes were lost and thus the zone-score decreased significantly.

Figure 11 shows this difference with respect to zone-stability for each team. As zone-stability takes into account the number of nodes in the zones, the two peaks in the zone-score of SMADAS-UFSC are also slightly reflected in the zone-stability graph. Nevertheless, zone-stability for Python-DTU is still much higher.

Achievements and Buying Strategy. During the second simulation, the buying strategy applied was the same as during the first one. This time, SMADAS-UFSC earned 68 achievement points and spent 14, whereas Python-DTU earned

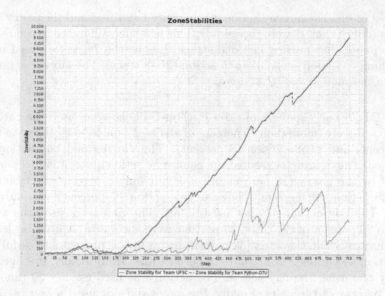

Fig. 11. SMADAS-UFSC vs. Python-DTU (Sim 2): Zones' Stability

66 and used 40. Nonetheless, as it can be seen in Figure 8, during this simulation the difference in achievement-points was not enough to compensate the difference in the zone-scores.

Actions per Role

SMADAS-UFSC. The *Explorers* of team SMADAS-UFSC used the `recharge` action in 61 percent of all cases, followed by `goto` (31 percent) and `probe` (8 percent). The `survey` action was only executed 10 times and the `buy` action was not used at all. Also, the *Sentinels* spend a lot of their time for recharging, i.e., the `recharge` action was used in 60 percent of all cases. Additionally, the main actions for this role were the `goto` action (31 percent) and the `parry` action (7 percent / 5 percent successful). Although the intended main purpose of the sentinel was to be used for surveying the edges the `survey` action was just used in 2 percent of the cases. Probably, because of the high visibility range of this role together with the information of the other roles these few executions were still enough. Finally, this type of agent did not `buy` anything. The behaviour of the *Saboteurs* was implemented in the following way. The `attack` command was executed 1302 times, i.e., in 43 percent of all cases, and was almost always successful (1123 times or 37 percent). The `recharge` action (37 percent) and the `goto` action (19 percent) were the second and third most used actions. The `survey` (25 times) and `buy` (7 times) action were only used sometimes, however the `buy` action was only used by this particular role. The main purpose of the *Repairers* was to go to some agents and repair them, therefore the `goto` (37 percent), the `recharge` (34 percent), and the `repair` (26 percent) action were used most often. The `survey` action was executed 42 times and the `parry` action 37 times (out of that 21 were successful). This is a huge difference to the Python-DTU Repairer that parried just one attack. Lastly, the *Inspectors* used mainly the `recharge` (72 percent) and `goto` action (25 percent). The `survey` action was used 53 times and `inspect` 20 times.

Python-DTU. The *Explorers* of team Python-DTU however used the `recharge` action extensively (more than 75 percent of all cases), followed by the `goto` action (14 percent) and `probe` action (8 percent). The `survey` and `buy` action were never used. The *Sentinels* executed the `recharge` action quite often (62 percent), followed by the `parry` (18 percent in total, but only 6 percent successful) and the `goto` action (12 percent). The `survey` action (7 percent) was only used seldom. The `buy` action was not used at all. The *Saboteurs* used the `attack` action in 39 percent of the cases. 33 percent were successful. A little bit less was the `recharge` action executed (33 percent in total / 30 percent successful). The `goto` action was applied in 27 out of hundred times. Additionally, this agent was the only one using the `buy` action. The action was used exactly 20 times, i.e., in 0.67 percent of the cases. Finally, the agent did not use the `survey` action once. The *Repairers* executed `goto` in 38 of the cases, followed by the `repair` (28 percent) and `recharge` action (33 percent in total / 31 percent successful). The `survey` action was used 17 times, the `parry` action just three times (out of that only one was successful) and the `buy` action was never executed. Finally, the *Inspectors* used mainly the `recharge` action (83 percent), followed by `inspect` (11 percent) and `goto` (5 percent). The `survey` action was executed 5 times and `buy` was never used.

4.3   PGIM vs. AiWYX – Simulation 1

The team *AiWYX* clearly won all simulations against *PGIM*. While the first simulation ended 81562 to 212016, the second resulted in 68748 to 107600 and the last in 75846 to 112466. The final position of *AiWYX* was 5 and *PGIM* got the 6th place.

During the beginning of the match both teams were at the same level. At step 170 *AiWYX* conquered an area of more than 640 nodes but was not able to keep it for a longer period (cf. Figure 14). At step 312 *AiWYX* finally stabilized its zone(s) (cf. Figure 16 and 15). The team *PGIM*, however, was not able to conquer zones larger as 160 nodes and got therefore only the achievement for holding 80 nodes at the same time.

AiWYX used a novel strategy (not seen in the competition so far) for building zones: Instead of trying to conquer a small zone, probing the nodes in order to increase the value of the zone and finally defending, the team was positioning itself around an opponent's zone and thereby isolating the opponents zone from the rest of the graph. Figure 14 shows such a zone. At step 312 *AiWYX* finally stabilized its zone(s) (cf. Figure 15 and 16). As one can see this resulted in very large zones, basically containing all nodes the opponents did not conquer.

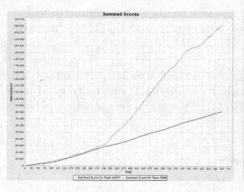

Fig. 12. PGIM vs. AiWYX (Sim 1): Summed scores

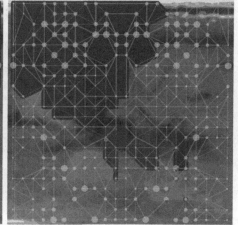

Fig. 13. PGIM vs. AiWYX (Sim 1): Step-scores and Achievement points

Fig. 14. Simulation after 170 steps

Fig. 15. Simulation after 312 steps

Nevertheless due to the lack of probing all conquered nodes the team $AiWYX$ did not score all possible points but only a small subset. Additionally, the strategy was highly depending on the size of the map and more effective on larger maps. That is probably the reason why the team $AiWYX$ scored the most points per simulation but did not reach a better place in the competition.

The complete visualization of the simulation can be downloaded from our webpage [12]. In the following, we will discuss this simulation in more detail.

Scores. The evolution of the zone scores and achievement points are depicted in Figure 13. While the development of the achievement points is similar (both teams did not invest the points for agent improvements), the flows of the zone

---

[12] http://www.multiagentcontest.org/downloads?func=fileinfo&id=1148

scores are different. From step 0 to 300 it was a head to head competition but after step 312 *AiWYX* was able to occupy a large zone and *PGIM* was not able to increase its zone score anymore.

Zone Stability. The zone stability of team *PGIM* was low, i.e., under 500 points per step. In contrast, the zone stability of *AiWYX* was quite good and was almost always higher than that for *PGIM*. This is one reason why the team *AiWYX* won the match.

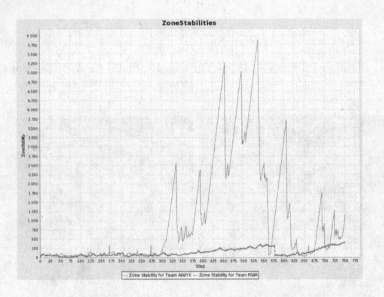

Fig. 16. PGIM vs. AiWYX (Sim 1): Zones' Stability

Achievements. The team *AiWYX* conquered a zone with an impressive value of 640 points, attacked 640 times the opponents successfully, probed 160 nodes, and surveyed 640 edges. Additionally, It inspected 20 times an opponent. An interesting fact is that the agents did not try to parry an attack.

The team *PGIM* made the following highest achievements: It conquered an area of 80 nodes, attacked 320 successfully, probed 80 nodes and surveyed 640 edges. It inspected 10 times an opponent and parried 40 times attacks successfully.

Actions per Role

AiWYX. The *Explorers* of team *AiWYX* used the `recharge` action extensively (more than 50 percent of all cases), followed by the `goto` action (35 percent) and `probe` action (10 percent). The `survey` action was just used in just 1.7 percent. The *Sentinels* executed the `recharge` action quite often (53 percent), followed by the `goto` action (32 percent) and the `survey` action (4 percent). The *Saboteurs* used the `goto` action in 42 percent of the cases, followed by the `attack` (35 percent) and `recharge` action (22 percent). The *Repairers* executed `goto` in 54 the cases, followed by the `repair` (26 percent) and `recharge` action (18 percent). Finally, the *Inspectors* used mainly the `goto` (41 percent) and `recharge` action (56 percent). The `inspect` was just used 18 times (0.6 percent). `survey` was executed in 1.73 percent of the cases.

PGIM. The *Explorers* of team *PGIM* however used the `goto` action in 56 percent of all cases. 19 percent of the time they executed the `skip` action which does not have an effect. It would be more efficient to use the `recharge` action instead. This action was used in 11 percent of the cases. Finally, `probe` and `survey` were executed 8 and 5 percent of the times. The behaviour of the *Sentinels* was not optimal. The `skip` action was the most often used action (49 percent) followed by a `goto` command (37 percent). `parry` (2 percent), `survey` (4 percent), and `recharge` (8 percent) were just used seldom. Also the behaviour of the *Saboteurs* was not implemented in a good way. The `skip` action was used 1304 times, i.e., 43 percent of all cases although a `recharge` (13 percent) would be more efficient. The `goto` action was executed in 27 percent of all cases, followed by `survey` (3 percent) and `attack` (14 percent). For the *Repairers* the `goto` action was the main action (48 percent). This was followed by the `repair` (18 percent) and `recharge` action (21 percent). The `skip` action was executed 296 times, that corresponds to 10 percent. `survey` was used 84 times, i.e., 2,8 percent. The *Inspectors* used mainly the `goto` action (55 percent), followed by `skip` (26 percent) while `recharge` (14 percent) would be the better option. `survey` was used in 4 percent of the cases and `inspect` just 21 times (0,7 percent).

5   Summary, Conclusion and Future of the Contest

This paper provides an overview of the most recent edition of the Multi-Agent Programming Contest. We have introduced the Contest in general, and we elaborated on the current scenario in a more detailed way. We have also introduced the teams that took part and evaluated their performance. We compared three of the more interesting matches using our new visualisation and statistics modules.

This is our third newly designed scenario that we will also use, with some modifications and lessons learned from the 2012 edition, for the Contest in 2013. It is time to lean back and consider what we have achieved so far. *What conclusions (if any) can we draw from the "Agents on Mars" scenario? Can we observe some trends in the quality of the teams? What is the impact on the ProMAS community?* While these are critical and difficult questions that might be answered differently by different people, we collect a few observations that we consider relevant.

- Both times a dedicated Multi-Agent Programming Language/Platform won, but runner-up was Python-DTU, which did not use a dedicated platform, but was inspired by MAS technology.

Nevertheless, other examples (e.g., the teams ranked 5–7 in this years edition) show that ad hoc implementations seem to perform worse than MAS inspired systems.

- The introduction of a qualification round increased the stability of the teams and therefore the whole contest a lot. This feature will be kept.
- Teams performing for the second time usually perform better. But the winners were both first time participants.
- The contest helped a lot to find bugs in the used platforms. This is an observation we made throughout the history of the contest. So it seems the scenario is demanding and most features of the used platform/language are indeed used (so that potential bugs surface). One team participated exactly because of this reason (testing their platform).
- We usually end up with as few as 7 to 9 teams that seriously want to participate. We believe this number could be much higher and does not really show a great impact on our community. On the other hand we have quite a variation: it is not always the same participants. Over the last 3 years, we had 20 different teams participating.
- The overall performance of the teams improved a lot with each new contest, although we increased the complexity considerably (size of the map, number of agents, difficulty of the task).
- Compared with the *cows and cowboys* scenario, we see much more cooperation among the agents, more dynamic behaviour, and a lot more interaction with the opposing team. In addition, the data to be handled (observing the environment, messages between the agents) has also increased a lot. While we have not yet excluded centralized approaches, the sheer amount of data makes it difficult for the systems to provide each agent with the central memory of the whole system.

    Also, in the current scenario, the computational costs of Dijkstra's algorithm is high so that it is not feasible for all agents to execute it at the same time.
- In the current scenario, there are indications that buying health and strength is much more important than investing the money for other reasons. Thus it may pay off to find a more balanced scenario that allows for more diverse strategies of the teams. This point makes us reconsider the precise values of the different parameter we have in our scenario.

The amount of work that went into implementing a team varied from one person with 250 person-hours to 6 people with 800 person hours and from 1500 to 10000 lines of code (the latter because no dedicated technology was used, interestingly, that was done by one single person).

It would be interesting to assess if it would be beneficial to steer the Contest into a more specialized direction in order to strengthen its niche in the research ecology. This includes but is not limited to focusing on the planning aspect of the competition, leaving behind path planning as the main facet of agent deliberation.

We could also focus on using a massive number of agents: lots of agents with different roles and thus different capabilities. This would allow us to take into account the scalability of agent-oriented programming platforms.

Additionally it would be worthwhile to focus on agent communication and to evaluate that aspect of the tournament by routing agent-messages through the *MASSim* server for proper evaluation.

Last but not least, the most important part of the contest are the contestants: We hope to attract more teams in the future — the contest is an excellent opportunity for a student project on Bachelor or Master level.

References

1. Behrens, T., Dastani, M., Dix, J., Köster, M., Novák, P. (eds.): Special Issue about Multi-Agent-Contest. Annals of Mathematics and Artificial Intelligence, vol. 59. Springer, Netherlands (2010)
2. Behrens, T., Dastani, M., Dix, J., Hübner, J., Köster, M., Novák, P., Schlesinger, F.: The Multi-Agent Programming Contest. AI Magazine 33(4), 111 (2012), https://www.aaai.org/ojs/index.php/aimagazine/article/view/2439
3. Behrens, T., Dix, J., Köster, M., Hübner, J.: The Multi-Agent Programming Contest: Environment Interface and Contestants in 2010. Annals of Mathematics and Artificial Intelligence, Netherlands, vol. 61(4). Springer (2011)
4. Behrens, T.M., Dastani, M., Dix, J., Novák, P.: Agent contest competition: 4th edition. In: Hindriks, K.V., Pokahr, A., Sardina, S. (eds.) ProMAS 2008. LNCS (LNAI), vol. 5442, pp. 211–222. Springer, Heidelberg (2009)
5. Behrens, T., Dix, J., Hübner, J., Köster, M., Schlesinger, F.: MAPC 2011 Documentation. Technical Report IfI-12-01, Clausthal University of Technology (December 2012)
6. Behrens, T., Dix, J., Hübner, J., Köster, M., Schlesinger, F.: MAPC 2011 Evaluation and Team Descriptions. Technical Report IfI-12-02, Clausthal University of Technology (December 2012)
7. Behrens, T., Hindriks, K., Dix, J.: Towards an environment interface standard for agent platforms. Annals of Mathematics and Artificial Intelligence 61, 3–38 (2011)
8. Behrens, T., Köster, M., Schlesinger, F., Dix, J., Hübner, J.F.: The Multi-agent Programming Contest 2011: A Résumé. In: Dennis, L.A., Boissier, O., Bordini, R.H. (eds.) ProMAS 2011. LNCS, vol. 7217, pp. 155–172. Springer, Heidelberg (2012)
9. Dastani, M., Dix, J., Novak, P.: The first contest on multi-agent systems based on computational logic. In: Toni, F., Torroni, P. (eds.) CLIMA VI. LNCS (LNAI), vol. 3900, pp. 373–384. Springer, Heidelberg (2006)
10. Dastani, M., Dix, J., Novák, P.: The second contest on multi-agent systems based on computational logic. In: Inoue, K., Satoh, K., Toni, F. (eds.) CLIMA VII. LNCS (LNAI), vol. 4371, pp. 266–283. Springer, Heidelberg (2007)
11. Dastani, M., Dix, J., Novák, P.: Agent contest competition: 3rd edition. In: Dastani, M., El Fallah Seghrouchni, A., Ricci, A., Winikoff, M. (eds.) ProMAS 2007. LNCS (LNAI), vol. 4908, pp. 221–240. Springer, Heidelberg (2008)
12. Köster, M., Schlesinger, F., Dix, J.: MAPC 2012 Evaluation and Team Descriptions. Technical Report IfI-13-01, Clausthal University of Technology (January 2013)

SMADAS: A Cooperative Team for the Multi-Agent Programming Contest Using Jason

Maicon Rafael Zatelli, Daniela Maria Uez, José Rodrigo Neri,
Tiago Luiz Schmitz, Jéssica Pauli de Castro Bonson, and Jomi Fred Hübner

Department of Automation and Systems Engineering
Federal University of Santa Catarina
CP 476, 88040-900 Florianópolis - SC - Brasil
{xsplyter,dani.uez,jrf.neri,tiagolschmitz,jpbonson}@gmail.com,
jomi@das.ufsc.br

Abstract. In this paper we describe the SMADAS system used for the Multi-Agent Programming Contest in 2012. This contest offers an useful context to evaluate tools, techniques, and languages for programming MAS. It is also a good opportunity to learn agent programming and test new features we are developing in our projects. Throughout the paper we highlight the main strategies of our team and comment on the advantages and disadvantages of our system as well as some improvements that still could be done. One important result from this experience regards the agent programming language we used, it provides suitable abstractions for the development of complex system and shows an increment in its maturity since no bugs was discovered this year.

1 Introduction

The empirical evaluation of proposals in the context of Multi-Agent Systems (MAS) is a quite complex task and the Multi-Agent Programming Contest [1,3][1] offers an useful context for doing this evaluation. In particular, the latest Mars scenario has emphasised solutions based on cooperation, coordination, and decentralisation which are important topics for our research. This contest is thus selected as the environment to evaluate the proposals being developed by the authors in their master and Phd thesis. Among the authors, we have one PhD student, three master students, and one undergraduate student. The main approach is (*i*) to develop a *base* MAS for the contest, then (*ii*) the master and PhD students will change the base system using their corresponding proposals, and finally (*iii*) each proposal can be evaluated and compared against the base system. In this paper we report the development and the main features of this base team, called SMADAS (the acronym of our research group). Another objective for attending the contest is to improve the experience in developing MAS. Since most of the authors are just beginning on the domain, the concrete experience is important for their overall learning and maturity in critical analysis.

---

[1] http://multiagentcontest.org

M. Dastani, J.F. Hübner, and B. Logan (Eds.): ProMAS 2012, LNAI 7837, pp. 196–204, 2013.

2   System Analysis and Design

For the analysis of our systems, we adopted a prototype driven approach instead of a well known software engineering methodology because the problem seemed quite simple to solve and we had no experience with them. Thus we decided that it was better to use our time developing the system than learning a methodology.

Based on the agent contest scenario description, we divided the overall problem in sub-problems, each one analysed in detail: exploration, exploitation, attack and defense, buy, repair, and inspection. A team member was engaged with programming each strategy discussed on biweekly meetings. Forty five versions of the system were produced in this phase. These versions were tested and compared with the best teams from the last contest [6,8,7,2] and also against our own versions of the system in order to select the most efficient one. In these preliminary tests, we identified some good strategies for the final implementation. To develop the SMADAS system, we spent about 500 hours, most of them testing the strategies.

The system has 20 agents of five types: repairer, saboteur, explorer, sentinel, and inspector. We considered two main distinct phases: exploration, in which the explorers identify all vertices and nodes in the map and find the best zones, and exploitation, where all agents try to conquest and defend these zones. During the match, if an agent senses a nearby enemy it calls a saboteur to attack it, and also if the agent is damaged it tries to find a repairer to be fixed.

Our agents are able to decide their own actions, however this autonomy produces some conflicting situations like two agents deciding to exploit different zones. These situations are solved using a centralized approach, which consists of a specific agent been responsible for the group decision. For example, one of the explorers defines the zones to exploit and one of the repairers defines the reparation order. Some conflicting situations are simply prevented by using a predefined priority order among the agents, where agents with higher priorities acts before agents with less priority.

The coordination among the agents is based on two communication mechanisms: blackboard and message exchanging. The blackboard is used to provide a global graph view to the agents, since some important information about the graph structure is synchronized in it. We decided to use a blackboard because the agents need an overall view of the scenario to be able to define the system exploitation strategy. The message exchanging is used to share information about the inspected enemies, the ally agent actions and damages, and about the map zones. The communication protocol used when a damaged agent needs to be repaired is shown in Fig. 1. It consists of the agent asking a repairer that contacts the other repairers to find out which one is the closest to the damaged agent. Then the other repairers inform their positions and the closest one is selected to repair the damaged agent. Thus, the selected repairer will send to the damaged agent the meeting path.

The SMADAS system is a truly MAS because the agents are autonomous, reactive, and proactive. They have autonomy to decide how and when to execute most of their actions, except the few conflicting situations explained before.

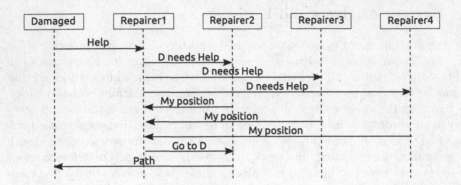

Fig. 1. A communication protocol used to define which repairer will repair a damaged agent. The damaged agent asks the `repairer1` for help, the `repairer1` then contacts the others repairers to find which one is the closest to the damaged agent. All repairer send their position and the `repairer1` elects the closest one. The selected repairer then sends the meet point to the damaged agent.

However, the agents also perform some actions in reaction to environment events, like the start of the step or a received message. Other reactive actions occurs when a saboteur attacks an enemy agent that is in the same vertex or when an agent runs away or defends itself from an enemy saboteur on the same vertex. Furthermore, the agents have a proactive behaviour, that shows up when they try to find a better vertex that improves the team score, contact the repairer when they are damaged, or look for enemies to attack.

3   Strategies

In our strategy both individual and group behavior are important. While the individual behavior is important when the agents are isolated in the map, the group behaviour is responsible for preventing redundant actions and for producing a coherent and cooperative global result. The agents are proactive in order to get achievement points and obtaining a good score. They also use their beliefs and the exchanged information to decide their next action.

As commented in the previous section, we consider two main strategies: exploration and exploitation. In the exploration phase the agents just explore the map and try to get as most achievement points as possible. After step 15, our agents go to a good zone to conquer it.

Since achievement points are important and they accumulate in each one of the 750 steps, it is desirable to obtain them as soon as possible. However, some achievements are more complicated to conquer after some time, hence they can be ignored. For example, it does not make sense to survey all edges in the graph, considering it takes a long time to be performed. Instead of it, our agents stay in a vertex getting more score by exploiting water wells. For the same reason we are not interested on inspecting all opponent agents, thus our inspectors only inspect them when they are near.

After the exploration phase, the exploitation phase starts. One of our explorers reasons about which are the two best zones in the map to be exploited. Exploiting two zones is advantageous since the map is symmetric and it is particularly important against teams that keep only one zone. In order to do that, we used a modified version of the BFS algorithm, that is run for all vertex, summing their values until some depth. The vertex with the highest sum represents where the best zone is (zone 1). After it, the algorithm tries to find the second best vertex to set the second best zone (zone 2), which may have some intersection with the first one. This algorithm is not optimal because its result is always a circular shape, when the ideal choice often has a free shape.

When the good zones are defined, an explorer organises the agents in two groups, one for zone 1 and another for zone 2. Each group has 10 members, with two agents of each type. The agents are then informed about the central vertex of its zone and how far they can go from it. The central vertex of an area is the one discovered in the exploration phase with the best sum. The distance they can go from it defines the border of the corresponding zone. After it, the agents are positioned in their zones. The non-saboteur agents take positions in vertices that have two neighbour vertices belonging to our team, but without anyone there. The saboteur agents scout their zones and attack opponents inside it, they also attack near enemy zones. We assume that if the enemy zone is not near, the opponent probably has a small zone and we do not need to attack them.

Table 1 shows the strategies and plans for each type of agent. There are plans with more steps (buy, repair, probe) and plans where the agents simply react (attack, parry, inspect, recharge, survey). We noticed that usually long-term plans are not a good idea, because the environment changes quickly. The strategies are explained in more details below.

- Buy: we concluded that it is be better to do not buy many things. We noticed it through tests between our MAS with a buying strategy where the agents buy more things against one where the agents just buy few things, and the second strategy won all matches in all simulations. Firstly the buying strategy consisted of only buying upgrades for the saboteurs: buy sabotage devices to have a strength equal to the highest enemy saboteur health value, and buy shields to have health one time greater than the highest enemy saboteur strength value. We did a second version of this strategy where just one saboteur (Hulk) buys upgrades, this had the benefit of decreasing our expenses while also making agent teams with a similar strategy waste money. Another improvement of the buying strategy was the addition of an agent named Coach, which received information about our enemies upgrades from the inspectors and used them to notice whether the enemy team is buying or not, if they were not buying anything this agent informs the agent Hulk to stop buying upgrades in the matches against this team and then save achievement points.

– Attack: the saboteurs always attack the opponent saboteurs first, and then the repairers. However, in the initial steps, attacking the explorers would be a good second option too, since it would be harder for the opponent team to explore the map. In order to prevent redundant attacks, there is a hierarchy defining which saboteur attacks first.

– Repair: the repair strategy consists of finding the closest available repairer to help a disabled agent, after it the repairer and the damaged agent move close to each other. If there are no available repairers the disabled agent moves to the closest repairer. If there is another closest disabled agent to repair or another repairer, they cancel the process and start it again with the closest agent.

– Parry: if there is an opponent saboteur in the same vertex that our agents, the formula $1/N$ defines the parrying probability, where N is the number of ally agents in the same vertex. This way we can prevent all agents from parrying the same saboteur. Our agents do not parry if there are more or the same number of ally saboteurs and opponent saboteurs, since the opponent probably will attack our saboteurs first. If an agent chooses not to parry, then it leaves the vertex.

– Probe: the explorers always probe the closest unprobed vertex and they repeat it until all vertices are probed. To avoid explorers probing the same vertex, there is a hierarchy which defines the explorers who act first.

– Inspect: the inspectors always inspects near enemies, the aim of inspection is to identify enemy saboteurs and to check if the opponent is using a buying strategy.

– Recharge: the agents always check if they have enough energy before doing an action, if they do not have or it is less than 2 points, then they recharge. They also recharge when they do not have any action to do.

– Survey: the agents only survey if there is an unsurveyed near edge. The sentinels are the main agents responsible for doing survey, but other agents do it too if they do not have anything to do in the step.

Table 1. Implemented strategies by agent type

Action	Repairer	Saboteur	Explorer	Sentinel	Inspector
buy		x(Hulk)			
attack		x			
repair	x				
parry	x			x	
probe			x		
inspect					x
recharge	x	x	x	x	x
goto	x	x	x	x	x
survey	x	x	x	x	x

Finally, there are strategies to expand the team zone and to stop expanding. The goal of the first one is to conquer more vertices in the same zone: when an agent is participating in a zone occupation and it can go to another vertex without breaking the zone, it will do it. The second strategy stops the agents from expanding when they have a high score and to wait for the opponents reaction.

4   Software Architecture

This section describes the technologies and frameworks that we used to develop our agents and how they are integrated. We used the EISMASSim framework [4] to communicate with the contest server, since the competition is built on Java MASSim platform and Java EISMASSim framework is distributed with the competition files. The programming language used to develop our agents is Jason (version 1.3.8) [5]. Its concept of BDI agents provided useful resources to build our agents, like plans and intentions, which allowed us to implement the strategies and to provide our agents with long-term goals. Another advantage of Jason is its interpreter that allow us to call Java methods, which simplifies the implementation of some algorithms and enables them to run faster. These methods are integrated with our Jason agents using internal actions. More specifically we implemented two algorithms as Java methods: Dijkstra algorithm to find the best path between vertices and Breadth-First Search algorithm to locate the best area in the graph.

A blackboard was used to share and build knowledge about the environment in the form of a graph. The process to update information in the graph has a high computational cost, lasting more than one step. Therefore, to avoid losing steps, the graph is updated and shared every three steps. The agent interaction is divided in two modes: agent-to-environment and agent-to-agent. In the first mode, in each step the EISMASSim framework receives an XML text from the server with the agents percepts, these percepts are then translated into Jason environment perceptions for our agents. This translation however does not happen when our team conquers the full map and the quantity of perception is so huge that the agents are not able to process them on time. In this case, perception is disabled and a default action (e.g. recharge) is sent back to the server. The actions of the agents are translated into text and sent to the server by EISMASSim. The Fig. 2 exemplifies how actions and percepts are exchanged. The agent-to-agent interaction uses Jason speech act based communication.

5   Results

We have tried to develop a system as complete as possible and we created several strategies for each system feature, like exploring, exploiting, buying, repairing, and attacking. Hence we developed many versions of the system, we exhaustively tested each one against the others to select the more efficient. We also tested our system during the contest test phase against the teams provided by the contest

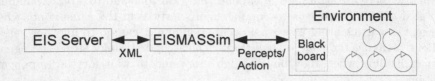

Fig. 2. Communication architecture

organisation. This approach was our main advantage in the contest and one of the reasons we played eighteen matches against six different opponents and won seventeen. However our system has a worse performance when it confronts a passive system because it is not so offensive. If our agents are in a good map zone they do not bother about the opponent: they assume that the opponent is not in a good area. Also, our agents have no focus on defending a conquered zone and this explains the match we lost against Python-DTU during the contest.

Two main strategies were responsible for the good performance of our system: the buying and exploitation strategies. The buying strategy was decisive because it forced our opponents to reinforce their agents spending a lot of their money. In a match against Python-DTU during the tests phase, for example, we conquered a small area but we won because we had more money. Fig. 3a shows the achievement points from this match. In the step 175 the Python-DTU (in blue) spent most of their money strengthening their agents and SMADAS (in green) spent only a part of its money. In the last 400 steps, from the step 350 to the 750, we had about 23 achievement points in each step, summing 9200 achievement points. In the end, this difference allowed us to win this match, as shown in Fig. 3b.

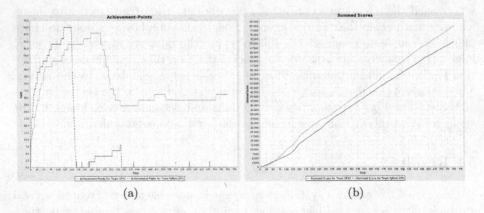

(a)   (b)

Fig. 3. From the step 350, SMADAS-UFSC (in green) has more achievement points than Python-DTU (in blue) (a). This difference has decided the match for SMADAS-UFSC system (b).

Our exploitation strategy chooses two good zones in the map. It was efficient because usually the opponents are concerned about finding and conquering just one good zone. Thus while part of our agents are under attack in one of these zones, the other part are scoring in another zone. This strategy earns less points in each step, because our agents are divided in two smaller zones, but it has better results against an offensive opponent. Fig. 4 shows a comparison from our system performance using these two exploiting strategies. The system in green tries to conquer one single zone and the blue system looks for two zones. The blue system has fewer points at the beginning because it gets two smaller zones. However after some steps where the green system loses many points disputing a single zone, the blue system has one fixed zone scoring without any attack. This strategy was decisive in the match against the AiWYX system.

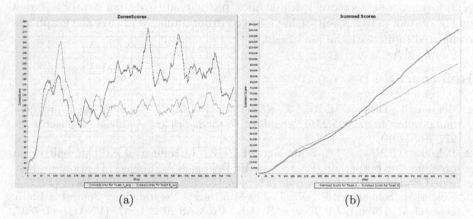

(a)   (b)

Fig. 4. The green system tries to conquer one single zone and the blue system looks for two zones. The blue system finishes the match with a highest score because it keeps scoring in a zone without disputing it with opponents.

6   Conclusion

Participating in the contest was a worthy experience for all the team, we learned a lot about MAS developing and about the tools and languages we used. The contest result, where our team got the first place, is due both to the dedication on developing the strategies described in this papers and to the tools we used. For instance, the Jason programming language supports agent programming with abstract concepts like plans, beliefs, and goals which are suitable for the problem and very expressive. Different from previous participations in the contest where several bugs in Jason were discovered and fixed [9], we did not identify any bug in Jason this year, which shows the maturity of this language. Although we can evaluate the used tools positively in general, some features are still missing. For example, it was very difficult to change, refactor, and debug the agents code since we have 5504 lines of Jason code and 20 agent instances running concurrently. The tools provided by Jason for debugging, like the sniffer and the mind inspector, are too specific and focused on the details. It is a hard task to identify a bug by looking at thousand of mind samples or message traces. High level abstractions and tools are required to help the debugging of complex MAS.

There is still a room for improvements in our system both in the strategies and the tools. Some of the improvements will be investigated in the authors' master and PhD thesis where proposals will be compared against the version of the system described in this paper. One particular drawback of the system is to be focused only on the agent aspect, all the code is "agent programming". More global aspects should be considered, for instance by organisation and interaction programming as first class abstractions. For that, new models and tools need to be developed.

For the current scenario of the contest, we would propose two improvements. (i) Inform opponent's score. It would allow participants to design strategies based on the current match result, rising more confrontations. (ii) Leave the graph less connected to increase the use of edges.

References

1. Behrens, T., Dastani, M., Dix, J., Köster, M., Novák, P.: The multi-agent programming contest from 2005-2010. Annals of Mathematics and Artificial Intelligence 59, 277–311 (2010)
2. Behrens, T., Köster, M., Schlesinger, F., Dix, J., Hübner, J.F.: The multi-agent programming contest 2011: A résumé. In: Dennis, L.A., Boissier, O., Bordini, R.H. (eds.) ProMAS 2011. LNCS, vol. 7217, pp. 155–172. Springer, Heidelberg (2012)
3. Köster, M., Schlesinger, F., Dix, J.: The Multi-agent Programming Contest 2012. In: Dastani, M., Hübner, J.F., Logan, B. (eds.) ProMAS 2012. LNCS (LNAI), vol. 7837, pp. 174–195. Springer, Heidelberg (2013)
4. Behrens, T.M., Hindriks, K.V., Dix, J.: Towards an environment interface standard for agent platforms. Annals of Mathematics and Artificial Intelligence 61(4), 261–295 (2011)
5. Bordini, R.H., Wooldridge, M., Hübner, J.F.: Programming Multi-Agent Systems in AgentSpeak using Jason. John Wiley & Sons (2007)
6. Carr, D., Russell, S., Pete, B., O'Hare, G.M.P., Collier, R.W.: Bogtrotters in space. In: Dennis, L.A., Boissier, O., Bordini, R.H. (eds.) ProMAS 2011. LNCS, vol. 7217, pp. 197–207. Springer, Heidelberg (2012)
7. Dekker, M., Hameete, P., Hegemans, M., Leysen, S., van den Oever, J., Smits, J., Hindriks, K.V.: HactarV2: An agent team strategy based on implicit coordination. In: Dennis, L.A., Boissier, O., Bordini, R.H. (eds.) ProMAS 2011. LNCS, vol. 7217, pp. 173–184. Springer, Heidelberg (2012)
8. Ettienne, M.B., Vester, S., Villadsen, J.: Implementing a multi-agent system in python with an auction-based agreement approach. In: Dennis, L.A., Boissier, O., Bordini, R.H. (eds.) ProMAS 2011. LNCS, vol. 7217, pp. 185–196. Springer, Heidelberg (2012)
9. Hübner, J.F., Bordini, R.H.: Using agent- and organisation-oriented programming to develop a team of agents for a competitive game. Annals of Mathematics and Artificial Intelligence 59(3-4), 351–372 (2010)

Reimplementing a Multi-Agent System in Python

Jørgen Villadsen*, Andreas Schmidt Jensen, Mikko Berggren Ettienne,
Steen Vester, Kenneth Balsiger Andersen, and Andreas Frøsig

Department of Informatics and Mathematical Modelling
Technical University of Denmark
Richard Petersens Plads, Building 321, DK-2800 Kongens Lyngby, Denmark
jv@imm.dtu.dk

Abstract. We provide a brief description of our Python-DTU system,
including the overall design, the tools and the algorithms that we used
in the Multi-Agent Programming Contest 2012, where the scenario was
called Agents on Mars like in 2011. Our solution is an improvement of
our Python-DTU system from last year. Our team ended in second place
after winning at least one match against every opponent and we only lost
to the winner of the tournament. We briefly describe our experiments
with the Moise organizational model. Finally we propose a few areas of
improvement, both with regards to our system and to the contest.

1 Introduction

This paper documents our work with the Python-DTU team which participated
in the Multi-Agent Programming Contest 2012 [7]. We also participated in the
contest in 2009 and 2010 as the Jason-DTU team [4,5], where we used the Jason
platform [3], but this year we use just the programming language Python as we
did in 2011 [6]. See http://www.imm.dtu.dk/~jv/MAS for an overview of our
activities.

The scenario is based on the scenario from 2011 and has only been changed
in a few ways. The most interesting change is the increase in number of agents
from 10 to 20 agents per team.

Our focus for the 2012 version of the contest has been on reimplementing
the system from 2011. Given that the scenario is very similar to that last year,
we decided to look into ways of improving our system. We have been exploring
the possibility of implementing an organization for the system using the Moise
organizational model [1] as part of a two-student bachelor project.

The paper is organized as follows. In section 2 we discuss some of the ideas
we have pursued. In section 3 we describe some of the facilities we have added
in the improved system. Section 4 describes in detail our strategies and how the
agents commit to goals. Finally, we conclude our work by discussing possible
improvements of our system and the contest in section 5.

---

* Corresponding author.

M. Dastani, J.F. Hübner, and B. Logan (Eds.): ProMAS 2012, LNAI 7837, pp. 205–216, 2013.
© Springer-Verlag Berlin Heidelberg 2013

2   System Analysis and Design

We chose to implement the system using Python as it is very fast and convenient to implement experimental systems in this language. Other useful features of Python are support of multiple programming paradigms, compact code and dynamic typing. We did not use any multi-agent programming languages because we wanted to have complete control of everything in the implementation. Last year we used Python 2 and we decided to upgrade to Python 3.

In order to make sure that our changes during the implementation phase improved our system, all new algorithms and architecture changes were tested against the older versions by comparing the data collected from the new statistics to see if the change made any differences.

2.1   Testing Moise

This year we wanted to try to implement some kind of organization for our system, so we made a substantial test implementation as part of a two-student bachelor project using the Moise organizational model [1]. We chose Moise because we have previous experience using it in combination with the Jason platform [3].

The Moise organizational model [1] is a formalism for organizational multi-agent systems where an organization is divided into three dimensions: structural, functional and deontic specification. The structural specification uses the concepts of *roles*, role *relations* and *groups* to build the individual, social and collective structural levels of an organization. Here, the roles an agent can enact are defined, and it is furthermore defined how roles are linked, e.g. by allowing agents enacting different roles to communicate. The collective level is specified using the notion of groups, in which it is determined which roles are allowed to be enacted and what links exists between agents both within internally in the group and with external agents. The functional specification specifies missions and plans using a so-called *social scheme* which is a goal decomposition tree that has as root the goal of that scheme. The responsibilities for each subgoal in a scheme are distributed in missions, which means that an agent choosing to commit to a mission effectively chooses to commit to the goals of that mission. The subgoals are created using the operators sequence, indicating that a goal is fulfilled when the sequence of subgoals are fulfilled, choice, in which a goal is fulfilled when a single subgoal is achieved, and parallelism, where all subgoals must be fulfilled, but no specific order is required. The deontic specification is the relation between the structural and functional specifications: it specifies on the individual level the permissions and obligations of a role on a mission. It makes it possible to specify that an agent enacting a certain role is obligated (or permitted) to commit to certain missions, and is therefore obligated (or permitted) to commit to the goals of that mission.

We follow the approach of S-Moise$^+$, which is an open-source implementation of an organizational middleware that follows the Moise-model [2]. Among other things it consists of a special agent, the *organizational manager*, which maintains consistency in the organization, i.e. by making sure that a single agent cannot enact two incompatible roles at the same time. This is done by letting the agents communicate with the manager when they want to join a group, enact a role or commit to a mission. If any such event is a violation of the organizational specification, the organizational manager will not allow it.

The plan trees and social schemes of Moise have a large potential, due to the fact that they will make sure that the right amount of agents will work together toward the best goal. We have chosen to only plan for a single subgoal for each agent, because of the very dynamic nature and the size of the map and number of agents. This makes the plans sufficiently small for the agents to coordinate themselves using direct communication, which makes the plan trees unnecessary.

It might be possible to split the agents into smaller groups to perform more coordinated plans, like finding the opponent's zones etc., but we did not have the time to try to implement groups. In the end we decided not to use Moise as we found that the benefits did not outweigh the needed effort to get the computation under the time limit, due to the quite large communication overhead of the organizational manager.

2.2   Agent Behaviour

Our resulting system is a decentralized solution with a focus on time performance. The communication between the agents relies on shared data structures as this is a very fast way to communicate for the agents. The `Runner` class which coordinates communication is described in more detail in section 3.3.

Instead of letting the agents find goals based on their own knowledge alone they use the distributed knowledge of the entire team. This does add some communication which in some cases is unnecessary but in most cases the extra knowledge will produce better goals for the agents.

In each step each agent will find its preferred goals autonomously and assign each of them a *benefit* based on its own desires (i.e. the type of agent), how many steps are needed to reach the location and so on. In order to make sure that multiple agents will not commit to the same goal they communicate in order to find the most suitable agent for each goal. This is done using our auction-based agreement algorithm which will be discussed in more detail in section 4.3.

The agents in this contest are situated in an inaccessible environment which means that the world state can change without the agents noticing from step to step, e.g. if the opponent's agents move outside our agents' visibility range. Hence our agents should be very reactive to observable changes in the environment.

The agents are only proactive in a few situations. The most important one being the communication between a disabled agent and a repairer. They use their shared knowledge in order to decide which of the agents should take the last step and who should stay, so that they eventually are standing on the same vertex instead of simply switching positions. This is implemented by considering the current energy for each agent.

Some of our agents also attempt to be proactive by for example parrying if an opponent saboteur is on the same vertex. Furthermore, repairers will repair wounded agents since they are likely to be attacked again.

2.3   Random Generation of the Map

Last year all maps had one high-valued area, indicated by numbers on the vertices, as seen in figure 1. For this setting we developed an algorithm which places the agents in defensive positions inside the area in order to defend it. For more information we refer to the paper about our system from 2011 [6].

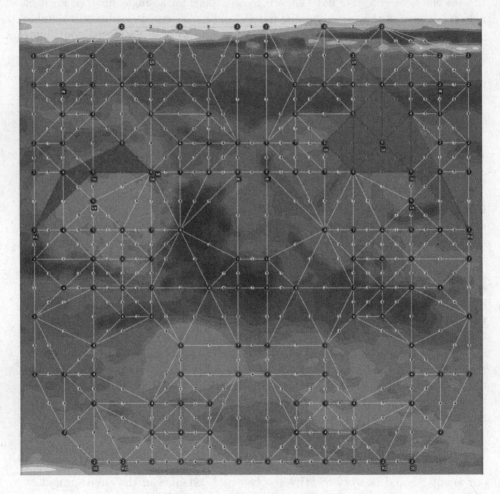

Fig. 1. An example of a map in the MAPC 2011

This year the map generation algorithm has been updated to create more than one high-valued area. An example of this can be seen on figure 2, where the size of a vertex represents its value. In some cases this lead to situations where our agents would protect a single good area even though it would be better to make smaller groups and have control over several areas. Therefore our previous solution would only be effective in special cases, so we have implemented a

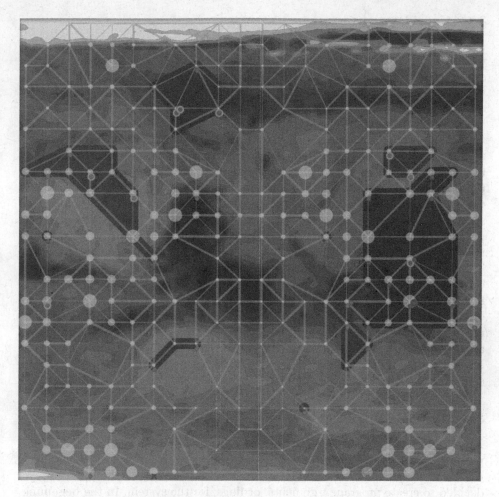

Fig. 2. An example of a map in the MAPC 2012

new algorithm which takes multiple areas into consideration. The new solution is actually much simpler and it works well for both maps with multiple areas and maps with a single, high-valued area. In section 4.2 we describe the main properties of this algorithm.

3   Software Architecture

The software architecture, including the auction-based agreement approach, is thoroughly described in the paper about our system from 2011 [6] and will only be described briefly here. The rest of this section will describe a few minor facilities added this year.

3.1 Considerations

The competition is built on the Java MASSim-platform and EISMASSim framework which makes it easy to implement a system quickly without spending time on server communication and protocols. However, we did not utilize this framework but chose to implement our system in Python exclusively to have better control and complete knowledge about the implementation. Another solution based on EISMASSim, ActiveMQ and the Java implementation of Python, called Jython, was implemented as well. This solution was discarded due to performance issues. We also considered using a multi-agent framework such as Jason, but due to prior experiences, we thought that the benefits where outweighed by the increased complexity and thus chose to implement our own framework. We chose Python as we think it is in many ways superior with respect to development speed and succinctness compared to Java, C#, C++ and other languages that we have experience with. Furthermore Python supports multiple programming paradigms, including the functional, which has quite effective for this setting.

Last year we used a decentralized solution where the agents shared their percepts through a shared data structures but each kept their own copy of the graph representing the environment. The increase in the number of agents and the size of the maps for this year's competition, forced us to rethink and reimplement the percept sharing. To efficiently handle the increased amount of information, all agents share a single instance of the graph. To avoid deadlocks, percepts that lead to updates in this graph are handled with synchronized queues which allow safe exchange of data between multiple threads.

3.2 Testing Using Flags

A lot of testing was required for verifying that our system was improved compared to our previous system, so we needed an easy way to select which algorithms to use. In order to be able to run several instances of the program, we decided to create program arguments, or flags, for the system. In the beginning we had a configuration file in which we set flags. This was not a very practical way to do it as we had to have multiple configuration files in order to run more instances of the program. These flags make it possible to specify which algorithms the system should use. The help page for our multi-agent system where the different flags are described is shown below:

```
$ python ./bagent.py -h
usage: bagent.py [-h] [-b] [-d] [-a] [-w] [-l] [-v {0,1,2}] {a,b,Python-DTU}

positional arguments:
  {a,b,Python-DTU}       agent name prefix

optional arguments:
  -h, --help             show this help message and exit
  -b, --buy              make the agents shop for upgrades
  -d, --dummy            dummy agents
  -a, --attack           do attack
```

```
-w, --weak_opp          attack EXP and INS in the start of the simulation
-l, --load_pickle       load vertices from pickled data
-v {0,1,2}, --verbosity {0,1,2}
```

The flags are used to start multiple instances of the system using different strategies. For example we can test whether it is better to use our buying strategy by starting the server and then start two instances of the system where the flag -b was passed to one of them. This was used to test whether it was beneficial to use our heuristics, but as we found that this was not the case we have removed them from the system.

3.3   Code Structure and Files

We briefly describe the main classes and files:

global_vars.py: We have all our global variables in this file. They are mainly used to make the implementation more dynamic and easier to maintain.

comm.py: This is the file where we have implemented the `Agent` class and the procedures used to communicate with the server. The `Communicator` class is implemented as processes such that all the agents can send and receive messages at the same time. The logic of the agents are implemented in the util.py and algorithms.py files.

bagent.py: This is where the main program is started and where the flags are parsed. It is also in this file that our `Runner` class is implemented. The `Runner` class starts and lets the agents do their calculations in a sequential fashion.

algorithms.py: Most interesting of our algorithms are implemented in this file, including:
- The *greedy zone control* which will be discussed in section 4.2.
- The *get goals algorithm* called by each agent. This algorithm is discussed in more detail in the paper about our system from 2011 [6].
- The *best-first search* used by each agent in order to find specialized goals according to their type.

util.py: We have implemented our graph representation of the map in this file. The file also includes a timer which was used to find bottlenecks in our code.

4   Strategies, Details and Statistics

In the competition each step of each achievement is exponentially harder to reach than the previous, thus our agents need a way to change their goals as the simulation progresses. We describe our strategy for getting achievements in section 4.1 and our zone control strategy in section 4.2. We describe how the agents decide what to do in section 4.3 and finally how communication works in section 4.4.

4.1   Getting Achievements

In the beginning every agent will work towards achieving as many type specific goals as possible in a more or less disorganized fashion, e.g. the inspector will inspect every opponent it sees.

We do this to achieve as many achievements as possible as fast as possible. We tried implementing different heuristics to improve the first part of the strategy. We considered the following heuristics:

Survey Heuristic: The agents always survey the vertex with the most outgoing edges if the steps needed to reach the vertex are the same (figure 3). The idea is to get survey achievements faster, but it turned out that even though we got the first few achievements faster, the last ones were achieved a lot later using this heuristic, so we did not use it.

Probe Heuristic: The agents probe the vertex with the highest valued neighbours (figure 4). This worked very well in the scenario from 2011, but in the 2012 scenario it can be more beneficial to first find a lot of potentially high valued areas which can be probed later. This can be achieved using a random walk, which will reduce the time in each area increasing the chance that the agents might find more areas in less steps. We chose not to use the probe heuristic since a random walk was more successful.

Attack Vulnerable Opponents: This heuristic is only applied in the first 80 steps (a simulation has 750 steps). We prefer to attack agents that cannot parry, as this will get us more successful attacks. Furthermore, as added value this will also lead to fewer successful parries for the opponent. This turned out to give us a slight advantage in the beginning of the simulation, so we chose to use it.

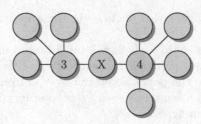

Fig. 3. Illustration of the heuristic values our agents would get trying to survey, standing on the green vertex. The vertex to the left has a heuristic value of 3 because it has three outgoing edges, whereas the one on the right has a slightly better heuristic value of 4.

After a certain number of steps the agents will proceed to the zone control part of our strategy. The sentinel is the only agent surveying after step 30. The explorers keep probing until step 150 and will probe in our target area for the next 50 steps to make sure we control as many vertices as possible. Afterwards they will follow the zone control strategy. All other agents begin zone control after step 150.

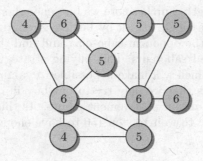

Fig. 4. Illustration of the heuristic values our agents would get trying to probe, standing on the green vertex where the blue ones are owned with the given value. The heuristic value of the red vertices are calculated by taking the mean of the known neighbouring vertices.

4.2   Zone Control

The zone control part of our strategy uses a very simple, but surprisingly effective, greedy algorithm. The algorithm works by first choosing the node with the highest value, and then by choosing a potential neighbour node. The potential value of choosing that node is then calculated as the value of the node plus the sum of all the neighbours which, according to the graph coloring algorithm [7], will be owned if the potential node is chosen. For each agent, the algorithm will choose the best node according to some parts of the graph coloring algorithm. If a vertex has not been probed the algorithm will use the value 1. This way we take some of the area coloring algorithm from the contest into consideration and as it is an inaccessible environment this is the best we could achieve.

This algorithm will to some extent choose the optimal area or several areas which are still fairly easy to maintain, even though our choices are limited by our (partial) knowledge of the map and the missing parts of the area coloring algorithm.

During the zone control part every type of agent has a specific job.

– *Repairers and saboteurs* do not directly participate in the zone control, instead they are trying to defend and maintain the zone.
– *Inspectors* keep inspecting from their given expand node, because the opponents might have bought something which we need to make a counter move against.
– *Explorers* will probe unprobed vertices within the target zone. When all vertices are probed they are assigned a vertex by the zone control strategy.
– The *sentinels* will stay on a vertex assigned by the zone control strategy and will parry if some of the opponent's saboteurs move to the sentinels position.

The last important change in the state of mind of the agents is that after step 150 the saboteurs start buying. They buy exactly enough extra health so that they will not get disabled by a single attack from an opponent saboteur that has not upgraded his strength. Furthermore we buy enough strength to disable any opponent saboteur in a single attack by buying strength for all our saboteurs every time we inspect the opponent saboteurs and find that it has more health than all other inspected saboteurs. This buying strategy is chosen in hope of dominating the map which will make it possible to gain control of the zone we want. The advantage is that we only try to out-buy in one specific field, thus we are unlikely to use all our achievement points. As this is a quite aggressive buying strategy we had to wait to step 150 to have enough achievement points to execute it.

4.3 Making Decisions

The agents need a consistent way of figuring out what to do. We do this by letting every agent find the nearest goals according to their type. They do this by using a modified best-first search (BFS) which returns a set of goals. To make sure that every agent always has at least one goal the BFS returns as many goals as we have agents. This is a very agent-centered procedure meaning the agents simply commit to the goal with the highest benefit, instead of coordinating any bigger schemes. However, since the goals are more or less dependent on each other there is some implicit coordination. For example the repairers will often follow the saboteurs as these search for opponents and thus more often will share a vertex with an opponent saboteur and get disabled.

To decide which goal to pursue the agents use an auction algorithm. Every agent can bid on the goals they want to commit to and will eventually be assigned the one they are best suited for. This results in a good solution, which however might not be optimal. For further details we refer to the paper about our system from 2011 [6].

Even though our planner calculates a few turns ahead the agents recalculate every turn. We do this to adapt to newly discovered obstacles and facts, such as an opponent saboteur or the fact that the agent has been disabled. The agents will not end up walking back and forth as their previous goal will now be one step closer, thus the benefit of the goal has increased. If another goal becomes more valuable it means that it is a better goal than the one the agent was pursuing, thus changing the commitment makes sense, so we do not lose anything on recalculating each turn.

4.4 Communication

Communication and sharing of information is extremely important in any multi-agent system. In our system every percept received by the agents are stored in a shared data structure so that all agents have access to the complete distributed knowledge of the team at all times.

Actual communication in our system only happens when the agents are deciding what to do. When they are figuring out what to do the auction-based agreement algorithm is used on conflicting goals and thus two agents will never pursue the same goal.

5   Conclusion

In the process of reimplementing and improving the Python-DTU multi-agent system we have analysed the changes to the competition and used our findings to design and implement better algorithms for the increasingly complex tasks. We have considered imposing an explicit organization upon the agents, and for this purpose we experimented with the Moise organizational model. While it had some advantages, such as the being able to ensure that the right amount of agents work together toward a certain goal using by use of roles and plan trees, we decided not to use Moise in the final version of our system, as its benefits did not outweigh the communication overhead caused by the organizational manager in the organizational middleware, S-moise$^+$.

All improvements to the algorithms are quite simple, but are nevertheless effective at reaching their goals. The simplicity and specialized approach is probably one of our strengths, as it makes it easy to implement special cases when certain improvements of the algorithms were necessary. Having aggressive saboteurs was also an advantage as it lead to the opponents being disabled often, which in turn gave us a larger zone score. Our greatest weakness was that our uncompromising attempt to have the strongest saboteurs could be countered by buying enough health on a single saboteur to make us use most of our achievement points for improving all of our saboteurs. This could lead to a large difference in step score gained from achievement points each step.

The many advanced programming constructs in Python, e.g. lambda functions, list comprehensions and filters made it possible to implement algorithms very efficiently.

One thing we have noticed during the competition is that it does not seem to pay off to buy anything other than health and strength. This meant that a lot of teams had more or less the same strategies. We think it could be interesting if many kinds of strategies could be sufficiently effective so that we might see the teams following different strategies. One idea could be to introduce ranged attacks which could be achievable through upgrades and should be limited by visibility range. This could allow for some other strategies, since the agents need to figure out where to hit the opponent a few steps in the future and how to avoid getting hit themselves. Furthermore, the teams will need to use their inspectors even more to find out whether or not to avoid possible ranged attacks from the opponent.

References

1. Hübner, J.F., Sichman, J.S., Bossier, O.: A Model for the Structural, Functional, and Deontic Specification of Organizations in Multiagent Systems. In: Bittencourt, G., Ramalho, G. (eds.) SBIA 2002. LNCS (LNAI), vol. 2507, pp. 118–128. Springer, Heidelberg (2002)
2. Hübner, J.F., Sichman, J.S., Boissier, O.: S-moise$^+$: A Middleware for Developing Organised Multi-Agent Systems. In: Boissier, O., Padget, J., Dignum, V., Lindemann, G., Matson, E., Ossowski, S., Sichman, J.S., Vázquez-Salceda, J. (eds.) ANIREM 2005 and OOOP 2005. LNCS (LNAI), vol. 3913, pp. 64–78. Springer, Heidelberg (2006)

3. Bordini, R.H., Hübner, J.F., Wooldridge, M.: Programming Multi-Agent Systems in AgentSpeak Using Jason. John Wiley & Sons (2007)
4. Boss, N.S., Jensen, A.S., Villadsen, J.: Building Multi-Agent Systems Using *Jason*. Annals of Mathematics and Artificial Intelligence 59, 373–388 (2010)
5. Vester, S., Boss, N.S., Jensen, A.S., Villadsen, J.: Improving Multi-Agent Systems Using *Jason*. Annals of Mathematics and Artificial Intelligence 61, 297–307 (2011)
6. Ettienne, M.B., Vester, S., Villadsen, J.: Implementing a Multi-Agent System in Python with an Auction-Based Agreement Approach. In: Dennis, L.A., Boissier, O., Bordini, R.H. (eds.) ProMAS 2011. LNCS, vol. 7217, pp. 185–196. Springer, Heidelberg (2012)
7. Behrens, T., Köster, M., Schlesinger, F., Dix, J., Hübner, J.: Multi-Agent Programming Contest — Scenario Description — 2012 Edition (2012), http://www.multiagentcontest.org/

Multi-Agent Programming Contest 2012 – TUB Team Description

Axel Heßler, Thomas Konnerth, Pawel Napierala, and Benjamin Wiemann

Technische Universität Berlin, Germany

Abstract. We describe our contribution to the Multi-Agent Programming Contest 2012, which has been developed by students and researchers of the DAI-Labor at TU Berlin, Germany, using the JIAC V agent framework and the agile JIAC methodology.

1 Introduction

Our team is called "TUB" and has participated consistently in the Multi-Agent Programming Contest [1–3] since 2007. Since our first participation, we consider the contest a very good opportunity to evaluate our platform and tools. The current team has been developed in the course "Multi Agent Contest"[1] by the following students: Pawel Napierala and Benjamin Wiemann, supervised by the following agent researchers: Thomas Konnerth and Axel Heßler (main contact). We have invested 640 hours approximately to create the contest version of our system and we are still not convinced that this version is competitive, although we have invested twice the time of last year's contribution.

2 System Analysis and Design

The methodology, which we have used during the course, borrows from the JIAC methodology, and can be described as bottom-up and agile methodology: we start with domain analysis, which is to build a first *ontology*: find the concepts of the domain, their structure and relationships with each other: agents, own team, opponents, nodes, edges, visited, probed, surveyed, weight.

As a second step the methodology says: make a *role model* and a *user interface (UI) prototype*. A role is specified by a number of capabilities or behaviours and the relationships with other roles. Identifying the roles was an easy task because they are easily collected from the scenario document. We then assigned simple and basic capabilities to the roles. As many of them were identical in each role, we created the generalised role of the *Mars invader*, which is a collection of the capabilities that all roles share, such as surveying, charging and moving. All other roles inherit from the invader role and add special capabilities such as probing, inspecting, and so on.

---

[1] Project 0435 L 774 at TU Berlin, Germany.

M. Dastani, J.F. Hübner, and B. Logan (Eds.): ProMAS 2012, LNAI 7837, pp. 217–223, 2013.

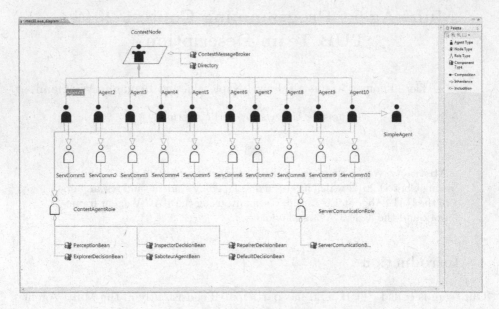

Fig. 1. TUB role model

The role model was subject to many iterations. In Figure 1, an intermediate version of the role model is shown that is very close to the final role model. In principle, every contest agent in this role model could take every role (the *ContestAgentRole*), but during this contest the roles are static properties given by the contest server to every agent in the team. Common capabilities (*goto, survey, buy, recharge*) are implemented to the *DefaultDecisionBean* component. Special capabilities (*probe, inspect, attack, repair*) are implemented in the corresponding role specific component (e.g. *ExplorerDecisionBean* or *SaboteurDecisionBean*). Every agent instance has a specialization of the *ServerCommunicationBean* component with the credentials for authentication. Finally, every agent is instantiated once on the *ContestNode*, which provides the infrastructure for acquaintance and inter-agent communication. The role model has been generated with the help of the *AgentWorldEditor (AWE)*, which is part of the JIAC V tool suite *Toolipse*. The AWE generates configurations for all agents and agent nodes that are used by the JIAC V runtime at startup.

The UI prototype is a simple visualisation of the world graph. The problem here is that we could not find a solution to draw the graph in a repetable way during preparation. As a workaround we have patched the contest server to send the coordinates that project the graph to a grid as used by the monitor tool. The next step is *implementing* the simple and basic behaviours and then *evaluating* their function. After several iterations, when the basic actions can be reliably achieved by the agent, more complex capabilities are added, such as finding the most promising node to occupy or calculate the shortest or fastest path to an arbitrary node, and so on. The system can be distributed over several machines if available, without changing any line of code, even at runtime. This is one of the features of the JIAC agent framework [5] that is usually used for MAS administration and self-administration [6, 7]. However, we could not use this feature during the contest due to a lack of available hardware.

The agent system that runs our bots is mostly decentralised. As we use a component framework to build our agents, the functionalities for the roles are implemented within a dedicated component for each role. However, in order to simplify configuration, we decided to equip all of our agents with all components. The agents then decide based on the first message from the server, which role they take and keep that role for the remainder of the match. This way, it was very easy for us, to expand the team for the 2012 contest. All we had to do was to add a number of additional agents, and they took their roles automatically.

During the match, the basic cycle of our agents was triggered by the perceptions from the server. Whenever an agent receives a new perception, it starts the decision making cycle. In this cycle, the current state is evaluated and the agent decides what to do, based on its role. This decision is then forwarded to all other team members. Afterwards the agent waits for some time, in order to receive the decisions from the other team members. Depending on circumstances, this may lead to a reevaluation of the decision. Afterwards, the final decision is send to the server.

The only centralized or hierarchical part of the team organization is the zoning calculation. While this calculation can be performed by every agent, we have instead decided to let only one agent calculate the Zoning and propagate the results to all agents that participate in the zoning. This agent is selected among and by interested agents that want to know where to position in the zone, using a simple voting protocol. The result is then calculated by the selected agent and shared with the other interested agents.

Regarding the communication strategy of our team, we follow our 2007 – 2009 successful approach (e.g. in [4]) to distribute all perceptions and intentions among all other agents, where we could reach an appreciable enhancement of the team performance. In theory this approach should not scale very well as the number of perceptions and intentions sent around is $2n * (n-1)$ per cycle. However, the JIAC V framework contains a messaging middleware that is capable of processing multicast messages for groups of agents. With this approach, each agent only needs to send one message that is then forwarded to all agents within the group. Thus the framework can handle the message very easily.

When it comes to coordination aspects we distinguish between explicit and implicit coordination. Implicit coordination can be achieved when the agents share their intentions. This notion of intention is often misunderstood when discussing the approach in the agent community. The intention in our case more often reflects a perform or achievement goal than the action that the agent has decided to execute. Taking the intentions of other agents into account, the actual agent can adopt the intention when it has a better utility or even dismiss its own decisions in case other agents will perform better. We have yet built only a few explicit coordination strategies into our agents, e.g. the collaboration between inspector and saboteur, or the unhealthy agent requesting the nearest repairer.

We have implemented general agent attributes such as autonomy, proactiveness and reactiveness as follows: JIAC V agents have their own thread of control and decide and act autonomously. We see the agents with low health level proactively seeking the repairer's help using a simple request, whereas probing or surveying has been implemented as a simple reactive behaviour: if the node is unprobed then probe.

Finally, our team was tested during the training matches that were organized by before the tournament in order to ensure that the agents run stable and can send their moves to the server within the allocated time.

3   Software Architecture

We have used the JIAC V agent framework to implement the contest MAS of our TUB team. For our agent researchers the contest is always an excellent reliability benchmarking of the framework, and also a test case for teaching principles of agent programming. We used a set of dedicated JIAC V plugins for the Eclipse IDE to create basic project structures and configurations. Then we added a number of components that were already available form last years contest, such as server communication and zone calculation functionalities. Finally, the biggest part of the work was invested in implementing and tuning the algorithms that control the actual actions of the agents. This was mostly done in Java, because the decisions and calculations are time critical, and we wanted to avoid the overhead from interpreting our declarative agent language.

As far as algorithms are concerned we experimented with Bellman-Ford and Dijkstra path finding algorithms for the movement calculations. However, the final team used a simple A-star algorithm, as other approaches proved to be to costly. They may become useful again, if we delegate the path finding to a dedicated agent that is not part of the team in future contests. Furthermore, the algorithm described in the contest scenario was used for the calculation of the zone scores.

4   Strategies, Details and Statistics

Every agents maintains its own world model (see Figure 2). Once the perception arrives, unknown vertices are added to the graph, which represents the physical world where the agents act in. Already known vertices are updated with the values from the perception. The perception is also shared with all other agents so that they can update their world model with information that is not visible to them.

The world model also contains a number of agent lists, i.e. team bots, enemy bots and special lists for interesting bots such as enemy's saboteurs and enemy's repairers (to either destroy or avoid them depending on the role of our agent).

Furthermore, the world model is updated by a number of Zones that support the decision process. The ownZones attribute is a list of zones that are held by the own team, enemyZones are the enemy's holdings as far as the own team can see them. A safe and a semisafe area are also calculated to give the bots a map of potential target vertices that are not reachable by enemy's saboteurs. The

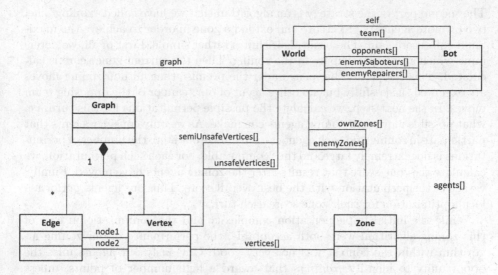

Fig. 2. Domain model

own saboteurs are more interested in the dangerous vertices because there are the first class targets to be destroyed: enemy's saboteurs.

The main strategy of our team is twofold: First, individual agents follows a simple, straightforward achievement collection strategy based on their roles. The behavior is as follows:

- **Explorer:** Explores the whole graph and if a node is not yet probed and the agent is situated on the unprobed node then it will try to probe until the probe action has been successfully achieved. If no probing is necessary, but there are unsurveyed edges connected to the current node, the agent will survey. Otherwise it will move to unprobed nodes.
- **Repairer:** If any agent is damaged and requires repairs, the repairer will move to that agent and repair it. Other repairers are repaired with a higher priority. If no repairs are necessary, the Repairer agents will participate in zoning.
- **Saboteur:** If any agents of the opposing team are detected, the Saboteur will try to catch them and attack them if possible. If no opposing agents are detected, or all agents are disabled, the Saboteur will participate in zoning. Furthermore, if enough achievement points are available, the saboteurs will buy increases for their attack-power and health attributes.
- **Sentinel:** Our strategy does not contain any special tasks for Sentinels. Therefore the Sentinels do always participate in the zoning.
- **Inspector:** The inspectors try to find agents of the opposing team and inspect them. This is mainly done to get the initial achievement points for the first ten inspects. When all opposing agents have been inspected, the Inspectors will stop inspecting and participate in zoning.

The second part of the strategy is an algorithm that we have called "zoning", i.e. two or more agents try to create and extend a zone in order to achieve the maximum zone score gain. The basic algorithm is rather simple. First of all, we determine which agents participate in the zoning. Then the current zone score is calculated. This calculation happens under the premise that all non-zoning moves are executed successfully but no other agent of our team or of the opposing team moves. In the next step, we calculate the possible permutations for this turn, i.e. what possible moves our zoning agents can make. As we only consider agents that participate in zoning and each agent can only make one step, the number of permutations is not extremely large and thus computable. For each such permutation, we calculate the zone score that results after the zoning agents have moved. Finally, we select the permutation with the best overall score. Thus our agents perform a local optimization for their zone score each turn.

While the initial implementation complexity and the computational cost of this zoning algorithm were both acceptable, the performance of our zoning algorithm within the contest was not very good. Obviously our agents miss the opportunity to identify *frontiers* that award a high number of points, unless these frontiers are already close to their current positions. This is likely the most important point for improvements on our strategy in future contests.

However, we should also mention that for the actual selection of both, targets for repairers and saboteurs, and for the zoning, we used greedy approaches. I.e. our agents simply take the closest target that maximizes utility. Unfortunately we could not find the time for the development of more elaborate strategies that achieve a global optimum – be it the discovery of a good border, or the detection of a high priority target for the saboteurs.

5 Conclusion

In summary, we are pleased withe the overall design and stability of our team. The agents worked flawlessly, did not break down, and submitted their actions in time to the server. However, the performance in terms of achieved scored is not what we had hoped for. Our strategy is probably too simple, and we need to improve the strategy for further contests. The most obvious points for this are the detection of globally optimal frontiers that our agents should occupy and a general improvement of situational awareness for all agents.

However, even though we think that our own performance in the contests could be improved, we wish to thank the organizers for the opportunity to test our framework and our agents. We think that the contests is a valuable addition to the multi agent community and hope that it will continue to be so for many years to come.

References

1. Behrens, T.M., Dastani, M., Dix, J., Köster, M., Novák, P.: The multi-agent programming contest from 2005-2010 - from gold collecting to herding cows. Ann. Math. Artif. Intell. 59(3-4), 277–311 (2010)

2. Behrens, T.M., Dix, J., Hübner, J., Köster, M.: Editorial. Ann. Math. Artif. Intell. 61(4), 257–260 (2011)
3. Behrens, T., Köster, M., Schlesinger, F., Dix, J., Hübner, J.F.: The multi-agent programming contest 2011: A résumé. In: Dennis, L.A., Boissier, O., Bordini, R.H. (eds.) ProMAS 2011. LNCS, vol. 7217, pp. 155–172. Springer, Heidelberg (2012)
4. Hessler, A., Küster, T., Niemann, O., Sljivar, A., Matallaoui, A.: Cows and Fences: JIAC V - AC'09 Team Description. In: Dix, J., Fisher, M., Novák, P. (eds.) Proceedings of the 10th International Workshop on Computational Logic in Multi-Agent Systems 2009. IfI Technical Report Series, vol. IfI-09-08. Clausthal University of Technology (2009)
5. Hirsch, B., Konnerth, T., Heßler, A.: Merging agents and services — the JIAC agent platform. In: Bordini, R.H., Dastani, M., Dix, J., El Fallah Seghrouchni, A. (eds.) Multi-Agent Programming: Languages, Tools and Applications, pp. 159–185. Springer (2009)
6. Kaiser, S., Burkhardt, M., Tonn, J.: Drag-and-drop migration: An example of mapping user actions to agent infrastructures. In: van der Hoek, W., Kaminka, G.A., Lespérance, Y., Luck, M., Sen, S. (eds.) The First International Workshop on Infrastructure and Tools for Multiagent Systems (May 2010)
7. Thiele, A., Kaiser, S., Konnerth, T., Hirsch, B.: MAMS service framework. In: Kowalczyk, R., Vo, Q.B., Maamar, Z., Huhns, M. (eds.) SOCASE 2009. LNCS, vol. 5907, pp. 126–142. Springer, Heidelberg (2009)

LTI-USP Team: A JaCaMo Based MAS for the MAPC 2012

Mariana Ramos Franco, Luciano Menasce Rosset, and Jaime Simão Sichman

Laboratório de Técnicas Inteligentes (LTI)
Escola Politécnica (EP)
Universidade de São Paulo (USP)
{mafranko,luciano.rosset}@usp.br, jaime.sichman@poli.usp.br

Abstract. This paper describes the architecture and core ideas of the multi-agent system created by the LTI-USP team which participated in the 2012 edition of the Multi-Agent Programming Contest (MAPC 2012). This is the second year of the Agents on Mars scenario, in which the competitors must design a team of agents to find and occupy the best zones of a weighted graph. The team was developed using the *JaCaMo*[1] multi-agent framework and the main strategy was to divide the agents into three subgroups: two in charge of occupying the best zones in the map, and the other one in charge of sabotaging the opponents.

Keywords: multi-agent system, multi-agent programming, JaCaMo, Jason, Cartago, Moise.

1 Introduction

The Multi-Agent Programming Contest (MAPC) is held every year in an attempt to stimulate research in the field of programming Multi-Agent System (MAS) [2]. This is the second year of the Agent on Mars scenario, in which the competitors must design a team of 20 agents to explore and occupy the best zones of Mars, represented by a graph with valued vertices and weighted edges.

The LTI-USP, located at the University of São Paulo is one of the most relevant research groups in multi-agent systems in Brazil. The group participated in the 2010 edition of the MAPC [3] and the previous Cows and Cowboys scenario was used in the last two years of the Multi-Agent course held at the Department of Computer Engineering and Digital Systems of the University of São Paulo.

For this year's contest the LTI-USP team was formed by Mariana Ramos Franco (M.Sc. Student) and Luciano Menasce Rosset (Undergraduate Student), supervised by Prof. Jaime Simão Sichman (Professor). The M.Sc. student fully developed the multi-agent system, while the undergraduate student helped with the tests and gave some suggestions during the discussions about the adopted strategy.

The main motivation to participate in the contest was to test and to analyze the *JaCaMo*[1] framework, in order to identify the weak and strong aspects of the platform, and its performance limitations.

---

[1] Available at http://jacamo.sourceforge.net/

M. Dastani, J.F. Hübner, and B. Logan (Eds.): ProMAS 2012, LNAI 7837, pp. 224–233, 2013.

JaCaMo [1] is a platform for multi-agent programming which supports all levels of abstractions – agent, environment, and organisation – that are required for developing sophisticated multi-agent systems, by combining three separate technologies: *Jason*[2] [4], for programming autonomous agents; *CArtAgO*[3] [5], for programming environment artifacts; and *Moise*[4] [6], for programming multi-agent organisations.

2   System Analysis and Design

For the development of this project, as the main developer of the team had not a lot of previous experience with any multi-agent methodologies, we preferred to follow an iterative approach, which consisted in a cyclic process of prototyping, testing, analyzing, and refining. In the testing phase, we run our team against a previous version, and against the test teams provided in the contest software package. Next, after fixing the observed implementation issues and performance problems, we analyzed how effective the current strategy was and collected new ideas to improve it.

The adopted solution is based on the centralization of coordination, that is, one agent is responsible for determining which the best zone in the map is, and then conduct the other agents to occupy this zone. The choice of centralized coordination was made to allow the rapid development of the team, since our principal motivation was to focus on the *JaCaMo* platform performance issues and not on the coordination aspects.

In our team, each agent has its own view of the world, and they communicate with each other for the following purposes: (i) informing the others agents about the structure of the map; (ii) informing about the agent's or the opponent's position, role and status; (iii) asking for a repair; (iv) asking an agent to go to a determined vertex.

The agents' communication occurs via the speech acts provided by *Jason* and, to reduce the communication overhead, agents broadcast to all others only the new percepts, i.e., only percepts received from the contest server which produces an update on the agent's world model are broadcasted. For this reason, there is a strong exchange of information between the agents in the beginning of the match due to the broadcast of new percepts, specially those related to the map, such as vertices and edges. However, the communication overhead decreases as the agents' world model starts to be more complete.

The agent architecture is based on the BDI model. Each agent has its own beliefs, desires, intentions and control thread. The agents are autonomous to decide by themselves the next action to be performed, but in cooperation with each other, particularly with the coordinator agent. The agents are proactive in the sense that they pursue their selected intentions over time.

---

[2] Available at http://jason.sourceforge.net/
[3] Available at http://cartago.sourceforge.net/
[4] Available at http://moise.sourceforge.net/

At each step, the agent decides which new plan will be executed to achieve a determined goal given only the state of the environment and the results of previous steps. There are no plans that last for more than one step and the plan's priority is determined by the order in which the plans were declared, i.e., the executed plan will be the first one to have its conditions satisfied. Some high priority plans can be considered reactive, such as the one which tells the agent to perform a recharge when running low on energy.

Approximately 300 man-hours were invested in the team development and, before the tournament, we participated in some test matches set by the organizers to ensure the stability of our team. Only during the competition did we discuss the design and strategies with the other participants.

3   Software Architecture

The prime requirement for this project was to create a MAS based on the *Ja-CaMo* multi-agent framework, making use of the *Moise* organisational artifacts. The architecture of the LTI-USP team is shown in Figure 1.

The agents are developed using the *Jason* MAS platform, which is a *Java*-based interpreter for an extended version of the *AgentSpeak* programming language for BDI agents [7]. Each agent is composed of plans, a belief base and its own world model. The plans are specified in *AgentSpeak* and the agent decides which plan will be executed according to its beliefs and the local view of the world.

The world model consists of a graph developed in *Java*, using simple data structures and classes. It captures every detail received from the MASSim contest server, such as: explored vertices and edges, opponents' position, disabled teammates, etc. At each step, the agent's world model is updated with the percepts received from the MASSim server, and with the information received from the other agents. The agent can access or change the state of its world model through the developed *Jason Internal Actions*. Some examples of internal actions are: `jia.closer_repairer(Pos)`, which returns to the agent the position of the closest repairer; and `jia.move_to_target(Pos,Target,NextPos)`, which tells the agent what the next movement to be performed is to achieve a desired position in the graph.

Some of the percepts received from the MASSim server are also stored in the agent's belief base, such as the agent's role, energy, position and team's money; allowing the agent to have a direct access to these information without a call for a *Jason Internal Action*. Percepts about vertices, edges and other agents were not stored in the belief base so as not to compromise the agent's performance, as it could be very expensive to update and to access the belief base with so much information. Moreover, since we wanted to update a belief when a new instance was inserted (instead of adding a second one), we decided to use the `IndexedBB` class provided in the *Jason* package, a customized version of the `DefaultBeliefBase` in which some beliefs are unique and indexed for faster access.

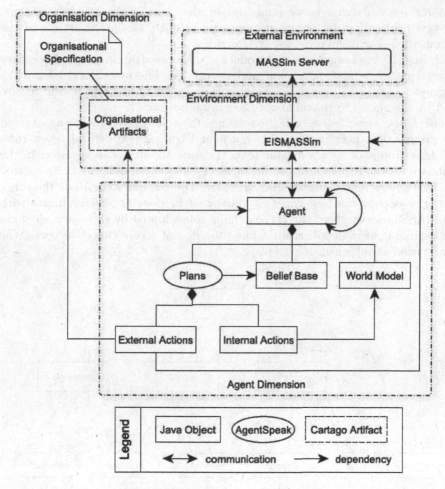

Fig. 1. LTI-USP Team Architecture

Agents communicate with the MASSim server through the EISMASSim environment-interface included in the contest software-package. EISMASSim is based on EIS[5] [8], which is a proposed standard for agent-environment interaction. It automatically establishes and maintains authenticated connections to the server and abstracts the communication between the MASSim server and the agents to simple Java-method-calls and call-backs. In order to use this interface, we extended the *JaCaMo* default agent architecture to perceive and to act not only on the *CArtAgO* artifacts, but also on the EIS environment as well.

CArtAgO is a framework for environment programming based on the A&A meta-model [9]. In *CArtAgO*, the environment can be designed as a dynamic set of computational entities called artifacts, collected into workspaces, possibly distributed among various nodes of a network [1]. Each artifact represents a

---

[5] Available at http://sourceforge.net/projects/apleis/

resource or a tool that agents can instantiate, share, use, and perceive at runtime. For this project, we did not create any new artifact; we only made use of the organisational artifacts provided in *Moise*.

Moise[6,10] is an organisational model for MAS based on three complementary dimensions: *structural, functional* and *normative*. The model enables a MAS designer to explicitly specify its organisational constraints, and it can be also used by the agents to reason about their organisation.

The *Moise structural specification* defines the roles played by the agents and the groups they take part in. As shown in Figure 2, we defined seven roles and four groups of agents for our team. Despite the five roles specified in the contest scenario (explorer, inspector, repairer, saboteur and sentinel), we created two other roles: `coordinator` and `martian`. The `coordinator` leads the other agents to occupy the best zones of Mars, and he does not communicate with the MASSim server. `Martian` is the default role adopted by the other agents in the beginning of the application, while they do not receive from the server the information about which role to play.

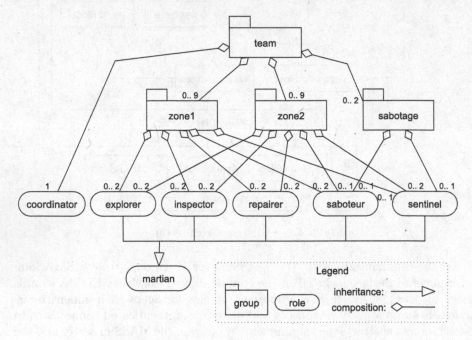

Fig. 2. *Moise structural specification* of the LTI-USP team

The agents are divided into three subgroups: `zone1`, `zone2` and `sabotage`. The two first subgroups are responsible for finding and occupying the best zones in the map, while the sabotage subgroup must attack the opponent's best zone. Each subgroup has a global goal associated to it.

The *Moise functional specification* is composed of a set of schemes. Each scheme decomposes global goals into simpler goals and distributes them by assigning missions to the agents. It also specifies how these mission are related to each other, i.e., if they should be achieved concurrently or in a certain sequence. We have four schemes for our team, in which the global goals associated to them are: `coordinate`, `occupyZone1`, `occupyZone2` and `sabotage`. In Figure 3, these global goals are represented as the root of the trees that represent the schemes, and the leafs are goals which can be achieved by the agents. The label which appears just above a goal represents the mission that the agent must be committed to in order to achieve the related goal. The missions are described in the next section.

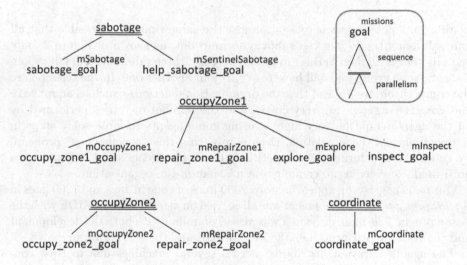

Fig. 3. *Moise functional specification* of the LTI-USP team

The *Moise normative specification* links the *structural* and *functional* specifications by defining which role has the obligation or permission to commit to each mission. The normative specification for the LTI-USP team is shown in Table 1.

When the team starts, the `coordinator` agent creates the organisational artifacts and adopts the `coordinator` role, while the other 20 agents connect to the MASSim server and wait for the beginning of the simulation to known what role to play. Despite the fact that the agent's role is defined by their identification/credentials, we assumed in our team that the agent will only be aware of its role during the competition.

Once defined its role, the agent communicates with the `coordinator`, who tells him which group to join and the missions to commit. We decided to make the `coordinator` responsible for distributing the groups and missions among the other agents, because by doing so we thus eliminate the performance issues caused by two or more agents trying to adopt the same role in a group, or trying to commit to the same mission. For example, in the beginning of the simulation,

Table 1. *Moise normative specification* of the LTI-USP team

Role	Mission	Deontic Relation
explorer	mExplore, mOccupyZone1	permission
explorer	mOccupyZone2	obligation
repairer	mRepairZone1, mRepairZone2	obligation
saboteur	mSabotage, mOccupyZone1, mOccupyZone2	obligation
sentinel	mSentinelSabotage, mOccupyZone1, mOccupyZone2	obligation
inspector	mInspect, mOccupyZone1	permission
inspector	mOccupyZone2	obligation
coordinator	mCoordinate	obligation

as all agents perceive their roles at almost the same time, it is possible that all four saboteurs try to join the `sabotage` group but, as shown in Figure 2, only one saboteur is allowed in this group. In this case, three saboteurs will fail to join the `sabotage` group and will have to try to join another one. In the tests before the competition, we noticed that the organisational actions - such as `adoptRole` and `commitMission` - are very costly, and the number of retries performed by all the agents could be very high, causing some agents to loose some steps in the beginning of the simulation. Even eliminating this "concurrency" problem, we could observe during the competition that some agents still lost some steps until finally succeeding to commit to a mission on the organisation.

Our team consists of, approximately, 2000 lines of code in Java and 1200 lines in *AgentSpeak*, and the development was all carried on using the Eclipse IDE with the *Jason* plugin. The main developer was already familiar with both the development and the runtime platforms, i.e. ,the Eclipse IDE and the *JaCaMo* framework.

The agents were not distributed across several machines due to time constraints, but is our intention to work in the future on a distributed team, since this is supported by *JaCaMo*.

4   Strategies, Details and Statistics

The team strategy is a combination of the organisational strategy, the role dependent strategies and the coordination strategy.

4.1   Organisational Strategy

As previously explained, one of the team's main strategy was to divide the agents into three subgroups: two of them in charge of occupying the best zones in the map, and the other one in charge of sabotaging the opponents. Below we describe the different missions related to each group.

- `occupyZone1`: Agents in this group have to occupy the best zone in the graph following the directions provided by the coordinator agent. In addition, one of the explorers works to probe the vertices of the graph to find the best zones to be occupied. In the exploration, he fixes the priority to the vertices belonging to the team's zone. Furthermore, one inspector has the mission of identifying the role of each agent in the opponent team. After the team has knowledge of all the opponents' role, the inspector joins the rest of the team for the mission of occupying the best zone in the graph.

- occupyZone2: All the agents on this group have the exclusive mission of occupying the second best zone in the graph, or to help the zone1 group to form a larger area. Whether this group must join the other group or not is determined by the coordinator.
- sabotage: This group is formed by one saboteur and one sentinel. The saboteur's mission is to attack the opponent who occupies a good vertex; and the sentinel helps with the sabotage by moving inside the opponent's zone.

4.2 Role-Dependent Strategies

The explorers probe every vertex and survey all edges on its path, while inspectors can perform an inspect action whenever an opponent is in a neighbor vertex.

The priorities to run away, parry or attack, when an opponent is on the same vertex, are set to each agent's role. The saboteurs should always attack any opponent agent in the same vertex. It should first target the saboteurs, then repairers, and finally, the other opponents. The sentinels should always parry in the presence of an opponents saboteur. The repairers will decide between running away and parrying, in the presence of an opponent saboteur, depending, respectively, on if there is another teammate in the same vertex or not. Inspectors and explorers should always try to run away if an opponent saboteur is in the same vertex.

Repairing a disabled or damaged agent may break the structure of the area occupied. Having that in mind the repairers should stay put on their own vertices and wait for damaged and disabled agents to come for repairs. The disabled or damaged agent locates the closest repairer and heads to it, but if this repairer already has three or more agents to be repaired, the damaged agent will proceed to the second closest, and so on.

At each step, the team's score is computed by summing up the values of the zones and the current money. Thus the money obtained by the team has a big impact on its score. For this reason, we decided to limit the buy action, allowing the agents to purchase extension packs (such as battery, shield or sabotageDevice) only when a defined amount of money is reached. Furthermore, there is a specific buying strategy for each role. For example, the saboteurs can buy sabotageDevices, while the other agents cannot buy it.

4.3 Coordination Strategy

The coordinator builds its local view of the world through the percepts broadcasted by the other agents. Whenever the world model is updated, it computes which the two best zones in the graph are. The best zone is obtained by calculating for each vertex the sum of its value with the value of all its direct and second degree neighbors. The vertex with the greatest sum of values is the center of the best zone. Zones with the sum of values below 10 are not considered in the calculation. The same computation is performed again to determine if there is a second best zone, but this time removing the vertices belonging to the first best zone from the analysis.

If two best zones are found, the coordinator agent will designate one first best zone for `zone1` group, and the second best zone for the `zone2` group. Otherwise, the same zone will be assigned for the two groups.

Given that the coordinator has assigned a zone for a group, all agents of the group are asked to occupy an empty vertex of the target zone. When all the agents are in the best zone, the coordinator starts to look to the neighbor vertices of the team's zone in which an agent can move, trying to increase the size of this zone.

5   Conclusion

Participating in the MAPC was a great opportunity to improve our knowledge of several multi-agent technologies by implementing a robust MAS through the *JaCaMo* framework. During the development, we had to deal with at least three different MAS technologies: *Jason*, *CArtAgO*, and *Moise*.

The team was built focusing to test the integration of these different MAS technologies, and not so much on the development of a better and decentralized strategy. Despite that, we believe that the team performed fairly well, finishing the competition in the fourth place.

Our greatest obstacle in the development of the team was to deal with the performance issues related to the use of the organisational artifacts. In a time limited context, as faced in this competition, the performance of a platform plays an important role, and we believe that these performance requirements may be a problem to the adoption of the *JaCaMo* in more real scenarios. Consequently, as future work we intend to perform a complete evaluation of the *JaCaMo* performance.

Besides these performance issues, the *JaCaMo* framework proved to be a very complete platform for the development of sophisticated multi-agent systems, by providing all the necessary features that we needed to developed our team.

Regarding possible extensions to the scenario, one idea is to change the score computation to consider only the sum of the zones values. In this way, the buying strategy will not impact directly the team score and it will be fairer to compare different strategies.

References

1. Boissier, O., Bordini, R.H., Hübner, J.F., Ricci, A., Santi, A.: Multi-agent oriented programming with JaCaMo. Science of Computer Programming (2011)
2. Behrens, T., Köster, M., Schlesinger, F., Dix, J., Hübner, J.F.: The Multi-agent Programming Contest 2011: A Résumé. In: Dennis, L.A., Boissier, O., Bordini, R.H. (eds.) ProMAS 2011. LNCS, vol. 7217, pp. 155–172. Springer, Heidelberg (2012)

3. Gouveia, G., Pereira, R., Sichman, J.: The USP Farmers herding team. Annals of Mathematics and Artificial Intelligence 61, 369–383 (2011), doi:10.1007/s10472-011-9238-x
4. Bordini, R., Hübner, J., Wooldridge, M.: Programming multi-agent systems in AgentSpeak using Jason (2007)
5. Ricci, A., Piunti, M., Viroli, M.: Environment programming in multi-agent systems: an artifact-based perspective. Autonomous Agents and Multi-Agent Systems 23(2), 158–192 (2010)
6. Hübner, J.F., Boissier, O., Kitio, R., Ricci, A.: Instrumenting multi-agent organisations with organisational artifacts and agents. Autonomous Agents and Multi-Agent Systems 20(3), 369–400 (2009)
7. Rao, A.S.: Agentspeak(l): BDI agents speak out in a logical computable language. In: Van de Velde, W., Perram, J.W. (eds.) MAAMAW 1996. LNCS, vol. 1038, pp. 42–55. Springer, Heidelberg (1996)
8. Behrens, T.M., Dix, J., Hindriks, K.V.: The Environment Interface Standard for Agent-Oriented Programming - Platform Integration Guide and Interface Implementation Guide. Department of Informatics, Clausthal University of Technology, Technical Report IfI-09-10 (2009)
9. Omicini, A., Ricci, A., Viroli, M.: Artifacts in the a&a meta-model for multi-agent systems. Autonomous Agents and Multi-Agent Systems 17(3), 432–456 (2008)
10. Hübner, J., Sichman, J., Boissier, O.: Developing organised multiagent systems using the MOISE+ model: programming issues at the system and agent levels. International Journal of Agent-Oriented Software Engineering, 1–27 (2007)

Conquering Large Zones by Exploiting Task Allocation and Graph-Theoretical Algorithms

Chengqian Li

Dept. of Computer Science,
Sun Yat-sen University
Guangzhou 510006, China
lichengq@mail2.sysu.edu.cn

Abstract. The Multi-Agent Programming Contest is to stimulate research in the area of multi-agent systems. In 2012, for the first time, a team from Sun Yat-sen University, Guangzhou, China, participated in the contest. The team is called AiWYX, and consists of a single member, who has just finished his undergraduate study. The system mainly exploits three strategies: strengthening action preconditions, task allocation optimization, and surrounding larger zones with shorter boundaries. With these strategies, our team is able to conquer large zones as early as possible, optimize collaboration, and ensure efficiency. The system was implemented in C++, and in this paper, we will introduce the design and architecture of AiWYX, and discuss the algorithms and implementations for these strategies.

Keywords: multi-agent system, distributing algorithm, task allocation optimization.

1 Introduction

The Multi-Agent Programming Contest (MAPC) [1,2] is held annually, in order for researchers to deepen the understanding about the cooperations and competitions among rational agents and also develop some powerful strategies in such environments. This year, for the first time, a team from Sun Yat-sen University, Guangzhou, China, participated in the contest. The team, called AiWYX, reached the fifth place in the contest. It consists of only one member: the author of this paper. I have just obtained my Bachelor degree and am now a PhD candidate. I am a member of the knowledge representation and reasoning group led by Professor Yongmei Liu. My motivation in participating in this contest was to gain experiences in designing multi-agent systems in order to facilitate my future research in this area. These years I am actively involved in the ACM International Collegiate Programming Contest (ICPC, see http://icpc.baylor.edu). Before this competition I had completed an undergraduate honors thesis on Squirrel World, which was proposed by Hector Levesque as an adaptation of the Monty Karel robot world written by Joseph Bergin and colleagues in Python (see http://csis.pace.edu/~bergin/MontyKarel). In Squirrel World, squirrels need to move around on a two-dimensional grid and gather acorns. Squirrels

M. Dastani, J.F. Hübner, and B. Logan (Eds.): ProMAS 2012, LNAI 7837, pp. 234–244, 2013.
© Springer-Verlag Berlin Heidelberg 2013

have both effectors (to do things in the world) and sensors (to gather information). Everything is known to the squirrels at the outset except for the locations of the acorns and some wall obstacles. The first squirrel or the first team of squirrels who gathers a certain number of acorns wins the game. I have adopted some of the strategies I developed for Squirrel World in the MAPC competition.

2   System Analysis and Design

I took part in the contest using the language C++, without using any multi-agent programming languages. There are two reasons for this. Firstly, my background is ACM/ICPC, so I am proficient in this language which is well-known for its efficiency and I did not program in Java which is not so efficient. Secondly, I did not have enough time to adapt myself to multi-agent programming languages.

We have exploited decentralization in implementing various strategies, however, the current implementation is restricted because we only deal with common knowledge [6]. When any agent's knowledge state is updated, other agents' knowledge state will be updated in precisely the same way, because of the assumption of common knowledge. Furthermore, we assume that communications between agents are perfect in this implementation. As to how to implement such strategies on a computer, we apply for a piece of main memory from the operating system, which stores the common knowledge. Hence, each agent has the same authority to access this memory space in order to communicate with other agents.

While such a team of agents is running in the competition, all agents have the goal that their team should reach a score higher than that of their rival. In any state of the world, any agent knows exactly what she should do next to achieve this goal and will start a new task immediately after completing one. In fact an agent can attain her goal by herself or through collaboration with others. Given a task, when there is only one agent intending to accomplish it, she will act by herself. However, if there are more, all such agents will collaborate to accomplish their task, that is, the task will be allocated to the agents in an optimal way. Moreover, the agents here are aggressive, that is, they keep exploring new areas of the world, never passively waiting for changes of the environment. Finally, in any state of the world, any agent is able to perform some action to achieve the goal, never lost in a dead-end.

To design and implement my system, I had spent about 250 hours. During this period, I did not discuss the design and strategies of my agent team with others, and I did not test my agents playing with other teams. I once tested my program by myself on a single computer, that is, I started a competition between two multi-agent teams, both of which were equipped with my own program. Both of them randomly selected a strategy at the beginning, thus they usually exploit different strategies, which helps me evaluate my team.

236   C. Li

3   Software Architecture

I used C++ as the programming language, because it is so efficient and various
mature data structures and algorithms are easy to code in C++. Each of the
agents runs a separate program which is designed at four different levels, from the
decision level to the physical level, as is described in Fig.1. Level 1 is the *decision
level*, which generates an action, or applies for joining a group, according to the
current state. Such a group are to accomplish a task which cannot be handled
by a single agent. For example, conquering a zone is a task, which cannot be accomplished by a single agent and need a group of them. If an action is generated,
the agent will herself perform it, otherwise she will join a group for coordinating
the task. If more than one agent applies for the same task, the first who applies
will become a manager responsible for coordinating this group of agents in an
optimal way. This manager agent produces the coordination in its program architecture at Level 2 (*scheduling level*), so Level 2 is responsible for scheduling
and allocating tasks to each of them. Level 3 is responsible for manipulating and
visiting the knowledge base (KB). When a percept is received by an agent, Level
3 will automatically update the knowledge base. On the other hand when being
asked about the current state, it will retrieve specific information from the KB,
so we call it *reasoning level*. Level 4 (*physical level*) contains various physical
implementations, including KB, network communication (TCP/IP), and special
algorithms such as string processing, Dijkstra algorithm [4], breadth-first search
algorithm [3], minimum cost flow algorithm [8] and Hungarian algorithm [5,7].

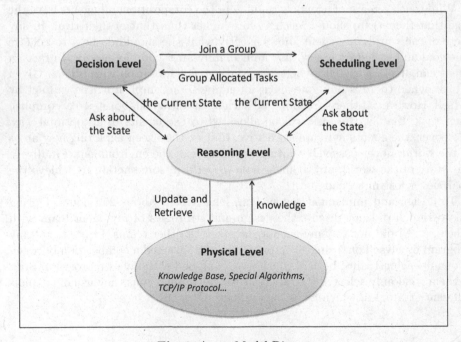

Fig. 1. Agent Model Diagram

To develop my system, I used Gedit Text Editor in Linux system, together with the g++ compiler. With the flexible C++ programming language, I was able to implement all the features of my system quite efficiently, so no features are lost in my implementation. Although I did not distribute the agents on different machines when I participated in the contest, I am actually able to do so with minor adjustments, that is, to modify the number of user names and passwords in the initialization file. When agents are on the same machine, they communicate with each other by sharing main memory, otherwise they do so via the TCP/IP protocol. In the receive-percept period, if an agent receives a new percept, she will immediately perform reasoning to figure out her current state and update her knowledge base. In the meantime any other agent will neither think nor perform actions, until this update is completed. In the send-action period, each agent reasons on her knowledge base to figure out her state, then reacts according to our previously computed classification, before the action is sent to the server. Furthermore a multi-thread TCP/IP sender will send the action to the server. Note that our program is so efficient that any agent is always able to send her action to the server before the next percept arrives. The most difficult part of the whole development process was the optimization of team strategies. That is, how to classify all the possible states and how to compute the optimal action wrt each specific class. Roughly I solved these problems after a series of observations, experiments, and comparisons. In classification, I considered roles, injury, emergency, etc, and in the end, there were nearly 100 specific classes. For example, suppose there is an agent who knows that her role is a repairer and that she is neither injured nor in emergency, e.g., her energy value is too low. And if there is an injured teammate in her location, she will retrieve all these pieces of information from her knowledge base and consider all these factors to compute which specific state she is in. And she will finally generate a reaction to repair the injured. To design agents who react responsively and effectively, I classified all possible states, and for each class, compute the optimal response beforehand. In total, I wrote 10,000 lines of C++ code for my system.

4   Strategies, Details and Statistics

The main strategy of my agent system is that the whole team survey the edges and probe the nodes of the whole map to search for available areas, and then they try to occupy areas with higher values. If any minor event occurs, such as encountering enemies or getting injured, the agent will abort her task. No matter whether they are exploring a map or trying to occupy some area, the agents will cooperate in an optimal manner, avoiding redundant work, so that they are able to accomplish the task with the lowest cost.

4.1   Task Allocation

Given a set of tasks $w[1,\ldots,n]$ and the same number of agents $a[1,\ldots,n]$, an arrangement can be denoted as a matrix $Ar_{n \times n}$, where $Ar_{i,j} = 1$ if task w_i is allocated to agent a_j, otherwise, $Ar_{i,j} = 0$. Here our strategy is that each of the agents is allocated exactly one task, so in each of the rows and columns of Ar, there is exactly one '1'. We use matrix $C_{n \times n}$ to denote the costs (the number of steps or energy value an agent needs to accomplish a task), where $C_{i,j}$ denotes the cost needed for agent a_i to complete task w_j. Considering all possible arrangements, we hope to find a minimal value v such that each agent accomplishes her allocated task with costs no more than v. Let S be the set of possible arrangements such that the maximum cost is minimal, and let T be the elements in S such that the total cost is minimal. Algorithm 1, as shown in the following, returns one element in T. It involves two procedures, Maximum_matching(Agents,Tasks,Edges) based on Hungarian algorithm [5,7], and Min_cost_flow(source, sink, Agents, Tasks, Edges, Cost) which is just the one in [8]. Table 1 shows the test results of Algorithm 1. Each row shows a specific type of 10 experiments, where the first three columns show the number of agents, tasks and edges respectively. The fourth here shows the average number of edges whose value is not greater than v . The last column shows the average running time.

We allocate each agent a unique task so that repetitive work is avoided so that we are able to minimize the total cost. As mentioned earlier, when any agent receives a new percept, any other agent will not perform any actions until this percept is passed to all of them. This ensures that all agents share a synchronized knowledge base based on the presumption of common knowledge. Each time an agent arrives at an unexplored location, she surveys this location, obtaining all adjacent nodes and the costs of respective edges. In this way, all locations explored form a connected component and the agents know all information about this subgraph, including the shortest path between any two nodes in this component. Their strategy now is to move to those nodes on the boundary, survey them and then continue this process again and again. This will accelerate the process of searching for more valuable areas. To avoid the case that two agents move to the same location to survey, and to minimize the total cost, we use Algorithm 1 to inform each agent where they should go. To communicate with the server, we use a multi-threaded TCP/IP protocol.

I have designed a particular strategy for each of the five roles in the game. When an agent realizes that she is acting in a certain role, say, repairer, she will follow the respective strategy. Only explorers will accept the mission of exploring the map and probing the value of the newly encountered node. After finishing exploring, they will join a group to conquer a large zone. Here sentinels will join a group to survey all the edges and after that, will join another group to conquer a large zone just as what the explorers do. If some enemies are found and the team does not know their roles and specific states, inspectors will join a group to inspect those enemies, to collect such information. Otherwise, they will join a group to survey all the edges and then join another group to conquer a large zone just as what sentinels do. If some injured teammates are found, repairers will run to them and repair them, otherwise, they will join a group to survey the edges and then another group to conquer a large zone in the same way.

```
input  : Agents, Tasks, Cost
output: arrangements
// binary search
low ← min_{x∈Agents,y∈Tasks} Cost(x,y) − 1
high  ← max_{x∈agents,y∈Tasks} Cost(x,y)
while low+1 ≤ high do
    mid ← ⌊(low+high)/2⌋
    Edges ← {(x,y)|x ∈ Agents, y ∈ Tasks, Cost(x,y) ≤ mid}
    if Maximum_matching(Agents,Tasks,Edges) == |Tasks| then
    // Hungarian algorithm
    |   high ← mid
    else
    |   low ← mid
    end
end
Edge ← {(x,y)|x ∈ Agents, y ∈ Tasks, Cost(x,y) ≤ high}
Edges ← Edges ∪ {(source,x)|x ∈ Agents} ∪ {(x,sink)|x ∈ Tasks}
Cost(source,x) ← 0// for all x ∈ Agents
Cost(x,sink) ← 0// for all x ∈ Tasks
Min_cost_flow(source, sink, Agents, Tasks, Edges, Cost)
for (x,y) ∈ Edges do
    if flow(x,y)==1 then
    |   // flow is defined in Min_cost_flow
    |   arrangements(x) ← y
    end
end
return arrangements
```

Algorithm 1. Min_max_cost_tast_allocation(agents,works,cost)

Table 1. Experimental results for Algorithm 1 (value of edge < 10000)

Agents	Tasks	Edges	Remaining edges	Time
20	300	3000	62	0.0039s
20	1000	10000	65	0.0088s
100	1000	50000	485	0.0571s
200	1000	100000	1243	0.1634s
500	1000	250000	3641	0.8317s
1000	1000	500000	8153	4.5360s

If some enemies are discovered, saboteurs will go to front line and fight with those enemies, otherwise, they just do what sentinels do in the same occasion.

4.2 Expanding Zones

Expanding a boundary node B, means adding all adjacent nodes of B, which are not occupied by the enemies, into the current zone. The agents first choose

```
input  : Nodes, Edges, value, Enemy_Nodes
output: Best_Zone
for x ∈ Nodes do
 |  Neighborₓ ← {y|(x,y) ∈ Edges}
end
Can_Not_Expand ← {x|x ∈ Enemy_Nodes or Enemy_Nodes ∩ Neighborₓ ≠ ∅}
// cannot be Expanded if an enemy is at or right beside
for i = 0 to p₂ − 1 do
 |  // p₂ is a prime number, assumed 1000007
 |  Hash_Zonesᵢ ← ∅
end
for start_node ∈ Nodes do
 |  Bound ← {start_node}
 |  Zone ← Bound
 |  while ∃x.x ∈ Bound ∧ (Neighborₓ − Zone − Enemy_Nodes ≠ ∅) do
 |   |  // there exists a non-enemy point right outside the boundary
 |   |  if Bound ⊆ Can_Not_Expand then // no point can be Expanded
 |   |   |  S ← {x| minₓ∈Bound |Eat_Nodesₓ|}
 |   |   |  // the set of points needing the least agents if eating
 |   |   |  T ← {x| maxₓ∈S Σ_{y∈Neighborₓ−Zone−Enemy_Nodes} valueᵧ}
 |   |   |  // set of nodes in S maximizing total cost
 |   |   |  Zone ← Zone ∪ {x|x ∈ Neighborᵧ − Zone − Enemy_Nodes ∧ minᵧ∈T y}
 |   |   |  // Select any point in T, expand it
 |   |  else
 |   |   |  S ← {x| minₓ∈Bound−Can_Not_Expand |Expand_Nodesₓ|}
 |   |   |  T ← {x| maxₓ∈S Σ_{y∈Neighborₓ−Zone} valueᵧ}
 |   |   |  Zone ← Zone ∪ {x|x ∈ Neighborᵧ − Zone ∧ minᵧ∈T y}
 |   |   |  // Select any point in T, expand it
 |   |  end
 |   |  Bound ← {x ∈ Zone|Neighborₓ ⊄ Zone}
 |   |  if Σ_{x∈Best_Zone} valueₓ < Σ_{x∈Zone} valueₓ then
 |   |   |  Best_Zone ← Zone
 |   |  end
 |   |  hash ← (Σ_{xᵢ∈Zone,0≤i<|Zone|} xᵢ × p₁i) mod p₂
 |   |  // p₁ and p₂ are prime numbers, p₁ is 1007 and p₂ is 1000007
 |   |  if Zone ∈ Hash_Zonesₕₐₛₕ then
 |   |   |  break
 |   |  end
 |   |  Hash_Zonesₕₐₛₕ ← Hash_Zonesₕₐₛₕ ∪ Zone
 |  end
end
return Best_Zone
```

Algorithm 2. Expand(Nodes, Edges, value, Enemy_Nodes)

Table 2. Experimental results for Algorithm 2

Nodes	Edges	Enemies	Time	Time (distributed)
100	300	20	0.0207s	0.002s
200	600	20	0.2910s	0.006s
300	900	20	1.2581s	0.013s
400	1200	20	3.5527s	0.023s
500	1500	20	7.4012s	0.034s
1000	3000	20	> 30s	0.128s

each node which is not occupied by enemies as a point zone and then repeat the following: find the boundary node P such that after expanding P the boundary increases the least (possibly by a negative number), and then, expand it. During the expanding process, we maintain the best zone found in the past, with the highest value. We say a zone B_1 is superior to another one B_2 if B_1 is more valuable than B_2. In details, we have the following Algorithm 2. The complexity of this algorithm is $O(N^2M)$, where N is the number of nodes and M is the number of edges in the graph. This is because the zone will only be expanded at most N times and at each expanding, at most M edges will be traversed. Table 2 shows the test results of Algorithm 2, where the first two columns show the number of nodes and edges respectively, and the third column shows the number of enemies, that is, the number of nodes occupied by enemies. The last two columns show the average running time for centralized and distributed algorithms respectively. Notice that in each type of experiments, the sum of the running time over all the machines for the distributed algorithm, is several times greater than the running time of the centralized algorithm, because in the centralized algorithm, we apply the hashing technique to examine whether a zone had already been computed before.

Note that Algorithm 2 can be made distributed, in that the expanding procedure can simultaneously begin at any number of nodes on the map. In particular, if we have as many machines as the nodes, we allocate each machine a unique node and instruct it to run a separate expanding procedure with that node.

4.3   Strategy Details

Formally below is the evaluation function for estimating the value of a zone:

$$\text{value}_{\text{Zone}} = \sum_{i \in \text{Zone}} \text{value}_i. \tag{1}$$

Our agents will calculate the most promising zone with Algorithm 2 and then move to the boundary of that zone and conquer it. Among them, the saboteurs always attack the nearest agent of the rival, so that this group of agents always attack the nearest area occupied by the enemies. If they are attacked by the enemies, they will recompute a new area not occupied by the enemies, and then move there. All agents are equipped with exactly the same program, however, at each step during the contest, the strategy can be changed with a relatively small probability. Intuitively given an area, the safest strategy is to fully cover its boundary, that is, each boundary node is occupied by an agent. However, we sometimes take some risk, hoping to occupy more with the same number of agents. One possible risky strategy is that there is at least an agent at any two adjacent boundary nodes. At the start of the contest, we exploit such risky strategy to conquer an area. If this area is often disturbed by enemies, we will recompute a new area with the aforementioned safe strategy and then move there. To summarize, two factors can trigger strategy changes: (1) whether a conquered area is often disturbed; (2) a relatively small probability. During the procedure of path finding, we exploit Dijkstra Algorithm and Breadth-First Search Algorithm, and we also use Algorithm 1 to prevent any two agents from exploring the same location. During the contest, there is a certain strategy that only saboteurs will buy sabotage device and shield, and the strength value will always be equal to the health value or one unit more. However, according to empirical results, it is best not to buy any facilities. Considering that this does not cause big problems, at the start we randomly make a choice between these strategies. In the contest, we value achievements, from which we are able to obtain some scores at each step, so we try to acquire achievements swiftly, never spending them.

As mentioned earlier, all agents in our team are rational and good team players, that is, each will always try to complete the mission of the group. Moreover, recall that all communications are perfect and all agents will not perform any actions when a certain percept is being passed in the group. In our team all the agents are armed with exactly the same program so that they have equal status. When a list of agents are applying for the same mission, one of them will become a temporary project manager, which is responsible for allocating the mission in an optimal way. Later this project manager will become an ordinary agent and each agent will accomplish her allocated mission separately. Hence we organize our agents explicitly and no hierarchy is exploited. When an agent encounters something emergent, she immediately interrupts her allocated mission and tell all others in the group. The group will possibly relax the team mission so that they are able to accomplish it without this agent. Agents are able to perform planning in path finding and they need complete knowledge about the (local) initial state. Here we do not call a planner, but exploit Dijkstra Algorithm to obtain a shortest path from the source to the destination. To synchronize with the server, the agents use multi-thread TCP/IP listeners to listen to the message from the server, and decide what actions to perform accordingly. Furthermore, a multi-thread TCP/IP sender will send the action to the server. Note that our program is so efficient that any agent is always able to send her action to the server before the next percept arrives.

5   Conclusion

The participation of this contest has greatly improved my knowledge of multi-agent systems and stimulated my interest in conducting research in this area. I have learnt some important strategies to improve the performance of my agent team. Firstly, agents should be trained beforehand to strengthen the preconditions of their actions in order to reduce the search space. For example, the agents would realize that any node should not be surveyed repeatedly so they strengthen the precondition of the survey action. Secondly, the agents should record some optimal solutions in some cases, then with the learned experiences, they will be able to make best responses in similar cases. For instance, if a saboteur encounters an enemy for the first time, she deliberates over the optimal strategy, attacks that enemy, and learns that experience. Then if similar cases happen next time, she will simply behave according to this experience, without deliberation. Thirdly, the agents should keep a balance between maximizing their worst outcome and minimizing the best outcome of their enemies in the meantime.

One strong point of our team is that we use Algorithm 1 for task allocation to avoid repetitive work, hence decreasing cost of the team. Also, Algorithm 2 ensures that our agents are able to search for a large area, and then occupy it. Another is that our team is efficient in that it only takes the team about 0.2 second to make all decisions, on the 300-edge and 800-node map, in a perfect network. This enables us to develop more complex strategies in future contests. The weaknesses of our team are that we do not have a good strategy for disturbing the opponents and we are not able to defend our own area effectively. Because there is a great number of agents and the map is complex, our programs have to run with great efficiency. Hence we choose C++, which is known for its efficiency and flexibility, supporting various data structures and algorithms. Next year we are going to exploit effective strategies to attack enemies' zone and protect our own zone. The performance this year is not so satisfactory and there are many reasons: this was the first time for us to participate, the team consisted of only one member, I have just finished my undergraduate study with little research experience, and I had not enough time to implement all the ideas. For the next year, some changes we would think beneficial include: (1) servers should never send repetitive static information so as to relieve the pressure of network communication; (2) a percept should contain no information about the teammates because the agents should communicate with each other to broadcast such information.

Acknowledgements. I thank Professor Yongmei Liu for introducing me to the Multi-Agent Programming Contest. I am deeply grateful to Yi Fan for his generous and valuable help with the writing of this paper. This project was supported by the Natural Science Foundation of China under Grant No. 61073053.

References

1. Behrens, T., Dastani, M., Dix, J., Köster, M., Novák, P.: Special issue about Multi-Agent-Contest I. In: Annals of Mathematics and Artificial Intelligence, vol. 59. Springer, Netherlands (2010)
2. Behrens, T., Dix, J., Köster, M., Hübner, J.: Special issue about Multi-Agent-Contest II. In: Annals of Mathematics and Artificial Intelligence, vol. 61. Springer, Netherlands (2011)
3. Cormen, T.H., Leiserson, C.E., Rivest, R.L., Stein, C.: Section 22.2: Breadth-first search. In: Introduction to Algorithms, pp. 531–539. MIT Press and McGraw-Hill (2001)
4. Dijkstra, E.W.: A note on two problems in connexion with graphs. In: Numerische Mathematik, vol. 1, pp. 260–271. Springer (1959)
5. Edmonds, J.: Maximum matching and a polyhedron with $0, 1$ vertices. J. of Res. the Nat. Bureau of Standards 69 B, 125–130 (1965)
6. Fagin, R., Halpern, J.Y., Moses, Y., Vardi, M.Y.: Reasoning about Knowledge. The MIT Press, Cambridge (1995)
7. Kuhn, H.W., Yaw, B.: The Hungarian method for the assignment problem. Naval Res. Logist. Quart, 83–97 (1955)
8. Orlin, J.B.: A faster strongly polynomial minimum cost flow algorithm. Operations Research 41(2), 338–350 (1993)

Author Index